The Concept of Belief in Islamic Theology

A Semantic Analysis of *Īmān* and *Islām*

Toshihiko Izutsu

The Concept of Belief in Islamic Theology

A Semantic Analysis of *Īmān* and *Islām*

KEIO UNIVERSITY PRESS

THE CONCEPT OF BELIEF IN ISLAMIC THEOLOGY
A Semantic Analysis of *Īmān* and *Islām*

Published by Keio University Press Inc.
19-30, 2-chome, Mita, Minato-ku
Tokyo 108-8346, Japan

Originally published in 1965 by the Keio Institute of Cultural and Linguistic Studies, Keio University.

We express our deepest gratitude to Mr. Seiji Masuda, a member of Shachu (Almnus), who financially supported publication of this work.

Printed in Japan.

First edition, 2016

CONTENTS

PREFACE vii

CHAPTER I THE INFIDEL (*KĀFIR*) 1
I The Khārijites and the origin of the problem 1
II The Khārijite concept of *kufr* 7
III The basic structure of the Khārijite thought 11

CHAPTER II THE CONCEPT OF *TAKFĪR* 19
I The danger of the free practice of *takfīr* 19
II Ghazālī's theory of *takfīr* 26

CHAPTER III THE GRAVE SINNER (*FĀSIQ*) 39
I The concept of the grave sin (*kabīrah*) 39
II The grave sinner (*murtakib al-kabīrah*) 45

CHAPTER IV *ĪMĀN* AND *ISLĀM* 63
I The relation between *īmān* and *islām* 63
II Is *īmān* identical with *islām*? 73

CHAPTER V THE ESSENTIAL STRUCTURE OF THE CONCEPT OF BELIEF 91
I The Murji'ites and the problem of *īmān* 91
II The essential structure of *īmān* 101

CHAPTER VI BELIEF AND KNOWLEDGE 113
I The predominance given to 'knowledge' in the definition of *īmān* 113
II Reason and Revelation 119
III Belief on the authority of others (*īmān bi-al-taqlīd*) 130
IV The locus of *īmān* 142

CHAPTER VII BELIEF AS ASSENT 147
I Knowledge and assent 147
II Ashʿarī's theory of *īmān* 152

CHAPTER VIII BELIEF AND VERBAL CONFESSION 159
I Which is more important, *taṣdīq* or *iqrār*? 159
II The Karrāmite theory of *īmān* 163

CHAPTER IX BELIEF AND WORK 171
I The Muʿtazilites and the Murjiʾites 171
II Ibn Taymiyyah's theory of *īmān* 178
III The increase and decrease of *īmān* 192

CHAPTER X 'I AM A BELIEVER, IF GOD WILLS' 207

CHAPTER XI CREATION OF *ĪMĀN* 217
I The origin of the question 217
II Ashʿarī's position 220
III The Māturīdite position 223
IV Creation of *kufr* 228

CONCLUSION 243

APPENDIX *KITĀB AL-ĪMĀN* 249
INDEX OF PERSONS AND SECTS 269
INDEX OF ARABIC WORDS 273

PREFACE

The present work is an analytic study of the concept of 'belief' or 'faith' in Islamic theology. It pursues a double purpose. On the one hand, it purports to present a detailed description of the historical process through which the concept of belief was born, grew up, and was theoretically elaborated among the Muslims. And on the other, it aims at making a careful semantic analysis of 'belief' and other related key-concepts together with the conceptual networks which the latter formed among themselves.

'Belief' was historically the first and the most important of all the theological concepts in Islam, and it raised in the first few centuries of Islamic culture a number of problems of real significance. Some of them were literally problems of life and death to the growing Muslim community. By methodically analysing these problems and the major concepts underlying them, we shall, I hope, be able to throw light upon one of the most interesting phases of the history of Islamic thought.

I must point out, however, at the very outset that this is a study of the concept of belief as it was theoretically elaborated by the theologians, and that Islamic theology did not and could not deal exhaustively with the problems of the belief that had been kept alive in the breasts of the Muslims through the ages. The present study looks at a very particular aspect of the matter from a very particular point of view. The utmost it can hope to do is to analyse and illuminate the scholastic aspect of the problem.

'Belief' is, by nature, a personal existential phenomenon. In this respect, one might say that it discloses its real depth only when it is approached from a non-scholastic point of view. And in this sense, the understanding of the same concept by the Mystics may be said to go far deeper into the very core of the matter. Nor do I hesitate to subscribe to this view.

And yet, on the other hand, Islamic theology is a pre-eminently *Islamic* phenomenon. The concept of belief as manipulated by the scholastic theologians, may very well be of such a nature that it merely touches upon the outward and formal side of the problem. But it is also undeniable that here as elsewhere the 'outward' is a direct self-manifestation of the 'inward'. In this sense, 'belief' as a theological concept reflects and reveals, albeit in a very particular way, the real nature of 'belief' as an existential event, i.e. as something actually lived and experienced in the course of history by the Muslim believers.

Be this as it may, I have done this study in the hope that it might prove not only a historico-philological analysis of one of the key-concepts of scholastic theology but also a modest but real contribution to the study of the essential structure of Islam itself as one of the most original and important religious cultures of the world.

The present work is based on the material which was originally prepared for a special seminar on Islamic theology I was asked to conduct in 1964 at the Institute of Islamic Studies, McGill University in Montreal.

It is my most pleasant duty to express my thanks to the Director of the Institute, Dr. Charles Adams for his unfailing sympathy and encouragement.

Thanks are also due to all those who attended my class; in particular to Mr. W. Paul McLean who, besides contributing a complete English translation of one of the earliest and most important documents (Appendix), has kindly gone over the whole manuscript with me, making helpful suggestions and useful hints. The final form of this work owes much to conversation with him.

I take this opportunity to offer my grateful thanks to Professor Nobuhiro Matsumoto for the active interest he took in my study and for what he has done to make possible the appearance of this book.

Lastly, I acknowledge my obligation to Yurindo Publishing Company for their generous offer to publish this volume and for the meticulous care with which it has been printed.

Toshihiko Izutsu

Tokyo, 12 April, 1965

CHAPTER I

THE INFIDEL (*KĀFIR*)

I The Khārijites and the origin of the problem

No one would deny that 'belief' or 'faith' is the core of religion. In the specifically Islamic circumstances, moreover, the problems relating to this concept are of paramount importance not only because they concern so vitally the very essence and existence of Islam as a religion, but also because the discussions that were aroused over the concept of 'belief' marked the starting point of all theological thinking among the early Muslims.

Stressing the historical importance of the problem of 'belief' *īmān*, the famous Ḥanbalite theologian, Ibn Taymiyyah, remarks[1] that 'the dispute on what these two words meant was the first internal discord to occur among the Muslims; because of this problem the Muslim community was divided into sects and factions, who came to differ on the Sacred Book and the Sunnah and began to call one another "infidels"'. And the first to enter the scene were the group, or groups, of people known as the *Khawārij* or Khārijites.

In order to gain an historical insight into the real nature of the problem, however, we have to keep in mind that the formulation given by Ibn Taymiyyah, which we have just quoted, is too abstract to do full justice to the concrete situation in which discussions were provoked by the Khārijites over this problem in such a vital and crucial way that it struck the young Muslim community, literally as a matter of life and death.

The early Khārijites were not primarily theoreticians. They did not raise their

1. Taqī al-Dīn Ibn Taymiyyah, *Kitāb al-Īmān*, Damascus, 1961, p. 142.

problems *in abstracto*. Certainly, all the key-concepts that were taken up and discussed by them were destined to develop sooner or later into a full-blown scholastic theology. But they themselves did not deal with them on a purely theoretic level. On the contrary, all those concepts were most closely bound up with the contemporary political situation. From our present-day point of view we might simply say that the problems were raised as political rather than as theological problems.

Only, to complicate the picture, the Khārijites talked about these problems in terms of religious belief. In other words, from their own subjective viewpoint, the Khārijī key-concepts were essentially of religious import. This would seem to suggest that all we can say about them at this preliminary stage is that the key-concepts dealt with by the Khārijites had in origin two different sides, each one of them pointing to an entirely different direction: political and theological. At first, that is, in the early Umayyad period, the political side was the more important, while, as time went on, the theological side came to be more and more prominent. Let us now consider the matter more closely and more concretely.

There is, indeed, something very peculiar about the way the Khārijites raised their basic questions concerning the concept of 'belief' *īmān*. At the very first, the center of all disputes was the problem of *Khilāfah* or 'Caliphate'. It is quite natural and understandable that the first grave question that faced the followers of the Prophet after the death of the latter was: To whom did or should the headship of the Muslim community belong? Who, in short, was to be the Caliph *khalīfah*? The word *khalīfah*, as is well-known, means roughly 'one who comes after', 'successor', 'deputy', or 'vicegerent'. But *khalīfah* of whom? That even this point was not yet clear in the minds of ordinary believers is easily seen from some of the early Traditions. In the *Musnad* of Ibn Ḥanbal, for example, we read:[2] Somebody addressed Abū Bakr as 'Caliph of God' (*khalīfah Allāh*). Thereupon Abū Bakr said, 'I am the *khalīfah* of the Messenger of God, and I am quite satisfied with this (title), I am quite satisfied with it, I am quite satisfied!'

The repetition of the last part of the sentence (*anā rāḍī bi-hi*) three times is obviously very significant. The fact that Abū Bakr had to emphasize so pointedly

2. *Musnad*, I, 1949, Cairo, Ḥadīth 59. The Ḥadīth 64 gives the same tradition in a slightly different form. There, instead of 'I am the *Khalīfah* of the Messenger of God', Abū Bakr says, 'No, *khalīfah* of Muḥammad!'

that he was content with the second title would seem to show that there were current at that time two different ways of interpreting the title of *khalīfah*: either as 'vicegerent of God' or as 'vicegerent, or successor, of the Prophet Muḥammad'. Abū Bakr emphatically denies the legitimacy of the first interpretation; he makes it clear that he himself chooses the second meaning, which he thinks the only right one, and is content with it.

Soon this problem was solved, apparently without much difficulty. The Ḥadīth just quoted itself bears ample witness to the fact. However, it left in its wake a far more difficult problem: Who, then, was to become legitimately the '*khalīfah* of the Prophet'?

The problem proved of far-reaching importance to the Muslim community particularly after the death of ʿUthmān. Widely opposing opinions were aroused, and three major 'parties' came into being. For one of them (known as the *Shīʿah*), it was ʿAlī and ʿAlī alone who was fully entitled to be the Caliph. The second party (the Umayyads or *Umawiyyūn*) held that it was Muʿāwiyah. The third said, 'neither this nor that (*lā hādhā wa-lā dhāka*).' Properly speaking, they asserted, there was no need for a Caliph; the Book of God was enough; but, they added, if there was no other way, then whoever was best qualified for it should be chosen from among the people 'even if he be an Ethiopian slave.' This was the representative view of the Khārijites.

As I have remarked above, this situation, viewed from the present-day standpoint, may be said to be essentially political. All these three groups with their differences on the problem of *khalīfah* are, as the late Professor Aḥmad Amīn observed in his *Ḍuḥà al-Islām*,[3] fully entitled to be called 'political parties' (*aḥzāb siyāsiyyah*), for the fundamental problem involved is after all that of the 'welfare' (*maṣlaḥah*) of the whole community. But they themselves did not discuss the problem as that of *maṣlaḥah*, i.e. as a purely political one, although they were keenly aware of all the immediate serious consequences that were bound to ensue from it. To their minds it was rather a theological issue that was at stake, and the problem roused passionate interest mainly in that sense. In short, it was for them an essentially religious problem.

This point will leap to the eye if we consider the particular form in which the problem was raised by the Khārijites. Trying to defeat and condemn their polit-

---

3. Aḥmad Amīn, *Ḍuḥà al-Islām*, vol. III, Cairo, 1963, p. 5.

ical opponents, the Umayyads and the Shīʿah, they formulated their basic question in this way. 'Is he who follows ʿAlī and supports him an "infidel" *kāfir* or a "believer" *mu'min*?' 'Is he who follows Muʿāwiyah and supports him an "infidel" or a "believer"?' The answer was of course evident from the beginning. Their argument was basically quite simple. ʿAlī, Muʿāwiyah and their supporters were all Kāfirs because they were 'grave sinners'. On a more theoretic level, the same question would assume the form of: Is a man who has committed a grave sin still to be regarded as a 'believer' *mu'min*, or is he by that very fact an outright 'infidel' *kāfir*? And it was only an easy step from the original formulation to this more theoretical one. Thus was created the famous theological problem of *murtakib al-kabīrah* or the 'grave sinner'.

Once the question was put in this form, one realized that it was impossible to justify one's position and to give an adequate answer to it without having a definite idea as to what it was 'to believe' and what actions made a man a 'grave sinner'. And this inevitably provoked theological discussions over the distinction between 'belief' *īmān* and 'unbelief' *kufr*. And this boiled down to the most fundamental question: What is Belief?

But even here, the Khārijites took up a very peculiar attitude which originated in their predominantly political concern, and from it ensued grave consequences both theoretical and practical. The first point to note about it is that, instead of attacking directly the problem of 'belief', they gave an almost exclusive attention to the concept of 'unbelief' *kufr*, and that in a personal form. In other words, they did not ask 'What is belief?', or even 'What is unbelief?' Rather they asked, '*Who* is an unbeliever or infidel?' This attitude naturally gave an extremely peculiar coloring to their pattern of thinking.

This particular approach to the problem of 'belief' from the rear, so to speak, should be considered in direct correlation with their primary concern in politics: excommunication from the Muslim community of certain persons—and certain *definite* persons at that. The fact that the Khārijites, at least in the earlier days of their politico-theological activity, had in mind the excommunication of certain definite men, is shown by what al-Baghdādī[4] has handed down to us as the central tenet of the Khārijites common to all the sub-divisions.[5] He gives two

4. ʿAbd al-Qāhir al-Baghdādī, *al-Farq bayna al-Firaq*, Cairo, 1910, p. 55. Throughout the present work, this book will be referred to as Baghdādī, *Farq*.

5. Baghdādī counts 20 sub-divisions (*firaq*, sg. *firqah*) among the Khawārij.

slightly different formulations, one by Kaʿbī and the other by Ashʿarī.

(I) Kaʿbī (in his *Maqālāt*): The main points on which all the Khārijites unanimously agree in spite of the fact that they differ from one another in other matters are that (1) they condemn as 'infidels' ʿAlī, ʿUthmān, the two arbiters,[6] those who took part in the Battle of the Camel, and all those who were satisfied with the arbitration of the two arbiters; (2) they condemn as an infidel, more generally, anyone who commits a grave sin; (3) they consider it incumbent upon all believers to revolt against the unjust ruler (*al-imām al-jāʾir*).

(II) Ashʿarī: (1) They regard as infidels ʿAlī, ʿUthmān, those who took part in the Battle of the Camel, the two arbiters, those who were satisfied with the arbitration, those who justified either the two arbiters or one of them; (2) they consider it incumbent upon all believers to revolt against the unjust ruling power (*al-sulṭān al-jāʾir*).

As we see, the only remarkable difference between the two versions is that Ashʿarī does not mention *takfīr murtakib al-kabāʾtr* 'regarding as an infidel a grave sinner'. This omission may be due, as it is generally thought to be, to Ashʿarī's having taken into account the fact that one of the most important subsects of the Khārijites, the *Najadāt* or Najdites,[7] did not share the same view. Perhaps a better way of explaining this omission would be to say simply that Ashʿarī gives here a more faithful picture of the early Khārijite thought which was so characteristically bound to the actual political conditions of the day, and which, consequently, left almost no place for pure theorizing. Kaʿbī's version probably represents the second stage in the development of the Khārijite thinking, at which people began to think about their problems on a more theoretical level.

Be this as it may, what is most important for our specific purpose is the fact that the concept of *takfīr* or *ikfār* 'condemning somebody as an infidel' was the

---

6. I.e. Abu Mūsá on ʿAlī's side and ʿAmr b. al-ʿĀṣī on Muʿāwiyah's side. Throughout the present work, a general knowledge of Islamic history, including incidents like that of the two arbiters, the Battle of the Camel, etc. is assumed on the part of the reader.

7. The followers of Najdah who was their leader from 686 to 692. Mention will be made of the view of this group later in the present chapter.

center on which revolved and evolved the main thought of the early Khārijites. Nay, it was the very origin of the Khārijite movement itself.

The first Khārijites, known as *al-Muḥakkimah* were some of ʿAlī's followers who regarded all those who admitted the authority of human decision (*ḥukm*) as downright infidels when in reality, as they claimed, there was no decision but God's. This last phrase, *lā ḥukm illā lillāh* 'there is no decision but God's', which is based on the Koranic verse[8] 'Whoever does not judge by that which God has revealed, such surely are infidels', worked as the ruling principle of their conduct. The phrase was understood by them in the sense that 'there can be no authority for arbitration for any man at all in the religion of God, in which God alone possesses the absolute authority'.[9] And in accordance with this principle, they judged that 'the two arbiters were Kāfirs, and ʿAlī himself became a Kāfir when he accepted arbitration'.[10] 'Besides', they said, 'the Koran admonishes us to "fight against that which does wrong till it return to the command of God" (XLIX. 9), but ʿAlī stopped fighting the wrong-doers when he accepted human arbitration. He, thus, abandoned the decision (*ḥukm*) of God and condemned himself to *kufr*'.[11]

We will do well to remember that this condemnation of ʿAlī was not merely a theoretical judgment on the part of the early Khārijites. This was a matter of immediate practical concern. And their fanaticism spilled the blood of thousands of the most innocent believers, as the following description by Malaṭī shows better than anything else.

Those *Muḥakkimah* used to go out with their swords to the marketplaces.

---

8. Sūrah V, 47, *Man lam yaḥkum bi-mā anzala Allāh fa-ulāʾika hum al-kāfirūn*

9. al-Malaṭī: *al-Tanbīh wa-al-Radd ʿalá Ahl al-Ahwāʾ wa-al-Bidaʿ*, ed. ʿIzzah al-ʿAṭṭār al-Ḥusaynī, Cairo, 1949, p. 51. In what follows this book will be referred to as Malaṭī, *Tanbīh*.

10. Ashʿarī, *Maqālāt al-Islāmiyyīn*, ed. Ritter, 2 ed., Istanbul, 1963, p. 452.

11. Ashʿarī, *ibid.* To this indictment against ʿAlī, by the way, the Rawāfiḍ (Shīʿah) replied, 'The two arbiters were certainly wrong, but ʿAlī himself was right, because he accepted the arbitration only for the sake of *taqiyyah* when his life was in imminent danger', Ashʿarī, p. 453. It will also be interesting to see at this juncture how later Orthodoxy replied to this kind of easy and arbitrary *takfīr*. One of the typical answers was the following. 'But he who bluntly declares the Muslims to be infidels and regards the best of the Prophet's Companions as infidels is much more *kāfir* than those whom he condemns', Baghdādī, *Farq*, p. 342 (reading *akfaru min-hum* instead of *al-kāfir min-hum*).

> And when the innocent people gathered together without being aware of it, they suddenly cried out '*lā ḥukm illā lillāh*!' and lifted up their swords against anybody they happened to overtake, and they went on killing people until they themselves were killed. … The people used to live in constant fear of them; it caused a terrible commotion. But fortunately not even one of them remains now on earth.

The rise of the Khārijite schism and the consequences of the excessive religious zeal of these people belong rather to the common stock of knowledge among all those who are interested at all in the history of Islam. And it is not our intention to allot an undue amount of space to the description of what they did in actual life. Enough has been said to show the political implications of the Khārijite phenomenon. Let us now turn to the conceptual side of their activity and see what were the real contributions they made towards the development of theological concepts in early Islam.

II The Khārijite concept of *kufr*

In order to simplify the explanation and also to clarify the true significance of the Khārijite movement from the specific point of view of conceptual analysis, I would begin by giving a schematic exposition of the radical change which affected the structure of the two key Islamic concepts: *īmān* (*islām*) and *kufr*.[13]

Īmān 'belief' (or *islām*) and *kufr* 'unbelief'—or the corresponding personal forms, *mu'min* 'believer' (*muslim*) and *kāfir* 'infidel'—are two of the most important terms in the Koran. They constitute the very center of the whole Koranic thought. The Khārijite theology inherits this conceptual pair from the Koran. Outwardly it would appear that no change has occurred in this semantic field. In reality, however, it is not in any way difficult to notice that, under the surface, a very profound change of values has occurred.

The Koranic system reveals a very simple structure based on a clearcut

12. Malaṭī, *Tanbīh*, p. 51. [ref. number missing in the original text.]

13. I have dealt with this same problem in my earlier work, *God and Man in the Koran*, Tokyo, 1964, pp. 52–57, as an illustration of a methodological principle of diachronic semantics. The following section is intended to give a slightly modified picture of the matter.

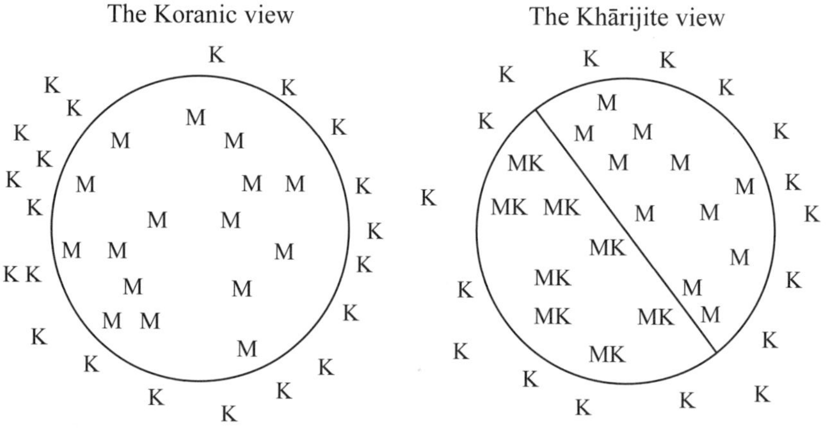

The circle symbolizes the Muslim community.
M=Muslim (or *mu'min*)
K=Kāfir

distinction between Muslims and Kāfirs. All Muslims are members of the community; that is, they are, diagrammatically, all within the circle. And they stand in a sharp opposition to those who remain outside the circle, i.e. all those who refuse to listen seriously to Muḥammad's teaching and to believe in God. In this simple structure there is no place for confusion or ambiguity. The *ummah* or '(*Muslim*) community', symbolized in our diagram by a circle, divides men neatly into two opposing sections. Man is either Muslim or Kāfir. And no Kāfir is allowed to come into the circle unless he 'surrenders', which is the original meaning of *islām*.

All this is, of course, but an idealized picture designed to show the conceptual structure of the Muslim community. In reality, however, since the formal procedure of this 'surrendering' was not a very rigorous one, many men of doubtful faith could easily come into the circle and become members of the community by simply pronouncing the formula of *shahādah* 'there is no God but Allah and Muḥammad is the Apostle of Allah!'

Now this thought that the space within the circle was not as pure and clean as it should be, that there were included within it an appalling number of doubtful and undesirable elements which were actually corrupting the purity of the ideal Muslim society—precisely this thought formed the starting point of the Khārijite movement. In their conception, the basic contrast that really matters is no longer between the members of the community (those who are within the circle), and the outsiders (those who remain outside the circle), but rather between a certain section of the community and the rest of it, that is, in short, the pure, real Muslims and the impure, false Muslims. The latter, in the Khārijite view, are only nominally Muslims; in reality they are nothing but Kāfirs. And those are the more dangerous elements precisely because they are nominally Muslims. They live within the circle, mixed with the real Muslims; they pass for real Muslims; they are allowed to enjoy all the privileges, spiritual as well as material, that should be given only to a pure Muslim.

Thus the Khārijites brought the concept of *kufr* right into the middle of the Muslim community. Formerly people were safe, so to speak, within the wall. Once they accepted Islam formally, they were treated as authentic members of the new community. Anyone who made an outward expression of the Islamic faith rendered thereby inviolable both himself and his possessions, for, as some Ḥadīths emphasize, 'you should not split open his heart to see the real motive from which he made such a confession'.[14] This, however, was exactly that upon which the Khārijites fanatically insisted.

With the rise of the Khārijites, an unexpected danger thus crept into the very compound of the 'community' *ummah*. The Muslims began to feel themselves vulnerable, both in a moral and a physical sense. Nobody, not even a devout and pious Muslim, was sure any longer whether he could keep the title of Muslim or 'believer' to the end of his life. A Muslim might be labelled at any moment as a Kāfir. And once he got this label, he was no longer considered a member of the *ummah*; such a Muslim was to be driven forcibly out of the compound. And this meant, in the understanding of the radical Khārijites, that he should be killed, and nothing could safeguard from the Khārijites word even his wives and children.

This situation made the concept of *kāfir* acquire inevitably a complex structure. Formerly, a Kāfir was a Kāfir, and nothing else. Now within the very wall of the Muslim *ummah*, *kāfir* is a double concept. Subjectively, that is, for himself, and also for the non-Khārijite believers, such a Muslim is still a Muslim, a 'believer', but from the particular standpoint of the Khārijites, he is a downright 'unbeliever'. In the diagram given above, this is indicated by the symbol of

14. Cf. for example, A. J. Wensinck, *The Muslim Creed*, Cambridge, 1932, Chap. II.

MK, standing for a Muslim-Kāfir.

Thus we see that exactly the same Koranic terms are used at this stage with the same sharp basic opposition of Muslim and Kāfir still intact, but the inner structure of them, particularly that of *kāfir*, and consequently that of *kufr*, has undergone a very radical change. To simplify the matter we might say that, in this new mode of thinking, a Kāfir is not so much an 'infidel' or a simple 'unbeliever' as a 'heretic'.

This subtle shift of emphasis in the connotation of the word *kāfir* from 'infidel' to 'heretic', occurring early in the history of Islamic thought is a very significant event, the importance of which cannot be too much emphasized. But the phenomenon itself is not in any way hard to account for.

In the days of the Prophet, the Kāfirs in the first sense of the word were the burning problem that confronted the Muslim *ummah*. It was still a small community, and its very existence was being threatened by the huge number of the Kāfirs who surrounded it. They were 'infidels' or 'unbelievers' who not only obstinately refused to 'surrender' themselves to God but, more positively, were firmly determined to fight with swords against the new religion. For the Muslims, they were the enemies who were either to be destroyed or won over to their side by persuasion. Besides, there was as yet no clear concept of 'heresy' in the community.

The situation greatly changed after the great conquests. All kinds of people came into the Muslim community with diverse cultural backgrounds. And in these new circumstances, in the so-called great Saracen Empire, the most dangerous enemies were no longer the Kāfirs outside of the wall, but the Kāfirs inside of the wall. The Kāfirs in the sense of those who do not accept Islam were now a matter of peripheral concern. The Muslim community was big enough and strong enough to stand on its own feet. At least, the infidels in their unbelief left Islam alone, and their existence beyond the far-off frontiers could do no harm at all to the firmly founded edifice of Islam. Their creeds were considered simply false and unimportant.

But the Kāfirs in the second sense of the word were quite different. They were formally and outwardly Muslims, to begin with. They accepted the basic principles of Islam. Only, they interpreted them, wilfully and on purpose in most cases, in a wrong way, and destroyed their value utterly by perverting them, and were undermining in this way the religion itself.

Thus it came about that the problem of *kāfir* in the sense of the 'wrong believer', not in the sense of the 'unbeliever', became a major concern of the thinking minds. The rise of the Khārijites was but a sudden outburst of this uneasiness that pervaded the community. But because of its explosive nature, it took, as we saw and as we shall see more presently, an extremely dangerous turn.

III The basic structure of the Khārijite thought

The Khārijites raised for the first time in the history of Islamic thought the problem of *īmān* 'belief' as a serious theoretic, theological problem. But they did so only indirectly, for they were not theorists or theologians if we take the word 'theology' in the technical sense of *'ilm al-kalām*. Besides, their approach to this problem was, as I remarked earlier, quite a peculiar one. In order to make this point fully understandable, I shall have to begin by saying a few words about the semantic structure of the concept of 'belief' itself. The real importance of this sort of schematic grasp will become more and more obvious as we proceed with the analysis of the key-concepts developed by those who come after the Khārijites.

Now, briefly speaking, the concept of 'belief' has semantically four points of reference: (1) its subject, (2) its object, (3) the act itself, and (4) the forms of its external manifestation. In other words, the problem of 'belief' may be approached from these four different angles.

The first approach, i.e. that of the 'subject', consists in asking about the person who believes. 'Who is the (true) believer?' is, in short, the major concern when we approach the problem from this angle. The second angle raises the problem of: What does or should the true believer believe in? The third concerns the inner structure of the act of 'belief' itself; in other words, the problem of: What is it to believe? The fourth approach is concerned with the problem of the 'works' that are expected to come out from the inner faith as its natural manifestations. The specific question raised in Islam in connection with this last approach was, as we shall see in a later chapter, whether 'works' constitute or not an integral part of 'belief'.

The Khārijites took the first approach. In other words, they raised and discussed the problem of *īmān* and *kufr* mainly—not exclusively, of course— in terms of the 'subject' of belief. However, they did so in a very characteristic way. Two features stand out clearly. First and foremost, their major concern was not so much with the theoretic nature of the individual 'subject' of belief, i.e. the individual believer, as with the problem of *ummah*, the ideal Muslim community formed by the true believers. 'Who are those that constitute the ideal Muslim community?' This was their main question. But instead of attacking the problem in this direct form, they approached it, as I have remarked earlier, from the reverse side and asked, 'Who are those that must be driven out of the existing community, which is corrupted and impure?' Hence the importance of the problem of excommunication, and hence the central position occupied in their thought by the concept of *kufr*. And this is the second remarkable feature of the Khārijite conception of religion.

Thus it comes about that the concept of *kāfir* plays in the Khārijite thinking a far more important role than that of *mu'min* 'believer'. Instead of trying to define *mu'min*, they tried to determine rigorously those who should be driven out of the Muslim community. Excommunicate by every means available all there is to be excommunicated; what remains will naturally be the ideal community of the believers! 'Excommunication' is here a rough English equivalent for the Arabic term *takfīr*, which, as we have observed, means literally 'declaring somebody—who, in this case, is an actual member of the community and passes for a believer—to be a Kāfir, and condemning him as such.' The key-concept *takfīr* was obviously the leitmotif of all Khārijite thinking in both theology and politics. But the Khārijites, we must keep in mind, were not a unified group; they were split into a number of sub-sects, and each sub-sect had something original to offer concerning this problem. Let us now turn to this aspect of the matter, and take a closer view of the different theories put forward by the most representative sub-sects of the Khārijites.

Reference has already been made to the earliest Khārijites, the *Muḥakkimah*, who deserted ʿAlī's camp when the latter, in his desperate fight against Muʿāwiyah, accepted arbitration, on the ground that ʿAlī followed a human *ḥukm* instead of obeying the Divine *ḥukm*. This acceptance of human judgment was, in their view, an unmistakable case of *kufr*. In other words, they exercised their first *takfīr* upon ʿAlī, and of course upon the two arbiters and those involved in this incident. On a more theoretical level, however, their *takfīr* is said to have stood on a very simple principle: Anybody who commits a sin or an act of disobedience (to God's commands) should be condemned as a downright Kāfir (*kāfir = kull dhū dhanb wa-maʿṣiyah*[15]).

The sub-sect, *Azāriqah* or the Azraqites, the followers of Nāfiʿ b. al-Azraq (d. 65/686), pushed this line of thought to its extreme conclusion both in theory and practice. They were known as the extremists of the Khārijites, 'the most fanatical of all, most horrible of all in what they did, the worst of all in what they were' as Malaṭī says.[16] Terrorism, in short, was what they were noted for.

This extremism had its exact counterpart in their theory of *takfīr*. To begin with, they introduced a more forcible term than *kāfir*, standing for something far worse and unpardonable than mere 'unbelief' or even 'heresy': the word *mushrik*.[17]

This word, as everybody knows, is one of the most important key-terms in the Koran which refers to it as *the* greatest sin to be committed against God, the sin of 'associating (other deities) with God', i.e. idolatry or polytheism. This is quite remarkable because it would mean that in the Khārijite view there were actually Mushriks—polytheists or idolaters—in the very midst of the Muslim community. Most probably, however, they simply discarded the original etymological meaning of the word, and used it mainly as an emotive term. To put it in a different way, they used the term as a sign for their subjective attitude of violent antipathy toward the worst thing imaginable from the point of view of religion as they understood it, retaining only the negative value that had been attached to the word.

Who, then, was to be considered a Mushrik (or Kāfir)? Their answer to this question, as it is handed down to us by the Muslim historians of heresiology, does not disclose much theoretic elaboration. Baghdādī,[18] for instance, points out three characteristic features of the Azraqite conception of the Mushrik. First, all Muslims who do not share their opinion in every detail are Mushriks. Secondly, all those, even if they agree with the Azraqites in theory, who do not make the 'sacred migration' *hijrah* to their camp are Mushriks. In the third place, the wives and children of these Mushriks are also Mushriks. And this im-

15. Baghdādī, *Farq*, pp. 56–57.
16. Malaṭī, *Tanbīh*, p. 167.
17. Baghdādī, p. 63.
18. *Ibid.*

plied that all those can be lawfully killed and their goods spoiled.

The first point simply means that in their view only the Azraqites are the true Muslims, that their camp is *the* Muslim community. They considered only their camp 'the abode of Islam' *dār al-Islām*. Hence the duty of all Muslims to migrate and join the Azraqite camp, instead of 'sitting still' *quʿūd* in the 'abode of unbelief' *dār al-kufr* (the second point). All those who 'sat still', whatever the reason, were condemned as Mushriks. According to Ibn Ḥazm,[19] however, this second point was established among the Azraqites 'only after the death of the man who first advocated it, whereas in his lifetime they did not exercised *takfīr* on those who opposed him on this point'. The *Muḥakkimah*, be it noted in passing, had not regarded as Kāfirs—much less as Mushriks—those who did not make the 'migration' to their camp if only they shared the Khārijite views basically.

Mention must also be made of the Azraqite practice of *istiʿrāḍ* based on the particular conception of the true religion just explained. The word means 'asking somebody to expose his personal view'.

> The Azraqites were of the opinion that, whenever they came across a Muslim who did not belong to their camp, they should ask him (at the point of sword) as to his religious conviction. And if he said 'I am a Muslim' they killed him on the spot (because there could be theoretically no Muslim outside their own camp), but they forbade killing anybody who declared that he was a Jew, or a Christian, or a Magian.[20]

And the word *istiʿrāḍ* became a symbol of terrorism and violence. This is, indeed, a strange and ironical situation. Muslims were killed in the name of the purification of Islam, while the Jews, Christians and even the Magians were spared. This seemingly strange phenomenon was but a manifestation in its concrete and extreme form of the Khārijites' preponderant—or exclusive, we might say—concern with the Kāfirs inside the community, which I have pointed out repeatedly; the unbelievers outside the wall were virtually forgotten.

Evidently the Azraqites went too far. The extremes to which they went and the devastating consequences led the other Khārijitesects toward modifying in some way or other the strict Azraqite view of religion, that is to say, toward

19. Ibn Ḥazm, *al-Fiṣal fī al-Milal wa-al-Ahwāʾ wa-al-Niḥal*, 2 vols, Cairo, 1317–1321, part IV, p. 189. This book will be referred to in what follows as Ibn Ḥazm, *Fiṣal.*
20. *Ibid.*

making the basic concepts more moderate and flexible. Even the Ṣufriyyah, the followers of Ziyād b. al-Aṣfar, for example, who, as a whole, still maintained the extremist Azraqite view that all sinners are Mushriks,[21] forbade at least the killing of the wives and children of those who opposed the Khārijite faith.

Some of the Ṣufriyyah took up a very peculiar attitude in regard to the problem of *takfīr*. The *takfīr*, they held, should be exercised only on those sins that have no particular and explicit *waʿīd* of God, i.e. those for which a particular punishment is not provided in the Koran. One who commits adultery, for example, the Koran explicitly names *zānī* 'adulterer'. Likewise, he who steals, *sāriq* 'thief', and he who accuses anybody unjustly, *qādhif* 'wrongful accuser', etc. These and the like are of God's *tasmiyah* 'naming', and no other name should be placed on them. A *zānī* 'adulterer' is *zānī*, nothing more nor less. He is punished solely in the capacity of a *zānī*, and not as a *kāfir*. In other words, he is neither a Kāfir nor a Mushrik. Such a man certainly goes out of the sphere of *īmān* 'belief', but does not go into that of *kufr-shirk*. But he who commits a sin for which there is no explicit mention of a particular punishment in the Koran, e.g. the non-performance of *ṣalāt*, the breaking of the Ramaḍān fast, etc., is a Kāfir, and his act is *kufr*.[22]

Some of the Ṣufriyyah put a further restriction on the exercise of *takfīr* even in cases of the last-mentioned kind. This seems to have been originally a theory put forward by the Bayhasiyyah.[23] According to this view, a man who commits a grave sin for which the Divine Law provides explicitly a definite punishment, should not be declared a Kāfir immediately. His case should be brought up to the ruler—Sulṭān (Ashʿarī), Imām (Ibn Ḥazm) or Wālī 'Governor' (al-Baghdādī)—and only after the latter has openly punished him for his sin is he to be condemned as a Kāfir. The *takfīr* should be exercised only through this legal procedure, and not arbitrarily.

---

21. Baghdādī, *Farq*, p. 70: *Qawlu-hum fī al-jumlah ka-qawl al-Azāriqah fī anna aṣḥāb al-dhunūb mushrikūn*. Ashʿarī (*Maqālāt*, p.118) says that according to Ṣufriyyah, 'all grave sin is *kufr*, and all *kufr* is *shirk*, and all *shirk* is the worshipping of Satan'.

22. Baghdādī (p. 70) attributes this theory to a sub-sect (*firqah*) of Ṣufriyyah. Both Ashʿarī (*Maqālāt*, pp. 101–102) and Ibn Ḥazm (*Fiṣal* IV, p. 191) mention it as a view held by 'a group of the Khārijites'.

23. See, for instance, Baghdādī, p. 70; Ashʿarī p. 119.

The Najdites, the followers of Najdah (d. 72/693), on the other hand, dropped as a general rule the concept of *shirk*, although in some particular cases they still used the label of *mushrik*. He who commits a sin, whether big (*kabīr*) or small (*ṣaghīr*), and persists in it (*muṣirr*) is a Kāfir-Mushrik. But even a grave sinner, if only he does not persist in it, is still a Muslim.[24]

Into the concept of *kāfir* they introduced, further, an important distinction: that of *kāfir niʿmah* and *kāfir dīn*. This distinction stands on the double meaning of *kufr*, which played an exceedingly important role in the Koran:[25] (1) 'ingratitude' or 'thanklessness' for a favor received, which was the original, pre-Islamic meaning of the word, and (2) 'unbelief', which developed fully only at the Koranic stage. In *kāfir niʿmah* 'Kāfir of Divine favor' obviously the *kufr* is taken in the first sense, whereas in *kāfir dīn* 'Kāfir of religion' the same word is taken in the second sense. It is worth remarking also that in the Koran, *kufr* in both its meanings is exactly of an equal negative value. Here in the Khārijite context, however, *kāfir dīn* is evidently considered to be far more serious than *kāfir niʿmah*. For *kāfir niʿmah* is nothing but a particular case of committing a sin—*kāfir fī kadhā* 'a Kāfir in such and such a matter' as they said—and to call somebody a Kāfir in this sense is, in reality, not to exercise 'excommunication' *takfīr*. Such a man is certainly a grave sinner, but he is not to be excluded from the community, although, to be sure, the Najdites, according to al-Baghdādī and others, applied this distinction only to those who took their stand by them and shared the Najdite view on the fundamentals of religion.[26]

A similar basic distinction between two kinds of *kufr* seems to have been made also by the Ibāḍiyyah, who, according to Ashʿarī, asserted that everything that God has imposed upon His creature as a moral duty is *īmān*, but every grave sin is but *kufr niʿmah* and not *kufr shirk* (which is the same as *kufr dīn* in al-Baghdādī's terminology), though (in the Hereafter) all grave sinners will be put into the Fire and will have to stay therein forever.[27]

---

24. Ibn Ḥazm, *Fiṣal* IV, p. 190.

25. This double meaning of the Koranic term *kufr* has been discussed in detail in my earlier work, *God and Man in the Koran*, Chap. IX.

26. Baghdādī, *Farq*, p. 56. See also Ibn Ḥazm, *Fiṣal* IV, p. 190, where we read: 'He who commits a grave sin, if he happens to be of their own camp is not a Kāfir, but if he happens to be of some other sect, then he is a Kāfir'

27. Ashʿarī, *Maqālāt*, p. 110.

Some other Khārijites elaborated the theoretic distinction between *kufr* and *shirk* (or Kāfir and Mushrik) in a somewhat different way. The Ḥafṣiyyah, for instance, an important sub-division of the Ibāḍiyyah, made *maʿrifah Allāh* 'knowledge of God' the sole standard by which to distinguish *kufr* from *shirk*. They asserted: He who knows God, and then disbelieves in any other thing, be it the Prophet, the Garden, the Fire, etc., or commits any or even all of the forbidden things (*muḥarramāt*) like murder, declaring adultery to be *ḥalāl*, etc., is a Kāfir, and not a Mushrik, because he knows God. Only he who does not know God and denies Him is a Mushrik.[28] In short, he who knows God is by that very fact free from *shirk* whether he believes in other things or not.

These are the main points made by the Khārijites regarding the problem of *kufr* and, as its reverse side, that of *īmān*. This is of course but a very simplified picture which hardly does justice to the complicated reality of minute details. But this is not the place to enter upon them. For, although they advocated various peculiar ideas in general, they did not go very far toward theorizing. The Khārijites were responsible for the introduction of some of the important theological terms, but theological thinking itself was not developed very much among them. The task was left to those who followed them.

28. Baghdādī, *Farq*, p. 83. Exactly the same thing is reported of the Ḥafṣiyyah by Ashʿarī in his *Maqālāt*, p. 102. Ashʿarī adds that the majority of the Ibāḍiyyah do not agree with the Ḥafṣiyyah on this point. See also Ibn Ḥazm, *Fiṣal* IV, p. 191.

CHAPTER II

THE CONCEPT OF *TAKFĪR*

I The danger of the free practice of *takfīr*

As we have seen in the foregoing, the problem of *takfīr* 'condemning as a Kāfir' was raised by the Khārijites in a most drastic way in close connection with the actual political situation of the day. For the theologians who succeeded the Khārijites, this was a grave theoretic problem involving the right definition of *kufr* and, consequently, of *īmān*. This theoretic aspect we shall see in the following chapters. More generally, however, *takfīr* was still largely a matter of practical significance, a handy tool of party-politics. And as such it proved an extremely dangerous weapon in the hands of those who were attached fanatically to their own sect.

The door, in any case, was now wide open for *takfīr*. And once the door was open, there could hardly be any limitation set as to how far one should go and where one should stop. In these circumstances a man could point to any one of his Muslim brethren and declare him to be an 'infidel' or even 'polytheist-idolater' on the slightest and most arbitrary ground. According to Ibn Ḥazm, for example, Bakr, the nephew of ʿAbd al-Wāḥid, a contemporary of the famous Muʿtazilite Wāṣil b. ʿAṭā, held the following view:

> Any sin, whether venial or mortal, even if it be a matter of taking wrongfully just a mustard-seed, even if it be a white lie told by way of pleasantry, must be considered *shirk bi-Allāh* 'polytheism' and the man who commits it is a Kāfir-Mushrik (infidel-polytheist) and will stay in Hell for ever. But if such a man happens to have taken part in the Battle of Badr, he goes to Paradise though he is still a Kāfir-Mushrik.[1]

Not content with condemning the contemporaries, people began to exercise *takfīr* even against the Prophets of remote past. According to Malaṭī[2] some of the Jahmites, for instance, thought that,

> Moses was a Kāfir when he asked his Lord for what was absolutely impossible, referring to Moses' having asked God to show Himself to him, which was absurd because, in the Jahmites' view, nobody could see God, not only in this world but even in the Hereafter.[3] Jesus also was a Kāfir, they went on to say, when he said (to God) 'Thou knowest what is in my soul, but I do not know what is in Thy soul (*nafs*). Verily, thou art the sole knower of the hidden world![4] Because to think that God has a 'soul' *nafs* is an act of *kufr*.[5] Thus their extremism led them to the *takfīr* of the Prophets, on whom be peace! Allah stands infinitely far above what those people say!

Quite apart from the absurdity of 'condemning the Prophets as infidels', the Jahmite position, on the problem of the visibility of God (*ru'yah Allāh*) which we have just mentioned, gives us a good insight into the historical process by which *takfīr* began to affect gravely the formation of Muslim dogmatics on a more serious, theoretic level. It is interesting to note that any article of creed, any dogmatic point asserted by a sect was likely to arouse the exercise of *takfīr* on the part of the opposing sects. And not infrequently, the exercise of *takfīr* was reciprocal. The doctrine of the visibility of God affords a good example.

The Muʿtazilites denied the visibility of God in the Hereafter (not to speak of the visibility in the present world), just as Jahm did, but on a more philosophic

1. Ibn Ḥazm, *Fiṣal* IV, p. 191. A few other versions of Bakr's view have been handed down to us, but this is not the place to discuss them.

2. Malaṭī, *Tanbīh*, p. 95.

3. The *Visio Dei* was a problem that provoked a hot controversy among the early Muslim thinkers. The orthodox hold that God is absolutely invisible in the present world, but in the Hereafter the Muslims will be allowed to enjoy the direct vision of God 'without any veil just as we see the moon in a full-moon night, or the sun on a cloudless day (Ḥadīth, Muslim, *Imān*, 299)' Jahm b. Ṣafwān (executed in 128 AH), the founder of the Jahmiyyah, flatly denied this on the ground that God is absolutely transcendent and has nothing at all to be correlated with human eyesight.

4. Koran V, 116.

5. Again this is based on the Jahmite concept of the absolute transcendence of God. God has nothing whatsoever in common with human beings.

ground. Philosophically, the Muʿtazilites held, a 'pure substance', i.e. an immaterial substance without any accidents, is absolutely invisible. Visible to our eyes are only accidents like colors and shapes; so to say that God is visible is to admit the existence of accidents in God.

In the eyes of those who kept themselves within the pale of Orthodoxy, this Muʿtazilite thesis was obviously *kufr*. All those who deny the visibility of God on the Resurrection Day go openly against the letters of the Koran and authentic Tradition; that is, they are Kāfirs. From the point of view of the Muʿtazilites, however, those who accuse them of *kufr* and assert the visibility of God are Kāfirs, for the thesis of the visibility of God is nothing other than *tashbīh* 'anthropomorphism'—more literally, 'making (God) similar to (man)'—and there is no doubt that *tashbīh* is a glaring case of *kufr*. Abū Mūsá al-Murdār, one of the leaders of the Baghdād school of Muʿtazilism, said:

> He who asserts that God can be seen with the eye, in whatever form he asserts it, is comparing God to His creature (which is nothing but *tashbīh*). And he who has doubt as to whether a Mushabbih[6] is a Kāfir or not and is not certain whether such a thesis is true or not, is also a Kāfir himself.[7]

In this way, as theology developed gradually, *takfīr* came to be exercised freely and, apparently, without any compunction, in regard to the minute details of dogmatics. So much so that, as we have just seen in the example of the problem of *Visio Dei*, one and the same dogma was often regarded by one sect as *kufr* and by another as *īmān*. Regarding the problem of the acts of man, just to give another telling example, the representatives of Orthodoxy emphasized very strongly that all human acts are created by God, for otherwise, they thought, man would be the creator of his own actions and this would be tantamount to admitting the existence of a creator besides the Creator. But precisely this thesis of the divine creation of human acts was condemned by the Muʿtazilites as *kufr*. Abū Mūsá al-Murdār—so writes al-Shahrastānī[8]—regarded as a Kāfir anybody who held that the actions of man were created (*makhlūqah*) by God'. It will be interesting to note that al-Shahrastānī in the same passage reports about this

---

6. Participial form of *tashbīh*, that is, in short, anthropomorphism.

7. al-Khayyāt, *Intiṣār*, ed. H. S. Nyberg, Cairo, 1925, p. 68.

8. al-Shahrastānī, *al-Milal wa-al-Nihal*, I, Cairo, 1948, p. 93. This book will be referred to in the following as Shahrastānī, *Milal*.

Muʿtazilite thinker, al-Murdār, that,

> He went so far in *takfīr* that he even asserted: Muslims were altogether Kāfirs though they confessed (outwardly) the unity of God. Once Ibrāhīm al-Sindī asked him as to what he thought of the whole of mankind. And al-Murdār replied that he regarded all of them as Kāfirs. Thereupon Ibrāhīm turned to him and said 'the width of Paradise covers the whole heavens and the earth. And yet nobody enters it except you yourself and three other men who hold the same opinion as you?' This made al-Murdār ashamed and he could not answer a word.[9]

Incidentally mention was made of the fact that al-Murdār considered a Kāfir anybody who doubted whether an anthropomorphist was a Kāfir or not. This attitude, however, was not at all peculiar to al-Murdār, but common to the thinkers of all schools. We all see from what al-Malaṭī writes about it that this seemingly small matter raised a serious problem among the theologians in particular connection with that of *takfīr*:

> All the Muʿtazilites, whether of the Baghdād school or of Baṣrah, nay, all the People of Qiblah do not differ from each other in regard to this problem. He who doubts whether or not a Kāfir is really a Kāfir is himself a Kāfir, for a 'doubter' *shākk* of *kufr* evidently has no (real) belief, being unable to distinguish *kufr* from *īmān*. Thus in the whole Muslim community, whether Muʿtazilites or others, there is no difference of opinion on this point, namely, that a doubter of a Kāfir is a Kāfir. The Muʿtazilites of Baghdād, however, go far beyond the Muʿtazilites of Baṣrah in that they assert that the doubter of the doubter (of a Kāfir) is also a Kāfir, and so also the doubter of the doubter of the doubter, and in this way *ad infinitum*. All of them, they say, are Kāfirs as much as the first doubter is a Kāfir. Against this the Muʿtazilites of Baṣrah—who, by the way, regard the Muʿtazilites of Baghdād as Kāfirs on this point!—hold that the first doubter is certainly a Kāfir because he doubts whether a Kāfir is a Kāfir, but the second doubter, who doubts only whether the first doubter is a Kāfir, is not a Kāfir, but simply a 'grave sinner' *fāsiq*[10] because he does not doubt that *kufr* is *kufr*, but doubts only whether the doubter com-

9. *Ibid.* p. 93.

10. On this technical term, and its particular connotation in the Muʿtazilite thought see the next chapter.

> mits *kufr* with his doubt or not. So he should not be treated in the same way as the first doubter. And this applies to the third doubter, the fourth doubter, etc. *ad infinitum*.[11]

Not only the *kufr* of the first grade is *kufr*, but any thesis which, however innocent and harmless it may look in itself, leads logically to *kufr* must also be considered *kufr*. Concerning the ontological status of the originated things (*ḥawādith*) before their origination, for example, the thinkers of Orthodoxy held that they are neither 'things' *ashyāʾ* nor 'entities' *aʿyān* nor 'substances' *jawāhir* nor 'accidents' *aʿrāḍ*.

> Against this the Qadarites[12] take the view that the non-existents (*maʿdūmāt*) are 'things' even in the state of non-existence. The Baṣrah School of the Muʿtazilah (going further in precision) maintain that substances are substances and accidents are accidents before being originated. This view, however, leads eventually to the (Aristotelian) thesis of the eternity of the world[13] (which is *kufr*). And any view which leads in this way to *kufr* is itself *kufr*.[14]

It is not to be wondered at that, in these circumstances, the theologians began to speak of *kufr* and non-*kufr* about each individual article of faith. Of ʿAbd al-Karīm b. Abī al-ʿAwjāʾ, for instance, Baghdādī says that he 'gathered four heretical views: (1) he secretly held to the dualist view of Manichaeism; (2) he believed in metempsychosis (*tanāsukh*); (3) he sympathized with the Rawāfiḍ on the problem of Imamate; (4) he professed a Qadarite view on the problem of Divine justice and injustice'.[15]

In a similar fashion, but on a more philosophic level, the people of Ortho-

---

11. Malaṭī, *Tanbīh*, p. 45. Malaṭī adds that in his view this second position is preferable to that of the Baghdād school.

12. I.e. the Muʿtazilites. We must remember that among the Muʿtazilites of Baghdād, al-Khayyāt was famous for the thesis here attributed by Baghdādī to the Baṣrah school, namely that 'substance is substance even in the state of non-existence and likewise accident is accident in the state of non-existence. … He even went so far as to say, for example, that black is black in the state of non-existence etc. until there remained only the attribute of existence… and origination itself' (Shahrastānī, *Milal*, p. 102)

13. The 'world' (*ʿālam*) in the terminology of the Muslim theologians means 'all things created'.

14. Baghdādī, *Farq*, p. 320.

15. *Ibid.* p. 225.

doxy (*ahl al-Sunnah*) condemned the great Muʿtazilite thinker al-Naẓẓām on several particular points of his theory. First, in the field of methodology,

> they consider al-Naẓẓām a Kāfir for his denial of the authority of the Consensus and the validity of authentic Ḥadīths and for his professing that it is quite possible that the whole Muslim community agrees on a mistaken view, because it is possible that those who have handed down an authentic Ḥadīth have agreed to make a lie pass for truth.[16]

Secondly regarding the atomistic philosophy,

> they (i.e. the Orthodox) declare al-Naẓẓām together with the Philosophers to be Kāfirs because they (deny the existence of atoms and) say that every particle (however small) is divisible into parts *ad infinitum*, for such an opinion implies that God's knowledge does not comprehend them and thus contradicts flatly His words: 'and He counts exactly the number of all things' (LXXII, 28).[17]

Thirdly, in the field of ontology,

> the people of Orthodoxy condemn al-Naẓẓām as a Kāfir for his view that the accidents (*aʿrāḍ*) are all of one class, that they are all movements (*ḥarakāt*) whereas the view held unanimously by the Orthodox is that accidents belong in diverse classes. They condemn al-Naẓẓām because he will be forced to admit by his own theory that 'belief' *īmān* belongs in the same class as *kufr*, knowledge as ignorance, speaking as silence, and the acts of the Prophet as the acts of the accursed Satan. On this ground, there would be no reason for him to get angry with one who curses him and abuses him, because, if his thesis were right, 'May God curse Naẓẓām!' would belong in exactly the same class as 'May God have mercy upon him!'[18]

As I said at the outset, once the door was open there could be no end to the practice of *takfīr* among the Muslims against each other. And the situation went on turning for the worse. The theory and practice of *takfīr* that developed

16. *Ibid.* p. 315.

17. *Ibid.* p. 316. It must be remarked that here the reason for the *takfīr* of al-Naẓẓām stands on a non-philosophical basis. But Baghdādī gives in another book, *Uṣūl al-Dīn* (Istanbul, 1928, p. 36) a logical refutation of the theory of the divisibility of things *ad infinitum*.

18. *Ibid.* p. 317.

among the *Qarāmiṭah* 'Qarmatians' will show better than anything else to what extremes it could go and what horrible consequences it could produce. Here is a passage from Malaṭī's *Tanbīh*,[19] which gives a detailed description of the Qarmatian theory of *īmān* and *kufr*.

> They believe and profess the transmigration of the spirit. And they assert that things like Paradise, Hell, the final Account, the Balance, the Punishment and the eternal Bliss, which God mentions in His Book, all concern the present world only, and are symbolic expressions for healthy bodies, beautiful colors, sweet tastes, pleasant smells, and lovely things at which rejoice the human souls; whereas 'chastisement' means illness, poverty, pains, sufferings, and all that torments the mind. This is the Qarmatian interpretation of the 'reward and punishment of the deeds'. They assert also that God has a human aspect in Himself, just as Christians do. As regards man, they say that he is 'spirit' *rūḥ* only, the body being like a garment which he wears temporarily. Further, in their view, everything that comes out of the body like mucus, phlegm, excrement, urine, sperm, blood, pus, ooze, and sweat—all these are clean, and there are some among them who even eat each other's excrement because of their conviction that it is pure and clean!
>
> They claim: only those who believe in all this and share the same view are 'believers'; their wives are 'believers'; they should not be killed, and their possessions should not be spoiled, whereas he who opposes them and does not share their belief is a Kāfir-Mushrik, and his blood and possessions are not safeguarded by the Divine Law. Thus they restrict the name of 'believer' to themselves. And among themselves they regard the wives of each other as 'religiously allowed', so also their children; that is, their bodies are just 'allowed' for any of them to enjoy, there being no prohibition, no restriction set. And this, in their view, is *īmān* itself, so much so that in case someone from among them demands of a woman her body, or of a man or a boy his body, if the person refuses to comply with the request, she or he proves thereby to be a Kāfir in their community, because such a person goes out of the Divine Law as they understand it.

Al-Malaṭī goes on to describe how these Qarmatians ran riot in the glorification of sensual pleasures and in the wildest sexual license, basing themselves on

19. *Op. cit.* pp. 20–28.

this strange definition of *īmān* and *kufr*. But this is not the place to follow up his description. Enough has been said, I believe, to show what fateful consequences could flow from the *takfīr* when it was left free and unbridled. And the Muslim thinkers themselves soon became keenly aware of the danger involved.

II Ghazālī's theory of *takfīr*

Reference was made in the last section to the Muʿtazilite thinker al-Murdār who was inclined to condemn almost all men as Kāfirs. He was not in any way an exceptional case. Ḍirār b. ʿAmr, for example, who was one of the prominent figures in the early history of Islamic theology is said to have expressed openly his suspicion of the nature of the belief entertained by the common people in the community. 'I am not sure', he said, 'perhaps the innermost hearts of the common people are nothing but *shirk* and *kufr*'.[20] This problem grows later into a serious one in theology and arouses there much heated discussion under the catchword of *al-īmān bi-al-taqlīd*, i.e. 'belief based on the authority of others', or *takfīr al-ʿāmmah*, i.e. 'condemning the belief of the common people as *kufr*'.[21]

Problems of this sort are after all a matter of pure theory. But when we take into consideration also the Qarmatian understanding of the concept of *īmān* and *kufr*, which, as we have just seen, were directly connected with the actual, concrete life of the people, we cannot help realizing how dangerous and serious the situation was. The latter theologians of the post-Ashʿarite times naturally felt the gravity of the matter. Trying to warn the Muslims against going too carelessly to the extremes in condemning their own fellow-believers, Taftāzānī says:[22]

---

20. Ḍirār was a contemporary of the Muʿtazilite Wāṣil b. ʿAṭā, an 8th century thinker. He was not a Muʿtazilite (see al-Khayyāt, *Intiṣār*, p. 133), though Ibn Ḥazm counts him among the Muʿtazilah. Baghdādī considers him the head of an independent sub-sect named after him *Ḍirāriyyah*. (*Farq*, p. 202)

21. Particularly interesting is the controversy provoked by this problem between the Ashʿarites and the Māturīdites. This will be considered in detail in a later context from a somewhat different point of view, when we come to discuss Ashʿarī's conception of *īmān*.

22. In his commentary on al-Nasafī's Creed, *al-ʿAqāʾid al-Nasafiyyah*, Cairo, 2 ed., 1939, pp. 343–344.

> He who asserts that man creates his own deeds[23] should not be labelled so lightly as a Mushrik, for *shirk* 'associating', in our view, is to posit an 'associate' to God in His God-ness, that is, in the necessity of existence, as the Magians do, or in the sense of deserving worship, as in the case of the idolaters. It must be observed that the Muʿtazilites in no way do such a thing. Nay, they do not exactly attribute to man the same power of creation as God's power of creation because (they admit that) man needs (in producing any deed) means and instruments that are created by God. The representative theologians of the Transoxiana[24] went so far in condemning them as heretics as to declare that even the Magians would be in a better state than the Muʿtazilites because the former recognized only one 'associate' (to God) while the latter recognized 'associates' without number.[25]

Pressing need for checking the abuse of *takfīr* was being felt on all sides. Something had to be done, and that not only practically but also theoretically, because to have attempted to lay restraints forcibly and unreasonably on the abuse of *takfīr* would simply have served to stir further emotive attitudes and aggravated the situation. In order to avoid this, a good theory of *takfīr* had to be formulated on the solid basis of reason and logical persuasion. As a typical instance of such an attempt, we shall take up here the theory advanced by Ghazālī on this problem.

The point from which he started was the deplorable situation which was unfolding itself before his own eyes, in which every group seemed to feel entitled to condemn all others. The Ḥanbalite, he says, condemns the Ashʿarite as a Kāfir on the ground that the latter denies, against the Prophet's explicit words, God's 'being above' and His 'sitting firm on the Throne', while the Ashʿarite, on his part, condemns the Ḥanbalite claiming that the latter is but an anthropomorphist and that he makes the Prophet a liar as regards the words 'there is nothing like unto Him'. The Ashʿarite, on the other hand, condemns the Muʿtazilite saying that the latter goes against the Prophet's teaching in denying the 'visibility of

23. Reference is of course to the Muʿtazilite thesis that man is the creator of his deeds, a thesis which intends to save the absolute 'justice' of God from the responsibility of creating all the evil deeds committed by man.

24. I.e. the Māturīdites.

25. I.e. in making out of men 'creators' of their own deeds.

God' and 'the existence of the Divine attributes like Knowledge and Power', But the Muʿtazilite condemns the Ashʿarite precisely because the thesis of the existence of (eternal) attributes (which is the theory held by the Ashʿarite) is simply tantamount to admitting the plurality of eternal entities and thus to making the Prophet a liar in his teaching of the Unity of God.[26]

In the face of such disastrous circumstances in which each sect, blinded by its fanatical party spirit, considers itself the sole representative of the Truth and treats all others as Kāfirs, Ghazālī begins by observing that

> he is a downright fool who, when asked to give his definition of *kufr*, answers: '*Kufr* is anything that is opposed to the Ashʿarite theory, or the Muʿtazilite theory, or the Ḥanbalite theory or indeed any other theory, (as the case may be)'. Such a man is more blind than a blind man, an uncritical follower of authority.[27]

And he goes on to prove the foolishness of such an attitude by a concrete example. Suppose, he says, here is a man of the Ashʿarite school, who is determined to regard anybody as a Kāfir who opposes Ashʿarī's teaching on any problem whatsoever. Is then Bāqillānī,[28] in his view, a Kāfir because he opposes Ashʿarī on the problem of the attribute of *baqā'* 'eternal existence'[29] and says that it is *not* an attribute which is distinguishable from, and accidental to, Divine essence? From where does he get the proof that Ashʿarī's view is the only truth in such a rigorous sense? If Bāqillānī is a Kāfir because he is opposed to Ashʿarī on this point, is it not equally possible to say that Ashʿarī is a Kāfir because he is opposed to Bāqillānī?[30]

Ghazālī goes on to give a more subtle example which concerns the problem of the Divine attributes, one of the pivotal points of Muslim theology since the rise of the Muʿtazilites.[31] The Muʿtazilites admit that God is the Knower who comprehends everything knowable and the Almighty who is capable of doing

---

26. *Fayṣal al-Tafriqah bayna al-Islām wa-al-Zandaqah*, ed. Sulaymān Dunyā, Cairo, 1961, p. 175.

27. *Ibid.* p. 131.

28. Abū Bakr Muḥammad b. al-Ṭayyib, al-Bāqillānī (d. 403/1013), one of the greatest names in the Ashʿarite school.

29. 'eternal' in the sense of 'eternal *a parte post*', that is, existence that will never come to an end.

30. Ghazālī, *op. cut.* p. 132.

31. *Ibid.* pp. 132–133.

everything possible; what they deny is the existence of the (eternal) attributes in God. So, Ghazālī asserts, the only difference between them and the Ashʿarites boils down to whether God is Knower and Almighty by Himself[32] or by an attribute distinguishable from (Himself).[33] Why then should we condemn the Muʿtazilites as Kāfirs? To this an anti-Muʿtazilite may reply: 'I condemn them because they assert that (what is there is only) one Divine Essence and from this one Essence are derivable Knowledge, Power and Life. But (I say that) all these are attributes which are quite different from each other both in definition and reality. And it is absolutely impossible for many ontologically different things to be united into one, or that the one Essence should take their place.'

But if we are to condemn the Muʿtazilite on such a ground, Ghazālī continues, then we would have to do the same thing with Ashʿarī, because he makes sometimes statements of exactly the same nature. Concerning God's Speech, for instance, he says: 'Speech is an attribute distinguishable from, and inherent in, God's Essence; and although it (i.e. Speech) is essentially one, it is, at the same time, the Torah, the Evangel, the Psalms, and the Koran; it is also (from a different point of view) Command, Prohibition, Information, and Interrogation'. This means that, in Ashʿarī's view, several different things are united into one to form Divine Speech. But how can one and the same thing—which is, in this case, Speech—allow sometimes of being affirmed and denied[34] and sometimes not?[35] In short, Ghazālī concludes, he who hastens without reflexion to the *takfīr* of those who happen to oppose Ashʿarī or anybody else is an ignorant and uncritical man.[36]

Errors of this kind, according to Ghazālī come ultimately from a basic misunderstanding of the nature of *takfīr* itself. Those theologians and jurists who exercise *takfīr* indiscriminately think that the basis of *takfīr* is Reason. They are wrong.[37] What, then, is the true basis of *takfīr*? What kind of problem is the problem of *takfīr*?

---

32. as the Muʿtazilites hold.
33. as the Ashʿarites hold.
34. as in the case of Information (or Predication).
35. as in the case of Command and Prohibition.
36. *Op. cit.* p. 201.
37. *Ibid.* p. 210.

In order to give a theoretically correct answer to this question, Ghazālī begins by elucidating what is really implied by the judgment: 'This man is a Kāfir'. This proposition means basically three things. First, (concerning his life in the Hereafter) that this man will be in the Fire, and that eternally. Secondly, (concerning his life in the present world) that his blood and possessions are not lawfully safeguarded, that he is not allowed to marry a Muslim woman, and that he is not protected by the law of vendetta. Thirdly, that what he says is a lie and his faith nothing but ignorance. In other words, the *takfīr* of a man means in short that he can be lawfully killed, his wealth spoiled, and that it is permissible for anyone to declare openly and without any reserve that he will be made to stay in the Fire forever.

Thus understood, it will be clear that *takfīr* is essentially a legal problem. Its basis is Revelation, not Reason. The judgment that a certain person can lawfully and justly be killed, his possessions confiscated, and that he fully deserves to be declared an eternal dweller of Hell, belongs to the domain of the Divine Law. But it is of the very nature of the Divine Law that it is absolutely free. In this domain it is, properly speaking, not impossible at all that God might declare that a liar (against God) and a man ignorant (of God) or one who gives the lie (to the Prophet) will be rewarded by Paradise instead of being punished in Hell, although it is impossible even in such a case that a lie should be declared to be truth, and ignorance knowledge. This implies that Reason is in this domain utterly powerless; there is no place for it to operate. Whether a man is a Kāfir or Muslim is judged solely by the evidence of revealed words (i.e. Divine Will) or *ijtihād*, that is, an analogical argument based on revealed words. In short, it is a matter of jurisprudence (*fiqh*). You cannot call anybody a Kāfir and condemn him as such on the ground that your Reason argues that way.[38]

What then is the basic criterion by which we can rightly judge a man a Kāfir? The question is ultimately reducible to the right definition of *kufr*. There may be conceivable several ways of defining the concept. But for the present purpose a very simple definition will suffice. Ghazālī offers the following one: '*kufr* is the *takdhīb* of the Apostle of God concerning any point of what he has told us'. The word *takdhīb* means literally 'giving a person the lie', 'regarding

38. Ghazālī, *al-Iqtiṣād fī al-I'tiqād*, Ankara, 1962, pp. 242–247. This work of Ghazālī will be referred to in the following as *Iqtiṣād*.

what he says as a lie', which is opposed to *taṣdīq* meaning literally 'regarding something as true', 'believing'. In this particular context, Ghazālī defines *īmān* as '*taṣdīq* of whatever the Apostle has told us'.[39]

So the basic criterion here in question is provided by the simple dictum: 'anybody who gives the lie to Muḥammad is a Kāfir', with the understanding that we take the dictum to mean nothing other than that such a person will go to Hell after death and remain there eternally, and that while he is alive, his blood and possessions are *ḥalāl*.

The only thing which goes to complicate the matter is that there are several degrees distinguishable in 'Kāfir-ness'. Ghazālī distinguishes six such degrees.[40]

(1) In the first place, the Jews and Christians (together with those who belong to some other religious communities, like the Magians and the idol-worshippers). They are notorious for the *takdhīb* of Muḥammad. The Koran itself constantly mentions them as Kāfirs, and there is also a unanimous Consensus of the Muslim community that such people are Kāfirs. So there can be no question about the *takfīr* of these people. This is the very 'root' (*aṣl*) of the whole question of *takfīr*, and all others are but corollaries.

(2) The 'Brahmans' and the 'Materialists'. The former deny not only Muḥammad but all Apostles in general, that is to say, they deny the principle of prophetic mission itself. For this reason they are more deserving of *takfīr* than the Jews and the Christians. The *Dahriyyah*, 'Materialists' or 'Atheists', are those who do not admit the existence of the Creator of the world. This means that they deny not only the Apostles but also Him who sends the Apostles. So they are even more deserving of *takfīr* than the Brahmans.

All those who advocate any theory which, by implication, leads to the negation of the truthfulness of Prophetic mission, and particularly of Muḥammad, fall under this second category.

(3) The Philosophers (*Falāsifah*) admit the existence of the Creator, the truthfulness of prophetic mission, and Muḥammad's being an authentic Apostle and Prophet. But they profess many things that go obviously against the words

---

39. *Fayṣal*, p. 134.

40. *Iqtiṣād*, pp. 248–253. In the *Fayṣal* he is content with mentioning only three classes that are fully entitled to *takfīr*: (1) the Jews and Christians, (2) the 'Brahmans' (*Barāhimah*), and (3) the 'Materialists' (*Dahriyyah*).

of Revelation. For example, they assert that the Prophet Muḥammad did not dare to disclose the real Truth (which coincides exactly with the teachings of Aristotle) and intentionally concealed it for fear that the common people with their poor intelligence might misunderstand and distort it. *Takfīr* must definitely be exercised against them without hesitation.

Their Kāfir-ness reveals itself nakedly in the following three points: (a) their refusal to admit the resurrection of the body, the chastisement (of the sinful) in Hell and the blissful reward (of the faithful) in Paradise with black-eyed maidens and all kinds of physical delights; (b) their view that God does not and cannot know the Particulars and the concrete details of what happens here on the earth, because He knows only the Universals, and because the knowledge of the Particulars is reserved to the Angels in Heaven; (c) their thesis that the world is eternal *a parte ante*, and that, therefore, God's precedence is (not in time but) in rank and order as the precedence of the cause over the caused.

All these three points are nothing other than an open *takdhīb* of the teaching of the Prophet. The Philosophers try hard with their sophistry to hide it, but in vain.

(4) The Muʿtazilites, the anthropomorphists, and other sects who stand outside the pale of the Muslim Aristotelians. They declare that they believe the veracity of the Prophet and his never having told a lie even for the sake of the good of the common people. They do resort, however, to *ta'wīl* 'the allegorical interpretation of the revealed words', and commit mistakes in arbitrary interpretation of this sort. Nevertheless, it may be questioned seriously whether or not *takfīr* should be practised against them.

As a general rule, Ghazālī thinks, we had better incline in such a case toward not exercising *takfīr*. It would be wise of you 'that you restrain your tongue as much as possible from condemning those who pray toward Mekka, and say: "There is no god but God and Muḥammad is His Apostle", without contradicting (by what they say and do) this confession of faith'.[41] The sin of leaving alive a thousand Kāfirs is far less grave than that of shedding just a few drops of the blood of one Muslim.

The sacred text itself provides us only with the rule that we should condemn as a Kāfir anyone who gives the lie to the Apostle (*takfīr al-mukadhdhib li-al-rasūl*), and nothing beyond that. And the people of the fourth category are not

41. *Fayṣal*, p. 195.

mukadhdhib in this sense. Besides, there is no definite text to the effect that a mistake in allegorical interpretation demands *takfīr*. The conclusion is that, except in case of an open straightforward *takdhīb*, the theologians are under the protective power of the confession of faith.

(5) Those who, though they do not make an open *takdhīb*, deny any one of the fundamental articles of the Sacred Law that can be traced back to the Apostle of God himself by an uninterrupted chain of reporters, and says; 'I do not know whether this really comes from the Apostle or not'. An example of this is a man who persists in his opinion that the five daily prayers are not a religious duty, however much we try (to make him understand the truth by) quoting from the Koran and Tradition, and keeps on saying, 'I am not sure if this really goes back to the Apostle of God; it may even be a wilful falsification!' Likewise a man who says, "I admit that the pilgrimage to Mekka is a religious duty, but I do not know where Mekka is, where the Kaʿba is, nor do I know if the place toward which the people face in their prayer and to which they go on pilgrimage is really the place which the Apostle of God visited and to which the Koran has referred'.

People of this category are obviously *mukadhdhib*, and therefore fully deserve *takfīr*, for the authentic Ḥadīths going back to the Prophet himself are naturally within the reach of the common folk, not to speak of the scholars. This rule of *takfīr*, however, does not apply to those who have been converted to Islam only recently, nor to those to whom any particular Tradition has not yet come regarding the specific subject in question.

Distinction must also be made in connection with this problem between the 'essentials' or 'fundamentals' (*uṣūl*) and 'non-fundamentals' (*furūʿ*). Everything that has no direct bearing on God, the Apostle, and the Last Day is a non-essential. And the rule must be: 'No *takfīr* at all in non-essentials (*la takfīr fī al-furūʿ aṣlan*)'. The regulations about Pilgrimage and Worship belong to the category of essentials, but the knowledge, for example, of Muḥammad's having married Ḥafṣah, daughter of 'Umar, and of the Caliph Abū Bakr's having really existed, etc., is a non-essential, and he who denies the veracity of Tradition in these matters is not liable to be condemned. Such a man forms properly the

---

42. The paragraph that follows is based on *Fayṣal*, p. 195, while the rest of the whole section dealing with the six degrees of *takfīr* is based on *Iqtiṣād*. [ref. number missing in the original text.]

object of *takhṭi'ah* 'declaring (something) to be a mistake' (in the case of legal problems), or *tabdīʿ* 'considering as an innovation *bidʿah* (in the case of the problem of the Imamate, for instance). A man who entertains a wrong idea of the Imamate is not a Kāfir. Ibn Kaysān,[43] for example, went so far as to deny the necessity itself of the Imamate. But this does not constitute a reason why he should be condemned as a Kāfir, for it does not lead to *takdhīb* of the Apostle. Ibn Kaysān is a Kāfir only to the fanatics of Shīʿah who attach such an importance to the Imamate that in their minds the belief in the Imām and the belief in God are of coordinate rank, which is of course absurd.

(6) Nor should we condemn a man lightly as a Kāfir simply because he denies something that has been established by the Consensus (*ijmāʿ*). The *takfīr* of such a man, according to Ghazālī, is very problematic. It is not easy to decide whether a man is a Kāfir or not, if he neither professes anything which is an open *takdhīb* of the Apostle nor denies anything established firmly by an authentic Ḥadīth going back to the Apostle in the domain of the 'essentials' of Islam, but denies something, the truth of which is based solely on the Consensus and for which there is no other proof than the Consensus. We are not even sure, Ghazālī says, as to whether we should condemn as a Kāfir the Muʿtazilite Naẓẓām who went a step further and denied the very authority of Consensus.

This hesitation to condemn one who doubts the Consensus rests on the fact that we are not so sure of the nature of Consensus as an absolute authority. It is open to serious question. The condition of the Consensus, if it is to act as an absolute authority, is that all the authoritative scholars (*ahl al-ḥall wa-al-ʿaqd*) of an age have agreed unanimously and openly on one and the same solution, and then have continued to agree for some time or, according to some, till the end of the age. Such absolute authority is achieved when the Caliph sends letters to every quarter of the earth and collects the formal opinions (*fatwá*) of all the authoritative scholars in one period and succeeds in showing the unanimous agreement of their opinions on a certain question in such a way that nobody will be allowed to repeal it or to oppose it.

This is possible in theory, but in practice extremely difficult to achieve if not absolutely impossible. Furthermore, even after the establishment of the Consensus of this nature, there still remains the question of whether we could

43. d. 320/932, or 299/911–12.

justifiably exercise *takfīr* against everybody who acts against it, because it is quite possible that the authorities consulted have agreed by mere chance, and some of them may withdraw from the Consensus later. But the withdrawal of even one member is enough to invalidate the agreement. Besides, how could we expect everybody to know immediately the Consensus on all matters? We come to know the points of agreement and disagreement among the authoritative scholars of the past gradually and step by step, through a long process of study. In other words, there are always many people to whom the Consensus has not come. When such a person has done or said something against the Consensus, he is simply a *jāhil* 'ignorant man' or a *mukhṭiʾ* 'one who has made a mistake'; surely he is not a *mukadhdhib*. And since there is no *takdhīb* involved, he cannot be condemned as a Kāfir.

The foregoing is an almost literal reproduction of a whole section in *Iqtiṣād* and *Fayṣal* dealing with the problem of *takdhīb*. What Ghazālī intends to do here is, as I said before, to check and bridle the excessive and inconsiderate use of *takdhīb* among the Muslims against each other. The entire theory is constructed, not for its own sake, but quite obviously with a view to providing a practical rule of right and reasonable conduct in matters that concern dogmatic positions. That is why the theory is based on an extremely simple principle, namely that *takfīr* must be exercised only and exclusively when there is *takdhīb*.

This simple principle, however, raised a very grave theoretic problem regarding the practice of *taʾwīl* because for many Muslim thinkers *taʾwīl* was nothing but a most obvious case of *takdhīb* against God and the Apostle.[44] Ghazālī allots a large space in *Fayṣal* to this problem. But it would take us too far beyond the scope of the present study to go into the details of his theory. We shall be content with giving here some of the most relevant points.[45]

Now *taʾwīl* is an 'allegorical'—or rather we should say 'non-literal'— interpretation of the sacred texts, both the Koran and the Ḥadīth. The point Ghazālī makes is, in the first place, that every *taʾwīl* does not necessarily constitute *kufr*. A man is not a Kāfir simply because he has practised *taʾwīl*, in interpreting

44. The *Iqtiṣād* does not go further into this problem. What follows is based on *Fayṣal* p. 200.

45. *Fayṣal*, pp. 175–199.

sacred words. So long as he keeps to the right norm of non-literal interpretation he is not to be condemned as a Kāfir. In fact Ghazālī takes the position that no one, not even one single Muslim, can do entirely without *ta'wīl*. Even Aḥmad b. Ḥanbal, who was admittedly the farthest removed from the practice of *ta'wīl*, had to resort to it occasionally. 'In Baghdād I heard personally from those who were considered the authorities of the Ḥanbalite school that Ibn Ḥanbal applied a non-literal interpretation to three Ḥadīths'. If Ibn Ḥanbal restricted the application of this type of interpretation to only three Ḥadīths, Ghazālī adds, it was merely because he was not a man who would go deep into logical thinking; otherwise he would have seen himself forced to extend *ta'wīl* to a lot of other Ḥadīths.

The first of the three Ḥadīths here in question, to give a concrete example, is: *al-ḥajar al-aswad yamīn Allāh fī al-arḍ*, 'The black stone (of Kaʿba) is the right hand of God on the earth'. The word *yamīn* 'right hand' must be understood metaphorically, and not literally, for a literal interpretation would inevitably lead to a crude type of anthropomorphism. One usually kisses the right hand of a man whom one desires to approach. Likewise the Muslim kisses the black stone as a means of approaching God. In this sense the black stone is similar to the right hand, 'not in its essence, nor in its essential attributes, but in one of its accidental attributes', and it is called 'the right hand' only in this sense. Ghazālī observes that, of all possible ways of non-literal interpretation, this represents the one which is a farthest removed from the 'literal' understanding of the words. 'It is remarkable that a man[46] who kept himself away from the non-literal interpretation was forced to have recourse to an interpretation which is as far away from the literal interpretation as possible'.

The basic condition of the right exercise of *ta'wīl* is that there should be a definite proof (*burhān*) showing the impossibility of the 'literal' *ẓāhir* interpretation. He who lays his hands on revealed words, particularly those that represent essential concepts of Islam, and changes the *ẓāhir* by an arbitrary interpretation, without any *burhān*, must be condemned immediately as a Kāfir. The philosophers who, by their sophistry, try to deny the literal truth of the Resurrection of the bodies must be considered Kāfirs, for there is no *burhān* at all that it is impossible for the spirits of the dead to come back to their former

46. I.e. Ibn Ḥanbal.

bodies on the Last Day. Likewise, the non-literal interpretation of the Garden and the Fire and other eschatological terms is liable to *takfīr*. These are all matters firmly established by an uninterrupted Tradition, and they do not allow of *ta'wīl*, for it is inconceivable that any *burhān* should be found in favor of an allegorical interpretation, which, in these cases, would amount to sheer negation of the eschatological facts.

But in case a key-concept essentially allows of such an interpretation, even a metaphorical interpretation far removed from the literal one, we must examine carefully its *burhān*. And if we find the *burhān* to be conclusive, we must profess it. However, even in cases of this sort, if our open profession of such an interpretation is likely to do more harm than good to the naive belief of the common folk, then making such a thesis public would constitute the sin of *bidʿah* 'innovation'. In case the *burhān* adduced for *ta'wīl* is not definitely conclusive but is not of such a nature that it might do harm to the religion, professing it is, again, *bidʿah*, and not *kufr*. The Muʿtazilites' negation of the visibility of God on the Day of Resurrection is an example in point. In case it is likely to do harm to the religion, the question must be regarded as subject to *ijtihād*;[47] it may or may not be condemned as *kufr* depending upon the view of the *mujtahid*.

When the non-literal interpretation proposed is completely arbitrary and goes beyond the bounds of the Arabic language, it is of course downright *kufr* and he who proposes it is a *mukadhdhib*, that is, Kāfir. Some of the *Bāṭiniyyah*, for example, understand the word *wāḥid* 'one' in the sentence 'Verily God is one!' in the sense of 'the giver and creator of unity', and the word *ʿālim* 'knower' as a divine name in the sense of 'one who provides knowledge', the word *mawjūd* 'existent' in the sense of 'one who gives existence to others' thereby denying that God Himself is the One, the Knower, and the Existent. When *ta'wīl* goes to this degree, it is no longer *ta'wīl*, because in Arabic the word *wāḥid* 'one' can never mean *ījād al-waḥdah* 'the creation of one-ness'. This is nothing other than *kufr*.

---

47. That is to say, recourse must be had to the opinion of an authoritative scholar (*mujtahid*) who has the right to make decisions.

CHAPTER III

THE GRAVE SINNER (*FĀSIQ*)

I The concept of the grave sin (*kabīrah*)

The Khārijites raised various questions around the central concept of *kufr*. Though most of the questions were still of practical significance rather than of a purely theoretic and theological nature, they gave an enormous impetus to the development of theological thinking among the Muslims and thus became the origin of many of the important theological concepts. One of them was *takfīr* which we have examined in the previous chapter. In this chapter we are going to take up for consideration another key-concept, 'the grave sin' *kabīrah*, which was brought to the foreground of attention in the Muslim community by what the Khārijites did and said.

The concept of the grave or mortal sin has direct scriptural basis in the Koran; namely, in Sūrah XLII, 37, the word *kabā'ir* (pl. of *kabīrah*) occurs in the sense of 'grave sins'.[1] The word *kabīrah* literally means 'big' or 'great'. And if there are 'big' sins, we must logically suppose that there are also 'small' sins, because the concept of a 'big' sin would be meaningless if it is not contrasted with that of a 'small' sin. Thus the distinction itself between grave and light sins stands, albeit indirectly, on a scriptural basis.

The real problem begins, however, when one begins to ask in a concrete situation as to whether a given act should be classified under the one or the other

1. … *wa-alladhīna yajtanibūna kabā'ira al-ithmi…*' and those who avoid the worst of sins'.

of the two categories. Drinking wine, for example, is surely a sin because it is an act of disobedience to God's command. But is it a 'big' sin or a 'small' sin? Only one thing is absolutely certain: *shirk* which, as we have seen in the foregoing, means 'associating anything with God' that is, 'polytheism' or 'idolatry', is a grave, unpardonable sin. The Koran makes this clear beyond any doubt when it declares:[2] 'Verily God will never forgive that anything should be associated with Him. But other than this He forgives whom He will'. But are we right in taking this to mean that the *shirk* is the only grave sin and, consequently, anything other than that (*mā dūna dhālika*) is a 'small' sin? Or are there many grave sins other than *shirk*? And if so, where should we draw the line of demarcation between the two categories? The Koran does not make this point definitely clear.

The extremists among the Khārijites, the Azraqites, as we have seen, simplified the matter by declaring that all those who did not belong to their camp are guilty of *shirk*. This, however, by no means solved the problem satisfactorily.

The concept of sin itself is not difficult to define in Islam. The Koran suggests that a sinner is one who disobeys God's commands. The sin, in other words, is an act of 'disobedience' (*maʿṣiyah*), which is the opposite of 'obedience' (*ṭāʿah*). The Islamic concept of sin is based on this opposition.

> *Ṭāʿah* means that a man acts in conformity with what somebody else has commanded him to do. Anyone who does so is 'obedient' *muṭīʿ*. It follows that *maʿṣiyah* means that a man acts against what he has been commanded to do, and does what he has been prohibited to do.[3]

The trouble is that 'disobedience' to God seems to have many degrees. In more concrete terms, although *shirk* and drinking wine, for example, are both evidently acts of 'disobedience', it is difficult to suppose that they represent exactly the same degree of sinfulness.

This situation is reflected in Tradition. A well-known Ḥadīth going back to ʿAbd Allāh b. Masʿūd reads:[4]

> A certain man once asked the Apostle, 'O Apostle of God, what is the greatest

2. Koran, IV, 116: *Inna Allāha lā yaghfiru an yushraka bi-hi, wa-yaghfiru mā dūna dhālika li-man yashā'u*. Cf. also IV, 50–52.

3. Baghdādī, *Uṣūl al-Dīn*, pp. 251–252.

4. Muslim, *Ṣaḥīḥ*, *Īmān*, No. 141.

> sin in the eyes of God?'[5] The Prophet replied, 'That you should worship anything with God, when He alone created you'. The man then said, 'And what comes next?' The Prophet replied, 'That you should kill your child for fear of his partaking (later) of your food.' The man went on to ask, 'And what comes next?' The Prophet said, 'That you should commit adultery with the wife of your neighbor.'

It is worthy of notice that in the Ḥadīth here quoted, no distinction is made between the purely religious sin (i.e. that of *shirk*) and crimes belonging to the domain of human relationships in the society. All these are 'big' sins, and the difference between them is a matter of degree rather than that of nature. This Ḥadīth is regarded by Wensinck[6] as representing the first stage in the development of the concept of *kabīrah*.

The second stage, in his opinion, is represented by Ḥadīth No. 144 of the same Book, in which seven grave sins are enumerated. This time the word actually used for the 'grave sins' is *mūbiqāt*, lit. 'destructive ones', that is, those sins that lead to perdition. The underlying idea is obviously the same as *kabīrah*. The seven 'mortal' sins mentioned are (1) *shirk*, (2) magic, (3) unlawful taking of human life, (4) spending the money of orphans, (5) usury, (6) desertion from the battlefield, (7) slandering chaste but heedless Muslim women.

It is thus clear that, from the very beginning, *shirk* was regarded by common consent not only as a 'big' sin, but the 'biggest' *akbar* of all big sins. And this has never been questioned in the history of theology. But this was also almost the only point of perfect agreement among the Muslim thinkers. Beyond this point, everybody took the way he liked, and opinion was divided.

The Khārijites, whose thought we studied in the preceding chapters, were not ignorant of the distinction between the grave sins and venial sins. The Najdites among them, for example, taught that grave sins were *kufr* and those who were guilty of them would be punished in Hell forever, while those who were guilty only of venial sins would be punished, but not eternally, perhaps

---

5. *Ayy al-dhanb akbar* lit. 'which of the sins in the greatest'. We must remark that the word *kabīr* 'big' 'great' itself is used here. In a variant another word *ʿaẓīm* is used with the same meaning. For an interesting use of the word *ʿaẓīm* in the sense of 'something disgraceful' 'shame' see *Dīwān al-Ḥamāsah*, Cairo, 1951, CDXXXI, v. 2. The Koran also uses it in this sense, XXXIII, 53.

6. *Muslim Creed*, p. 39.

in Hell, perhaps not. But the distinction itself was not elaborated by the Khārijites theoretically. As we have observed more than once, they were much more concerned with the immediate practical consequence of a man's committing a grave sin than with the problem of how to define the concept of the grave sin itself. Those who have committed a grave sin, whatever it is, are to be excluded from the Muslim community as being no longer Muslims; they are Kāfirs (or Mushriks), and are, therefore, liable to be killed lawfully. This equation of grave sin and *kufr*, with all the consequences of the equation, dominated their thinking. As to the conceptual structure of the grave sin, they did not take the trouble to analyze it theoretically.

The Murji'ites (*murji'ah*), who succeed the Khārijites in the history of Islamic theology, made a remarkable contribution toward the development of theological thinking among the Muslims by theorizing on the problem of the concept of 'belief' *īmān*, as we shall see presently. But they do not seem to have made any major contribution regarding the concept of the grave sin. Ashʿarī writes about the Murji'ites:[7]

> There are two main currents among them on this particular problem. According to one, every act of disobedience constitutes a grave sin, that is, whenever a man disobeys God in any matter, there is a *kabīrah*. (This was the opinion of Bishr al-Marīsī[8] and others). According to the other, the acts of disobedience are two kinds: great and small.

But beyond this point Ashʿarī does not give us any information, except about a few points of minor importance. He remarks, for example, that opinion was divided among the Murji'ites into two on the question of sins committed by the Prophets. 'All acts of disobedience', one party held, 'done by a Prophet are grave sins'. People of this group declared furthermore that it was possible for a Prophet to commit any *kabīrah* such as murder and adultery. The other party held that 'all acts of disobedience done by a Prophet constitute only small sins'.[9]

The Muʿtazilites in general recognized the basic distinction between 'big' and 'small' sins. And some of them explained this conceptual pair by saying:

> Everything for which there is *waʿīd* (lit. 'threat', i.e. a divine chastisement

7. *Maqālāt*, p. 150.
8. On this Murji'ite thinker more will be said in the following chapter.
9. *Op. cit.* p. 151.

> definitely stated in the Revelation) is 'big', whereas any act of disobedience for which there is no *waʿīd* is 'small'. Others took the view that not only everything which is the direct object of *waʿīd* is 'big' but so is also everything which is similar to it in degree, and that everything for which there is no *waʿīd* or anything analogous to it can be either 'small' entirely or partly 'small' and partly 'big', but it can never happen that such an act should be neither 'small' nor even partly 'small'. Jaʿfar b. Mubashshir of the Baghdād school taught that all intention (to commit a sin) was a 'big' sin, and all those who committed an act of disobedience intentionally were grave sinners.[10]

Al-Jubbāʾī had a somewhat different thing to tell about the distinction between these two kinds of sin.[11]

> It is of the nature of a 'small' sin that the man who has committed it will obtain the right to be pardoned if he avoids 'big' sins, whereas all 'big' sins are such that they will nullify whatever Divine reward a man deserves for his belief; but the avoidance of 'big' sins nullifies Divine punishment for 'small' sins. Moreover, he used to say, the resolution (*ʿazm*) to do a 'big' sin is itself a 'small' sin; likewise, the resolution to do *kufr* is *kufr*. Abū Hudhayl held a similar view, namely, that anyone who has made a resolution to do something is just the same as he who has done it.

The emphasis upon 'resolution' points to the importance attached by the Muʿtazilites to intention in ethico-religious acts. Before the Muʿtazilites, however, the Murjiʾites had already put forward a sort of motivation theory in ethics, as we shall see in the following chapter. Dr. Albert Nader in his study of the philosophical system of the Muʿtazilites[12] points out with great emphasis as another remarkable characteristic of the Muʿtazilite theory of sin, the supremacy given in it to the Law of Reason (*al-sharīʿah al-ʿaqliyyah* as he calls it) over against the Divine Law (or *al-sharīʿah al-nabawiyyah* 'the Law of the Prophet'). Dr. Nader points out that to commit a grave sin means, in the Muʿtazilite system, to violate something which Reason has judged to be good. 'Disobedience' *maʿṣiyah* means here primarily 'disobedience against the natural Law of Reason'. This interpretation squares quite remarkably with the general tendency of the Muʿtazilite thought. And yet the words of Ashʿarī quoted above

10. The following passage is taken from Ashʿarī, *op. cit.* pp. 270–271.
11. Ashʿarī, p. 270.
12. *Falsafah al-Muʿtazilah*, II, 1951, pp. 111–112.

about the Muʿtazilites' having made *waʿīd* the basic criterion of 'big' and 'small' sins, would seem to show that the matter was not in reality so simple.

Be this as it may, it is clear that even the Muʿtazilite thinkers did not work out an elaborate and sophisticated theory of the grave sin.

They had a far more important problem to occupy their minds in connection with the concept of *kabīrah*. We shall examine this problem in the second half of the present chapter.

But before we turn to it, we shall give here an English translation of a whole paragraph from Abū ʿUdhbah's famous book,[13] which will provide us with a fairly accurate picture showing to what extent the intellectual spokesmen of the wider Muslim community went in theorizing systematically on this problem.

> (The definition of) *kabīrah* is that for which a definite legal punishment has been fixed as obligatory. (Several degrees are recognizable in it:) the 'biggest' of all 'big' sins is associating something with God (i.e. *shirk*), and the 'smallest' of them all is the drinking of wine.
>
> Some expand the above definition and assert that a sin which is in itself 'small' *ṣaghīrah* constitutes also a 'big' sin in case one persists in doing it. This is based on a Ḥadīth to the effect that there is no *kabīrah* with *istighfār* (asking pardon, i.e. when one repents sincerely and asks God's forgiveness) as there is no *ṣaghīrah* with *iṣrār* (persistence). …
>
> Some add the remark that (there is no fixed number of the grave sins;) as to some Ḥadīths in which a definite number is mentioned like the one in which the Apostle admonishes 'to avoid seven mortal sins',[14] they show only that the Apostle acted in accordance with some particular situation, in that particular time, in which the personal circumstance of the man who asked the question called for a definite number in the answer. And this does not by any means suggest that there is no other grave sins than that.
>
> There is a man who made a classification of the grave sins according to the parts of the human body. It is the great Master Abū Ṭālib al-Makkī.[15]
>
> His theory is as follows:
>
> The grave sins are seventeen in number. (A) Four of them are in the heart

13. *al-Rawḍah al-Bahiyyah fī-mā bayna al-Ashāʿirah wa-al-Māturīdiyyah*, Haydarabad, 1904, p. 60.

14. See above, p. 37.

15. Abū Ṭālib al-Makkī (d. 996), the famous author of *Qūt al-Qulūb*.

(*qalb*): (1) *shirk*, (2) persistence in any act of disobedience to God, (3) feeling perfectly secure from God's stratagem (4) sheer despair of God's mercy. (B) Four in the tongue (*lisān*): (5) perjury, (6) slandering chaste women, (7) swearing a false oath, (8) telling a lie. (C) Three in the belly (*baṭn*): (9) drinking wine, (10) eating orphans' wealth, (11) 'eating usury'. (D) Two in genitals (*farj*): (12) adultery, (13) sodomy. (E) Two in the body (*badan*): (14) murder, (15) theft. (F) One in the foot (*rijl*): (16) running away from the battlefront. (G) One in the whole body (*jamīʿ al-badan*): (17) disrespectfullness toward one's own parents.

Once you know what *kabīrah* is, (you know automatically what *ṣaghīrah* is:) any sin that is not *kabīrah* is *ṣaghīrah*.

II The grave sinner (*murtakib al-kabīrah*)

The foregoing has, I think, made it clear that the early theologians did not elaborate very much the theory of the grave sin. They did not care to analyze the concept itself of *kabīrah* because their major concern lay elsewhere. Leaving this concept in a somewhat nebulous state, they were engaged mainly and positively in discussing the problem of the exact status of a man within the Muslim community who has committed a grave sin. In other words, *murtakib al-kabīrah*, and not *kabīrah*, was for them the key-concept in their thinking. Is a Muslim who has committed a grave sin still truly a Muslim? If not, how should we properly classify such a man? These were the pivotal questions. Clearly, this is nothing other than a continuation and a further theoretical development of the vital problems raised by the Khārijites in such a drastic and brutal way.

Four different interpretations of the grave sinner appear in the early history of Muslim theology:

I Such a man is a downright Kāfir or even a Mushrik (the Khārijites).

II He is still a Muslim, a believer (the Murji'ites, and later, Orthodoxy.)

III He is neither a Muslim nor a Kāfir, belongs to an independent category between the two (the Muʿtazilites).

IV He is a hypocrite (Ḥasan al-Baṣrī).

Let us now examine these four positions in detail. The Khārijite position has already been discussed in the preceding chapters. The briefest and most widely accepted formula for it is: 'Anyone who has committed a sin is a Kāfir' (Baghdādī),[16] or 'He who has committed a grave sin, nay even a light sin, is a Kāfir' (Taftāzānī).[17] To be exact, such a formula does not by any means do full justice to the historical reality, because it was not the case that all Khārijites agreed with each other on this point. As we have seen, there was considerable divergence of opinion among them. Baghdādī himself admits immediately after giving the above formula that the Azraqites took the view that a grave sinner was not only a Kāfir but a Mushrik, while the Najdites declared that a grave sinner was merely a Kāfir 'of favor'—i.e. a Kāfir in the sense of one who is ungrateful for the Divine favor received—and not a Mushrik. To this we may add the following information given by Ibn Ḥazm.[18] The Ṣufriyyah, a sub-sect of the Khārijites, he says, hold that in case the sin committed is a grave sin the man is a Mushrik just as any worshipper of idols, but if it is a light sin he is not even a Kāfir. And according to the Ibāḍiyyah, Ibn Ḥazm goes on to say, even if the sin committed is a grave one, the man is a Kāfir 'of favor' and the relations of inheritance and marriage between him and other Muslims are to be regarded as lawful, and the animal slaughtered by him is not *ḥarām*; he is, properly speaking, neither a pure believer nor a pure Kāfir.

And yet we must admit that, on the whole, and viewed from some distance the short and concise formula of Baghdādī or Taftāzānī does represent the very gist of the Khārijite thesis in its most typical aspect. And as a matter of historical fact, the later theologians, when they attacked the Khārijites for their fanatical *takfīr*, usually held before their minds' eye the thesis in the form of some such formula.

Malaṭī, for example, argues against the Khārijites in the following way, focusing his attack upon two points: (1) the Khārijites' *takfīr* of all grave sinners, and (2) their not making any distinction between *kabīrah* and *ṣaghīrah*.[19]

> We would ask them in respect of their *takfīr* of people: 'Why do you regard as a Kāfir a man who acknowledges God, His Apostle and His religion, as soon as he commits a grave sin?'
>
> They will answer: 'By an inference from God's own words like "Whoever

16. *Uṣul al-Dīn*, pp. 249–250.
17. *Op. cit.* p. 412.
18. *Fiṣal* IV, p. 229.
19. *Tanbīh*, pp. 52–53.

denies the faith (*īmān*), vain indeed is his entire work" (V, 5), "He it is who created you, but some of you are Kāfirs and some of you are Believers" (LXIV, 2). It is clear that God has not put between *kufr* and *īmān* a third term. And he who has renounced his belief and made his entire work vain is nothing but a Mushrik. Belief is the most important of all acts, and is the very first religious duty to be fulfilled. Whoever does not do what God has commanded him to do, nullifies his own work and belief, and whoever nullifies his work is a man without belief, and a man without belief is no other than a Mushrik-Kāfir'[20]

This argument (Malaṭī continues) is based on an erroneous interpretation of the Koran, for the latter affirms that a man who has committed a grave sin (*fāsiq*)[21] is a third category between Muslim and Kāfir. "and those who accuse chaste woman (of adultery).... are indeed Fāsiqs". (XXIV, 4) Here God does not regard as Kāfirs those who falsely accuse chaste women,[22] nor does He put them in the category of Believers in spite of their sinful act.[23] He simply attaches the name of Fāsiq to them. So this kind of people are Fāsiqs, neither Believers nor Kāfirs.[24] Besides, the Muslim community as a whole is at one in applying the name of *fisq* to those who have committed a grave sin. The community is also agreed that *fisq* is an intermediate category between *kufr* and *īmān*.

(As regards the Khārijites' not making any distinction between grave and light sins,) we may ask them, 'Why do you lump together *kabīrah* and *ṣaghīrah* in one class, whereas God Himself has made a clear distinction between the two when He says "If only you avoid the *kabā'ir* (pl. of *kabīrah*) of what you

---

20. Note that in this argument the importance of 'work' *'amal* is very much emphasized. Indeed, this is one of the most remarkable theoretical consequences of the Khārijite position. The Khārijites, as we have seen, used to judge people by what they did. Theoretically this would mean that inner faith alone is not enough to make a man a real Muslim, his faith must be corroborated by his work. This theoretical implication of the Khārijite position, however, was made clear and manifest only by the Murji'ites when they took the opposite view on this problem and asserted the essential irrelevance of work to belief. This point will be dealt with fully in the following chapters.

21. *Fāsiq=murtakib al-kabīrah.*

22. as the Khārijites do.

23. as the Murji'ites do.

24. As we shall see presently, this is the Mu'tazilite position on this important problem.

> have been forbidden to do, We will surely forgive all other evils of yours" (IV, 31)?'
>
> The Khārijites thus regard all sins indiscriminately as *kabā'ir*, but they can never justify their position by Reason nor by Revelation.

Many Ḥadīths have come down to us showing how the early non-Khārijite Muslims reacted to this Khārijite attitude. One of the most interesting is Ḥadīth 29 given by Bukhārī in the Book of Belief. This Ḥadīth is extremely interesting and important because both the circumstance described and the wording used show that it represents in all probability the Prophet's own attitude to this problem which was going to arise immediately after his death.

> (Abū Dharr said: Once I went to the Prophet and made the following confession): 'I have inveighed against a man (one of my servants). I have reviled him by (reviling) his mother'[25] The Prophet said to me, 'O Abū Dharr, have you reviled him by (reviling) his mother?! Indeed, you still keep in yourself a remnant of Jāhiliyyah! (Remember that) your servants *are* your brethren'.

Bukhārī adds to this a personal remark which puts this Ḥadīth in direct connection with the Khārijite position. 'All acts of disobedience', he says, 'pertain to Jāhiliyyah.[26] (In other words) he who has committed such an act should not be immediately labelled as a Kāfir, except in case it happens to be *shirk*. This (interpretation) is based on the Prophet's words (just quoted) "you still keep in yourself a remnant of Jāhiliyyah" and also on the words of God: "Verily God will never forgive that anything should be associated with Him. But other than this he forgives whom He will". (IV, 116)' What Bukhārī wants to assert here is that Abū Dharr, though he committed an act of disobedience, was none the less a real Muslim, for the Prophet himself called his act an act of Jāhiliyyah, not *kufr*. By the strict standard of the Khārijites, such a pious Muslim as Abū Dharr would have been condemned as a Kāfir.

Now we turn to the Murji'ite position, which, in its extreme form, is dia-

---

25. Reviling a man by reviling his mother was to hurl against him the most unbearable invective.

26. For a detailed discussion of the meaning of 'Jāhiliyyah' see my *God and Man*, Chap. VIII, p. 198 sqq.

27. *Ṣaḥīḥ al-Bukhārī* (with com. by al-Kirmanī) vol. I, Cairo, 1939. [ref. number missing in the original text.]

metrically opposed to the Khārijite thesis, and which Ibn Ḥazm formulates as follows:[28] 'A grave sinner (*murtakib al-kabīrah*) is a Believer with his belief intact. It is all the same if he has never done a single act of good and has never refrained from doing evil acts'. In reality, however, already in the latter phase of Khārijism, a strong tendency toward moderatism is clearly discernible. The intransigent idealism of the early Khārijites ran against the solid wall of reality. And the later Khārijites were forced to admit willy-nilly that it was a better policy to act more moderately in accordance with the demands of the actual political situation in which they were living. Murji'ism, in its origin, was but a development and actualization of this spirit of moderation.

The name itself of the Murji'ites, *murji'ah* in Arabic, is quite significant. It comes from the verb *arja'a* (infinitive *irjā'*) meaning 'to defer' or 'to postpone'. We may distinguish two distinct stages in the development of this concept among the Murji'ites. At the first stage, that is, in origin, the concept of *irjā'* was marked with a singularly political coloring. It meant 'postponing or suspending judgment' on the question of whether a particular individual was a Believer or a Kāfir. But it was not a simple matter of general principle. When they declared that one should 'suspend judgment' on this matter, they had in mind concretely the Umayyad rulers who were notoriously irreligious in their way of life. In other terms, *irjā'* meant at this stage taking up the attitude of non-commitment, or refusing to condemn as Kāfirs the rulers whose injustice was so obvious to every pious Muslim.

This attitude furnished the opponents of the Murji'ites with a good occasion to make the latter a target of most furious abuses. Nawbakhtī, for example, reports that their opponents describe them as 'those who attach themselves servilely to the ruler of the day regardless of whether he be just or unjust, comply with the government, make friends with all kinds of people indiscriminately, and assert that the People of Qiblah are all Believers because of their outward verbal acknowledgment of belief, and wish for all of them Divine forgiveness'.[29] The Murji'ites in the eyes of their opponents were political and religious opportunists.

But the Murji'ites, on their part, could easily justify themselves not only by

---

28. *Op. cit.* p. 229.

29. *Firaq al-Shī'ah*, Istanbul, 1951, p. 6. Nawbakhtī was one of the leading theologians of the Imāmiyyah sect of the Shī'ah.

pointing to the devastating effects produced by the reckless and extreme *takfīr* practised by the Khārijites, but also by adducing an essentially religious basis for their position. It is presumptuous of a man, they declared, to pass ultimate judgment on his fellow men. For how could one disprove the sincerity of a Muslim who openly professes belief? The final judgment rests with God, and God alone. In this world, even an evil-doer, if he professes Islam, is to be considered a member of the community. This was the basic thought underlying the concept of *irjā'* in the first stage.

Soon, however, the problem came to be transferred to a far more theoretical level. The Murji'ites began to theorize systematically on the nature of 'belief' in an attempt to put their 'suspension of judgment' on a solid basis. Later they apparently became interested in establishing a theory of 'belief' itself. Unlike the Khārijites, the leading thinkers of the Murji'ites proved to be excellent theoreticians equipped with keen intellect and remarkable capacity for analysis. They marked the real beginning of Muslim theology.

It is important to observe that at this second stage, the word *irjā'* no longer means 'suspension of judgment' but 'postponement', not in terms of time but in terms of ranking. More concretely, it means the 'postponement' of *work*, i.e. 'regarding it as of secondary importance', by comparison with inner *faith*. The basic idea is that the concept of 'belief' stands solely and exclusively on that of inner faith, and that what one does, whether good or evil, does not count essentially. This aspect of the Murji'ite thought, which marks one of the most decisive moments of the whole history of Muslim theology, will form the subject matter of the two following chapters. We may notice in passing that the later historians of Muslim theology usually explain the name 'Murji'ah' by this second sense. Baghdādī, for instance, says:[30] 'they are called Murji'ah simply because they put "work" after "belief" in importance'. To the main topic of the present chapter, however, the concept of *irjā'* in its second stage is rather irrelevant. What is relevant is the general Murji'ite thesis that 'sin does not do any injury where there is *īmān*, just as acts of obedience are of no use where there is *kufr*'.

It is important to remark also that Orthodoxy as a whole follows the Murji'ite tradition on this particular problem, albeit with noticeable modifications. The

30. *Firaq*, p. 190.

31. *Fiṣal* IV, p. 229. [ref. number missing in the original text.]

orthodox position is, we might say, a sort of moderate Murji'ism. Here is Ibn Ḥazm's formulation: 'The People of Sunna and Tradition and the Fuqahā hold that a man who has committed a grave sin is still a Believer; (only, he is not any longer a *perfect* Believer) he is a Fāsiq, imperfect in belief'. It is obvious that this represents also Ibn Ḥazm's own position, which is based on the usual tripartite conception[32] of 'belief' *īmān*: (1) 'assent' *taṣdīq*, (2) 'verbal confession' *iqrār*, and (3) 'work' *'amal*. Ibn Ḥazm's idea is that a grave sinner is a Believer in his 'assent' and 'verbal confession', but Fāsiq in his 'work'. It will be interesting to note that Māturīdism takes up the same attitude, but it does so from a very peculiar point of view. The Māturīdite commentator of *al-Fiqh al-Akbar*[33] says: 'The locus of belief is the heart, whereas the locus of the acts of disobedience are bodily members. In other words they occur in two entirely different places, and so they do not nullify each other. This Māturīdite, whoever he may be, makes the above remark in connection with the Article I of the *al-Fiqh al-Akbar* which runs as follows: 'We do not exercise *takfīr* against anyone because of a sin (he has committed), nor do we deny anyone his belief'.[34]

This is exactly the same as Ash'arī's thesis. In both his *Kitāb al-Ibānah* and *Maqālāt*,[35] Ash'arī, representing the People of Truth and Sunnah, declares: 'We profess that we do not exercise *takfīr* against any member of our community because of a sin he has committed, like adultery, theft, drinking wine etc.' To this *Ibānah* adds an important remark, which is not found in *Maqālāt*, that 'a man who commits any of the grave sins like adultery, theft etc. considering it licit (*ḥalāl*) and not believing it to be forbidden (*ḥarām*), must be considered a Kāfir'. On this last point, too, Māturīdism agrees with Ash'arism.

Thus we see that the orthodox position is historically a continuation of the Murji'ite thesis as far as concerns the basic attitude of refraining from the *takfīr* of grave sinners. The difference between the two, however, comes out with clarity when it comes to deciding whether such a Muslim, i.e. a Believer who has committed a grave sin, will be allowed to enter Paradise in the Hereafter. The

32. The following chapter will deal with this tripartite conception in detail.

33. *Fiqh Akbar* I, as Wensinck called it, Haydarabad, 2 ed. 1365 A.H. p. 3. The emphasis on the 'locus' *maḥall* is very characteristic of the Māturīdites, including Māturīdī himself, as we shall see later.

34. *Lā nukaffir aḥad bi-dhanb wa-lā nanfī aḥad min al-īmān*, p. 2.

35. *Kitāb al-Ibānah*, Haydarabad, 2 ed. 1948, p. 7, *Maqālāt*, p. 293.

Māturīdite just mentioned states about this problem that for the Murji'ites, the final abode of a Believer will surely be Paradise, even if he commits all sorts of *kabā'ir* and disobedience, because nothing affects his destiny if he has 'belief' in his heart. But, he adds, for the Māturīdites the only proper attitude in such cases is 'hope' and 'fear'; in other words, they sincerely hope and wish for such a Muslim that he will be allowed to enter Paradise, but, at the same time, they cannot help feeling an intense fear as to his destiny.[36]

The attitude of the Muʿtazilites toward this problem is almost a commonplace among those who have ever studied the history of Islamic culture. It is generally known as *al-manzilah bayna al-manzilatayn* 'the (intermediate) position between the two (extreme) positions'. And the anecdote of Wāṣil b. 'Aṭā' who separated himself from the circle of Ḥasan al-Baṣrī because of the difference of opinion on this point is too well-known to be repeated here. Ibn Ḥazm[37] describes the Muʿtazilite position as follows: 'In case what has been committed happens to be a grave sin, the man is a Fāsiq, neither a Believer nor a Kāfir, nor, indeed, a Munāfiq (hypocrite).[38] This implies that, according to the Muʿtazilites, the normal relations of marriage and inheritance are considered licit between such a man and other Muslims, and that the animal slaughtered by him is *ḥalāl* to others. In case the sin happens to be only a "small" one, the man remains a Believer unconditionally'.

What is most important to note is the fact that the Muʿtazilites made out of the Fāsiq an independent category having its proper place as an intermediary between the Believer-Muslim and the Kāfir. In ordinary conditions, the word *fāsiq* simply means a 'sinner', and in theology it is, as we saw above, a synonym of *murtakib al-kabīrah* 'one who has committed a grave sin'. Such a person may still be a Believer (i.e. Believer-Fāsiq); or he is a Kāfir (i.e. Fāsiq-Kāfir). The Fāsiq, in other words, does not constitute a third, independent category. On this point, the Muʿtazilites differed from all other schools.

---

36. *Op. cit.* p. 16.

37. *Fiṣal* IV, p. 229.

38. This addition of Munāfiq is made in particular reference to Ḥasan al-Baṣrī's thesis which we will examine in the next section. As the name itself of *al-manzilah bayna al-manzilatayn* indicates, usually two categories only, Believer-Muslim and Kāfir, are taken into account in defining the Muʿtazilite concept of Fāsiq.

This does not mean that the Muʿtazilites denied the existence of a modicum of 'belief' in the heart of a Fāsiq. 'Even in a Fāsiq there may be belief, but we do not call him a Believer because of that belief. Likewise in a Jew there may be belief, but we do not call him, because of that, a Believer'.[39] On this point, the great Muʿtazilite thinker Jubbāʾī put forward an interesting original theory. The following is a passage from Ashʿarī's *Maqālāt*.[40]

> Muḥammad b. ʿAbd al-Wahhāb al-Jubbāʾī used to make the following assertion. Having faith in God[41] consists of all that God has imposed upon His servants as religious duties,[42] though those of a supererogatory nature are excluded therefrom. Each one of the constituent elements (*khiṣāl*) which God has commanded man to observe is part of the faith that man puts in God, and it is also belief in God (*īmān bi-Allāh*).
>
> A Fāsiq of our community (may sometimes be) a Believer, if we are to name him as a mere matter of language, because of any act of belief he happens to do.
>
> Jubbāʾī used to distinguish between 'naming as a matter of language', and naming as a matter of religion'. The names of the former class are those that derive from individual acts; they pass away as the acts themselves pass away, whereas a name of the latter kind is one by which a man is named not only during the act itself but after the passing away of the act.[43] In this sense a Fāsiq of our community is a Believer, which is, in this case, a name as a matter of language, and this name passes away from him as soon as he ceases to do that particular act of belief. Such a man cannot be given the name of a Believer as a matter of religion. Jubbāʾī used to say: even in a Jew there is belief,

39. Ashʿarī, *Maqālāt*, p. 270.

40. p. 269.

41. The original expression used is *al-īmān li-Allāh*. A fine distinction is made here between *īmān li-Allāh* and *īmān bi-Allāh*. Kirmānī (Comm. *Ṣaḥīḥ al-Bukhārī*, I. p. 70) explains it in the following way: *īmān li-* means to consider somebody as truthful, to believe what somebody says, while *īmān bi* means doing so with an additional connotation of acknowledgment, formal avowal.

42. This is an explicitly anti-Murjiʾite position, as we shall see in the following chapter, the basic idea being that 'belief' does not consist in 'inner assent' alone, but comprises all 'good works'. In other words, 'belief', in such a view, has a number of 'constituent parts' (*khaṣlah*, pl. *khiṣāl*) into which it is divisible.

43. I.e. it remains behind the act as a permanent label for the man who did it.

by which we may call him a Believer and Muslim, but only as a matter of language.

Now the Muʿtazilites adduced Koranic verses and Ḥadīths in support of their thesis, namely that the Fāsiq or grave sinner constitutes a third independent category between the Believer and the Kāfir (e.g. Sūrah XXXII, verse 18).[44] Their opponents, however, could also adduce a number of verses with which to combat the Muʿtazilites. In any case, there will be in the Hereafter only the Garden and the Fire, and no third place. All Believers will enter the Garden and all Kāfirs the Fire. There will be no special place prepared for the Fāsiqs as an independent category. Under which of the two recognized categories then are we to classify the Fāsiqs (grave sinners)? Except in the case of *shirk*, which is admittedly the 'biggest' of all sins,[45] the Fāsiq belongs in the category of Muslim-Believer. A famous Ḥadīth has come down to us, in which we see Abū Dharr arguing obstinately with the Prophet about this very problem.[46] Abū Dharr, in discontent with the Prophet's words: 'Whoever says that there is no god but God and dies in this belief, will surely enter the Garden', asks him, 'Even if he commits adultery? Even if he commits theft?' This is repeated three times. Finally the Prophet puts an end to the conversation by saying, 'Yes, (such a man will enter the Garden) even against the will of Abū Dharr!'

As the Ḥadīth itself tells us most eloquently, this was not a kind of solution that would satisfy everybody, particularly the very pious Muslims represented by Abū Dharr. And yet, neither the Khārijite thesis nor the Muʿtazilite could win a victory over it. And it ended by becoming the standard orthodox conception of the Fāsiq. It goes without saying that in this process, the conception was elaborated more theoretically.

Here I give, as a concrete example of this kind of elaboration, Ibn Ḥazm's interpretation of the matter.[47] The gist of his argument is that a Believer who has committed a sin loses his belief only in that particular point. In other words,

---

44. *A-la-man kāna muʾminan ka-man kāna fāsiqan* 'Is the Believer the same as the Fāsiq?', where the Believer is clearly contrasted with the Fāsiq. But of course the anti-Muʿtazilite could easily dispose of this verse by saying that the word *fāsiq* is in this verse completely synonymous with *kāfir* (see Taftāzānī, *op. cit.* p. 414).

45. *aʿẓam al-fusūq*, Taftāzānī, p. 413. Only in this case, the sinner—Fāsiq—is a Kāfir.

46. Muslim, *Īmān*, No. 154.

47. *Fiṣal*, pp. 233–234.

by committing a sin he does not lose his belief in its entirety, but only the particular part of his belief which corresponds to that particular sin. 'Such a man is a Believer as regards his good acts, but a non-Believer as regards his evil act'. This interpretation stands on the basic idea—to which reference has been made, and which will be dealt with more specifically in the following chapter—that 'belief' consists of inner faith or assent (*taṣdīq*) and deeds (*aʿmāl*). What Ibn Ḥazm wants to say, in the light of this basic conception of belief, is that, when a Believer commits a sin, his *taṣdīq* itself remains quite unaffected in its core, but that his qualification for the title of Believer gets impaired in one of the works.

Ibn Ḥazm interprets in this sense the well-known Ḥadīth: 'No adulterer can commit adultery while being at the same time a Believer.'[48] The meaning of this, he says, is that such a man is not 'obedient' (to God's command) insofar as he commits adultery, but he is still a Believer insofar as he obeys God in other acts. True, in the Koran (X, 33), God Himself distinguishes clearly between *fisq* and *īmān* and says, 'Thus has the word of thy Lord come true concerning those who do wrong (*fasaqū*): that they do not believe (*lā yu'minūna*)'. But this, Ibn Ḥazm says, does not argue for the Muʿtazilite position. We know with certainty that *fisq* is not *īmān*, and that he who has done wrong (*fasaqa*) is no longer a Believer. But he is a non-Believer only in regard to that particular act which is *fisq*. God has never said that such a man is no longer a Believer in any respect.

Belief is a complex structure including all pious acts. *Fisq* in one act does not invalidate the merit of all the remaining acts of *īmān*, just as *īmān* in all the remaining sections does not atone for the *fisq* done in one section. Ibn Ḥazm says in conclusion, 'Our thesis is this: All Kāfirs without exception are unjust disobedient Fāsiqs, but not all unjust disobedient Fāsiqs are Kāfirs; some of them are Believers.'

Last, let us examine the thesis which classifies a Fāsiq neither as a Believer nor as a Kāfir, but as a 'hypocrite' *munāfiq*. Formally this position resembles that of the Muʿtazilite. For the Muʿtazilites, too, a Fāsiq is neither a Believer nor a Kāfir, but belongs to an independent intermediate category. But the people to whom we turn now gave a particular twist to the problem by identifying the Fāsiq as a 'hypocrite'.

48. *La yaznī al-zānī ḥīna yaznī wa-huwa mu'min* For the full form of this Ḥadīth, see Muslim, *Ṣaḥīḥ*, *Īmān*, No. 100.

Now the word *munāfiq* (or its verbal form *nifāq*) occurs very frequently in the Koran. Briefly it refers to a man who professes his belief in God and the Prophet, thereby concealing *kufr* which remains deep in his mind and which dictates to him all his actions. In the Koranic conception, the Munāfiqs form a particular section within the large category of Kāfirs.

In the post-Koranic period, the concept was discussed by some of the Khārijites. According to Ashʿarī,[49] the Ibāḍiyyah, an important sub-sect of the Khārijites to which reference has been made in the foregoing, were interested in this problem, and three different views developed among them. (1) The Munāfiq is free from *shirk*, although he is not a Believer. He is a man who is constantly fluctuating between *kufr* and *īmān*, an idea based on Sūrah IV, 142. (2) The Munāfiq is a Mushrik, because he is against *tawḥīd* 'considering God as essentially One'. (3) The Munāfiq is a name, or a fixed label which God Himself attached to certain definite persons. So we should not remove it from the place and apply it arbitrarily to those whom God did not call by that name.

But quite obviously the Ibāḍiyyah did not discuss the concept of 'hypocrisy' in terms of *fisq* and grave sins. The thesis that the grave sinner is a Munāfiq (*ṣāḥib al-kabīrah munāfiq*) is represented by the great thinker of early Islam, Ḥasan of Baṣrah. From the very early days it was famous as Ḥasan's position and was propagated under his name. In Muslim theology (in the sense of *ʿilm al-kalām*) Ḥasan al-Baṣrī occupies an important place as the representative of this position.

It is not at all sure, however, that in reality Ḥasan al-Baṣrī advanced such a simple equation. As a matter of fact, such a simple equation, would seem to disfigure and distort the deep personal piety of this great ascetic. That the equation *murtakib al-kabīrah* = *munāfiq* is the result of a mere 'Schematisierung' has been shown by Professor H. Ritter in his careful study of the early history of Islamic piety.[50] In any case it seems to be certain that the above equation is a very particular theoretical elaboration by the later theologians—and, most probably, not by Ḥasan himself—of his more general conception of the Religious Man, which, in its turn, grew out of his deep religious experience.

49. *Maqālāt*, p. 105.

50. Hans Ritter, *Studien zur Geschichte der Islamischen Frömmigkeit I* (Der Islam, XXI, 1933), to which I am greatly indebted for the following description of Ḥasan's basic thought.

Just as Ḥasan was against the Murjiʾites in the political field, so he was against their fundamental optimism in the field of theological thinking. There was, at the bottom of the Murjiʾite minds, a sense of security, a feeling that man is safe from the Divine wrath if only he believes in God. Ḥasan was opposed to such a view. Man, according to him, cannot be too fearful of the Divine wrath and punishment. Nowhere is there a final guarantee for his safety. However much he tries, however much he is pious, he cannot attain, if he is sincere, to an absolute conviction that he is going to the Garden after death.

Hence the great importance attached to 'works' *aʿmāl* in Ḥasan's thought in striking contrast to the Murjiʾite view which, as we shall see in the next chapter, tended to make light of 'works' in the conceptual structure of 'belief'. But by 'works' Ḥasan did not mean only outward works of obedience. What was of primary importance in his view was that each one of the acts should be a natural manifestation of a pure heart—a deeply pious and absolutely pure heart concerned with nothing other than the Hereafter. The cultivation of such a heart, which he calls *qalb ṣāliḥ* or *qalb salīm*, should be man's sole task throughout his earthly life. Since, however, such an absolutely pure heart is but an ideal never to be achieved completely, man should always and constantly be in the subjective state of fear (*taqwá*, *faraq*, or *khawf*). This, in brief, is Ḥasan's idea of the Perfect Man.

All those who do not consciously strive to attain to this ideal of *homo religiosus*, Ḥasan calls 'hypocrites' (Munāfiqs). In other words, a Munāfiq is a man whose concern is with the present world (*al-dunyā*) rather than with the world to come (*al-ākhirah*), who is not fearful of Divine chastisement in his life at every step. A man of this type is a 'hypocrite' because he is merely nominally Muslim; he does not take *īmān* seriously, and thus there is necessarily a discrepancy between what he says and what he does.

> The *Ṣaḥīḥ* of Bukhārī has a special section[51] devoted to this very problem, 'Concerning the fear of the Believer that his work might lose its value without his being conscious of it,'
>
> Ibrāhīm al-Taymī said: Whenever I examine what I say in the light of what I do, I cannot help feeling a profound fear that I might prove a liar. And Ibn

51. *Bāb khawf al-muʾmin min an yaḥbaṭa ʿamalu-hu wa-huwa lā yashʿuru* in the Book of Belief.

> Abī Mulaykah said: I used to know personally thirteen of the Prophet's Companions. All of them without exception were very much afraid of committing 'hypocrisy' *nifāq* against themselves. Not even one of them ever said 'My belief stands on a par with that of Gabriel and Michael.'[52]
>
> Ḥasan (al-Baṣrī) is reported to have said: No one fears Him except Believers, and no one can feel completely safe (from His chastisement) except Munāfiqs.

According to *Ḥilyah al-Awliyā*, Ḥasan classified all men under three heads: (1) Believer, (2) Kāfir, and (3) Munāfiq. The following is the explanation of these three terms by Ḥasan himself, as it is given in this book.[53]

The Believer is a man who is the best of all men in regard to work, the most fearful of all men. He is a man of such a nature that the more he does good works, pious deeds, and acts of serving God, the greater the fear he feels within himself, and feels that he will not be saved. The Munāfiq is a man who says, 'There are so many people around me (i.e. who are doing the same thing). I shall be forgiven. Nothing bad will happen to me'. Thus he goes on doing evil while indulging a hope that God (will forgive him). Ḥasan saw Munāfiqs all around him; every place swarmed with them. 'If all the Munāfiqs were to go out of Baṣrah', he said, 'the city would remain vacant'.

As regards the concept of Kāfir, Ḥasan was rather indifferent, because he saw no hope at all for real Kāfirs. His major concern was with the Munāfiq who, he taught, should not simply be excluded from the community (or killed as the Khārijites used to hold), but must be encouraged and aided to amend his way of life, for otherwise, he was in grave danger of going to perdition.

If such was the teaching of Ḥasan in its real form, then it is obvious that the formula 'grave sinner is Munāfiq' does not in any way do justice to it. However, it is also true that Ḥasan's thought entered into the main current of Muslim theology and occupied a definite place there precisely in the form of such a formula.

As a very interesting and quite an original example showing how Ḥasan's conception, thus formulated, entered into theological thinking and raised important questions, I shall give here the argument which Ibn Ḥazm brings forth

52. 'This is said against the Murji'ites who assert that the belief of even the worst type of sinner is equal to the belief of the angel Gabriel'. (Kirmānī, p. 188)

53. *Ḥilyah al-Awliyā* quoted by Ritter, p. 43.

against it. After having declared that from the viewpoint of the religion of Islam, there can be either *īmān* or *kufr*, and no third category[54]—an argument which applies equally well to the Muʿtazilite position—he begins by asking those who support Ḥasan's view, 'What is the meaning of the word *munāfiq*?'

> The only possible answer to this question is: Munāfiq is a man who has *nifāq* as his predominant attribute, the word *nifāq* here being taken in the sense of 'manifesting *īmān* while concealing (in the soul) *kufr*, which is its meaning in the Divine Law.... But who can know, except God alone, that which is in the soul and the soul itself which contains it? So we are not in a position to pronounce a judgment of *kufr* on the faith of others unless they acknowledge their own *kufr* by the tongue or unless it is confirmed by God's Revelation. And he who tries to know what is inside the souls is a man who dares to probe the Unknowable. Such probing is evidently a mistake, known as such immediately by everybody. And a thesis that will lead to an evident absurdity is the worst kind of thesis.
>
> There is reported in the Ḥadīth the following incident. Somebody said to the Prophet: 'A great many of those who participate in the ritual Worship say with their tongue what is not in their heart'. The Prophet replied: 'I assure you, I have not been sent (to you as the Messenger of God) in order to split open the hearts of men'.
>
> Again, there is in the Koran (IX, 101) the verse which reads: 'There are among those around you of the Bedouins Munāfiqs, nay even among the people of Medina there are some who persist in *nifāq*, whom thou (Muḥammad) knowest not. But We know them'. If even the Prophet was ignorant of *nifāq*-nature of those among whom he lived, how much more should this be the case with those who are not Prophets.
>
> Besides, calling something by a particular name (*tasmiyah*) in matters that pertain to the essentials of Islam—for example, calling the grave sinner *munāfiq*—belongs to God alone and to no one else. (This view of 'naming', by the way, is the very basis of Ibn Ḥazm's theology.) And if we examine the matter in the light of this basic principle, we find that nowhere does God call a grave sinner a Munāfiq. The following objection may be raised to this. By the Ḥadīth we know that the Prophet pointed out a certain number of the

54. *Fiṣal*, pp. 231–232. The following description is based on a passage extending from p. 244 to p. 246.

Munāfiq-making properties, and asserted that whoever had in himself those properties is a Munāfiq, however much he fasts and prays, however much he insists that he is a Muslim.

(To this objection Ibn Ḥazm replies, applying his original method of linguistic interpretation): 'Hypocrisy' *nifāq* in this particular Ḥadīth is not 'hypocrisy' in the technical, i.e. the particularly Islamic, sense. It is but an occurrence of the word in accordance with the common linguistic usage. *Nifāq* etymologically means 'the hole of a field-mouse' *nāfiqā' al-yarbū'*; it is a small entrance to the burrow, which the animal has covered with a little bit of earth. So Munāfiq means generally 'anybody who hides something behind him'. When the Prophet, in the Ḥadīth, applies the name of Munāfiq to those who have properties like telling lies, betrayal etc., he is using the term simply in its no-technical sense.

This usage of the word corresponds to the Divine use of the word *kuffār* (pl. of *kāfir*) in the Koran: *ka-mathali ghaythin a'jaba al-kuffāra nabātu-hu* (LVIII, 20), in which God calls the farmer a Kāfir in the non-technical sense (of 'one who covers the earth with seeds'). Since this obviously does not mean the religious *kufr* (the etymological meaning of which is said to be 'covering up the Divine favors'), so the word *nifāq* which occurs in the above-mentioned Ḥadīth does not mean *nifāq* as defined by the Divine Law.

Aside from all these linguistic considerations, we might ask: Is there anybody in the whole world who has never committed a grave sin? Even with regard to the absolute impeccability of the angels and the Prophets there is among the Muslim scholars no unanimity. If, in spite of this, there is a man who claims that he has never committed a grave sin, he is guilty of self-glorification which is so sternly forbidden by God in the Koran. Self-glorification is itself a grave sin. More generally, do we doubt God and the Prophet, even in the very moment when we are actually doing evil? Is it not rather that, even while committing a grave sin, we still firmly believe in God and the Prophet, and have the consciousness of doing something evil, something wrong? If this is true, then we must admit that committing a grave sin does not make anybody a Munāfiq.

The conclusion to be drawn from all this is that such a man is a Muslim, a Believer, but that he is at the same time a Believer-Fāsiq, that is, a Believer whose *īmān* is less than that of a Believer who is not a Fāsiq.

In the early history of Muslim theology, there is another name associated with the idea here in question, that is Bakr, the nephew of ʿAbd al-Wāḥid, a contemporary of the first Muʿtazilite thinker Wāṣil b. ʿAṭā' (beginning of the eighth century). Of Bakr's conception of the grave sinner, two entirely different versions have come down to us. One of them has already been given in the preceding chapter. According to that version, Bakr asserted that a Muslim sinner was a Kāfir to the same degree as an idol-worshipper, or even worse.[55] Another version as given by Ashʿarī runs as follows:

> All the grave sins (*kabā'ir*) committed by the People of Qiblah are acts of *nifāq* without exception. A member of the Muslim community who commits a grave sin is a worshipper of Satan (*ʿābid li-al-shayṭān*), giving God the lie (*mukadhdhib*), disavowing Him (*jāḥid*). He is a Munāfiq, who, if he dies without repentance, will be put in the lowest depth of the Fire to remain there forever. In the heart of such a man there is no veneration, no reverence for God, and yet, in spite of all that, he is a Muslim-Believer.[56]

The basic difference, despite the seeming resemblance, between Ḥasan and Bakr is quite clear. Here the grave sinner is called a Munāfiq, which is the same as in Ḥasan's case. But unlike Ḥasan, Bakr identifies the Munāfiq as a Satan-worshipper and ascribes to him all the qualities that are generally considered most characteristic of *kufr*. Particularly noticeable in this connection is the mention of *takdhīb* 'giving the lie to God', which, as we saw in the foregoing chapter, is an immediate reason for *takfīr* even in the moderate theory of Ghazālī. In other words, the Munāfiq in Bakr's terminology is nothing more nor less than a downright Kāfir. And yet, Bakr insists that the Munāfiq *is* a Muslim-Believer. Analyzed in this way, Bakr's thesis discloses its semantic inconsistency, being based on an entirely arbitrary interpretation of the term *nifāq*. But whether this second version really represents what Bakr taught is another question.

---

55. Maqrīzī, *Kitāb al-Khiṭaṭ*, Cairo, 1270 A.H., II, p. 349.
56. *Maqālāt*, p. 286.

CHAPTER IV

ĪMĀN AND *ISLĀM*

I The relation between *īmān* and *islām*

'What is Belief (*īmān*)?' 'What is Islam?' 'What does it mean, in the specifically Islamic context, to believe?' This was one of the most important theoretical problems that faced the newly-born Muslim community. The situation is quite understandable. It is clear that some formulation was needed most urgently. The need was made more urgent and more pressing by the rapid expansion of Islam. So many people with so divergent cultural and religious backgrounds came into the community, some willingly, others by force. In either case it was necessary for those new members of the community to be told what conditions they had to fulfil in order fully to bc cntitled to the name of Muslim. What were they to believe inwardly, and how were they to act outwardly? The minimum essential requirement for being a Muslim must have been a big question not only for those who had just joined the community but for those pious Muslims who had been converted to Islam during the lifetime of the Prophet, once they became conscious of themselves as Muslims surrounded all round by unbelievers.

Thus the question was raised and efforts were exerted as early as in the lifetime of the Prophet. This is faithfully mirrored in the Ḥadīth. According to what the Ḥadīth tells us, the question seems to have been raised in the earliest period of Islam in two basic forms, both of which were very concrete and close to the actual life of the Muslims, quite different in nature from the elaborate scholastic treatment of the subject in the hands of the professional theologians. (1) What should we do in order to enter Paradise in the Hereafter? The form of the question is naive and simple, but it forebodes already the more theoretical formulation that is to come later, namely; What is the structure of the concept of *īmān* in the Islamic sense? (2) What should we do in order to render our blood (i.e. life) and possessions lawfully inviolable? Compared with the first one this is much more practical and of direct political import.

The answers given in the Ḥadīth to these two questions are, as is easy to understand, practically the same. In the typical Ḥadīth[1] relating to the first form of question, the Prophet mentions, as the essentials of Islam, five commandments: (1) belief in God alone, that is, witnessing that there is no god but God and that Muḥammad is the Apostle of God, (2) correct performance of Worship, (3) handing over the *zakāt*, (4) keeping the Ramaḍān fast, and (5) paying the fifth from booty. The answer to the second form of question is given in the Ḥadīth in various forms. The most typical one reads:[2]

> (The Apostle of God said:) I am commanded to fight people until they confess 'There is no good but God and Muḥammad is the Apostle of God', and perform correctly Worship, and hand over the obligatory *zakāt*. Whoever does so has thereby rendered inviolable to me his blood and his possessions except for some particular justifying reasons (for killing and confiscation) provided by Islam. As to the real accounting of the people, God alone is able to handle it.

It is worthy of notice that, as the Ḥadīth itself clearly states, the *shahādah* (witnessing the Unity of God and the prophethood of Muḥammad) and the rest, of the rites and religious duties mentioned are but the formal conditions of Islam. In other words, anybody who performs them is thereby recognized *formally* as a member of the Muslim community. The answers given by the Prophet here do not go deep into the inner structure of belief.

Much more important and interesting from the theoretical point of view is the very famous Ḥadīth[3] connected with the questioning of Muḥammad by the angel Gabriel. Here in answer to the question of Gabriel, the Prophet gives the following definitions.

(1) 'Islam' consists in your serving God and not associating anything with Him, your performing correctly the prescribed Worship, paying the obligatory *zakāt*, and keeping the Ramaḍān fast.[4]

---

1. Bukhārī, *Ṣaḥīḥ*, *Īmān*, No. 50.
2. *Ibid.* No. 24.
3. Muslim, *Ṣaḥīḥ*, *Īmān*, No. 5.
4. A variant adds 'and the pilgrimage to Mekka when there is a means thereto'.

(2) 'Belief' *īmān* consists in your believing in God, His Angels, His book (or books), meeting with Him (in the Hereafter), His Apostles, and the final resurrection.[5]

(3) 'Perfection' *iḥsān*—that is, being a perfect Muslim[6]—is that you serve God (always) as if He were before your own eyes; for if you do not see Him, He sees you.

The concluding sentence of the same Ḥadīth tells us that Gabriel came to the Prophet and asked him these questions with the intention of teaching the Muslims what their religion (*dīn*) was. This means that the religion of Islam should, according to this Ḥadīth, be defined in terms of these three fundamental concepts. Evidently there is a certain definite structure putting the three concepts together into a system. The explanation given by Ibn Taymiyyah seems to me to be most logical and illuminating.

The three concepts, he says, form three graduated degrees in the concept of religion as understood in the Islamic sense. The highest degree is *iḥsān*, the middle *īmān*, which is followed by *islām*. Thus every *muḥsin* (man of *iḥsān*) is a *mu'min* (man of *īmān*, or Believer), and every *mu'min* is a *muslim* (man of *islām*, or Muslim), but not every *mu'min* is a *muḥsin*, nor is every *muslim* a *mu'min*.[7] In other words, the term *iḥsān* is, 'in itself (*min jihah nafsi-hi*)—i.e. in more modern terminology, as a matter of 'intention' or 'connotation'—the widest of all, and with regard to 'those who are qualified by it' (*min jihah aṣḥābi-hi*)—i.e. as a matter of 'extension' or 'denotation'—is the narrowest of the three. It is connotatively the widest because the meaning of *iḥsān* comprises within it all the characteristics or attributes of both *īmān* and *islām*. Indeed, it is the perfection of these two. Denotatively, however, it is the most narrowly delimited

5. A variant puts 'believing in the Divine foreordination regarding both good and bad' instead of 'meeting with Him'.

6. Wensinck (*Muslim Creed*, p. 23) translates *iḥsān* wrongly, I think, as 'righteousness', which makes the structure of the whole Ḥadīth incomprehensible. The word *iḥsān* in this context must be taken in the sense indicated by the common phrase used in describing a perfect Muslim: *aslama fa-ḥasuna islāmu-hu* 'he accepted Islam, and proved a perfect Muslim', not in the sense of 'doing good'. The Koran uses the word in these two senses (e.g. II, 112, II, 190 in the former sense, and XVI, 90, XVIII, 30 in the latter)—cf. Bayāḍī, *Ishārāt al-Marām min 'Ibārāt al-Imām*, Cairo, 1949, pp. 64–65. This point will be discussed more in detail presently.

7. Ibn Taymiyyah, *Kitāb al-Īmān*, Damascus, 1961, p. 4.

concept because it applies naturally to fewer people than *īmān* and *islām*.

Exactly the same relation obtains between the last two. So *iḥsān* contains *īmān*, and *īmān* contains *islām*, but the Muḥsins are more particular than the Mu'mins, and the Mu'mins are more particular than Muslims. Ibn Taymiyyah adduces as a telling example of the same nature the conceptual relation between Apostleship (*risālah*) and Prophethood (*nubuwwah*). The Prophethood is contained in the Apostleship, and the latter in its intention is wider than the former, but in its extension it is more delimited. Thus every Apostle is a Prophet, but not every Prophet is an Apostle.[8]

To this Ibn Taymiyyah adds an extremely important observation based on his own semantic theory. In reading the Koran and the Ḥadīth, he says, we must be careful to distinguish as a general rule between the absolute (*mujarrad*) mode of the usage of a term and the delimited and conditioned usage of it. When, for example, the Sacred text uses the word *īmān* in the former way, i.e. without any delimitation, then it must be understood in its natural, widest sense comprising within it the meaning of *islām*, that is, 'good works'. To believe, in this sense, is not only to believe inwardly but also to act in accordance with what the belief dictates. But when the words *īmān* and *islām* occur side by side, the meaning area of *īmān* is thereby delimited. In that case *īmān* means only and specifically the inward act of the heart, that is, as the above-mentioned Ḥadīth tells us, believing in God, His angels, His books, His Apostles, and the Last Day. And the outer side of the matter—external works—is relegated altogether to the realm of *islām*. These external works, according to the Ḥadīth, would include witnessing to the Unity of God and the Apostleship of Muḥammad, worship, *zakāt*, fasting, and Pilgrimage. And this, Ibn Taymiyyah says, is the meaning of the Ḥadīth handed down by Aḥmad b. Ḥanbal: '*Islām* is an external matter, while *īmān* is in the heart.'[9]

The theory of *iḥsān*, *īmān* and *islām* put forward by Ibn Taymiyyah is a very interesting one, stemming from his penetrating analysis of the semantic structure of language, to which we shall have occasions to return in later contexts. If all the theologians of Islam had taken up such a flexible and dynamic attitude toward the problem of *īmān* and *islām*, the problem of the relevance of

8. *Op. cit.* p. 7.

9. *al-Islām ʿalāniyah wa-al-īmān fī al-qalb* (quoted also by Wensinck, *op. cit.* p. 23), Ibn Taymiyyah, p. 10.

'work' to 'belief' would not have caused so much trouble to the early thinkers, and consequently the following chapters would not have been written. Things, however, did not actually happen that way. Let us now leave Ibn Taymiyyah for a moment and go back again to the earlier part of the history. It is important to note here that the concept of *iḥsān* which, as we have just seen, occupied such an important place—it being recognized as the highest element of the Islamic religion—was not, strangely, destined to be elaborated theoretically by the theologians. It did not develop into an authentic theological concept in Islam.[10] The minds of the theologians were almost exclusively occupied in this field by the remaining two concepts. So in this book, too, we shall be, from now on, concerned only with *īmān* and *islām*.

The establishment in final form of the so-called five Pillars (*arkān*), i.e. the five essential constituents of Islam, was a truly significant event in the earliest period of the history of Muslim theology.[11] The conception crystallized in the form of a Ḥadīth: 'Islam is based on five things' (*al-islām 'alá khams*). This determined in outline the way in which the relation between *īmān* and *islām* must be conceived, and introduced a certain organization into the rather nebulous conceptual relations. The five basic items mentioned in this Ḥadīth[12] are: (1) belief, (2) worship, (3) *zakāt*, (4) pilgrimage, and (5) the fast of Ramaḍān.

The conception of the five Pillars of Islam is extremely important in connection with the problem we are now discussing, because it regards *īmān* as one of the constituents of *islām*.

As the diagram on the left side shows, *islām* is here made the comprehensive and the widest idea, within the whole region of which *īmān* occupies only one, albeit the most important, section. It is to be noticed also that all the remaining

10. What Baghdādī (*Uṣūl*, p. 269) calls 'authentic belief' *ṣiḥḥah al-īmān* may be regarded as a theoretical elaboration of the earlier concept *iḥsān*. But it is not, in any way, a key-concept.

11. The process by which this thought came to be established in this form is admirably described by Wensinck, *Muslim Creed*, Ch. II.

12. The Ḥadīth came down to us in a number of slightly different forms. Bukhārī, for instance, (*Īmān*, No. 7) mentions 'witnessing that there is no god but God and that Muḥammad is the Apostle of God'—i.e. *shahādah*—in place of 'belief', while Muslim (*Īmān*, No. 20) gives as the first of the five, 'serving God (alone) and disbelieving in anything other than God'.

four items are 'works', that is, ritual duties. This point is of primary significance in view of the fact that the theological activity of the Murji'ites was to raise a little later in history the problem of the relation between one's inner belief and one's acts, as we shall see in detail in the next chapter.

In any event, the conception of the five Pillars made *īmān* one of the elements (*khiṣāl*) of *islām*. This position is represented perfectly well by Bāqillānī's dictum:

> *Islām* means 'yielding' *inqiyād* and 'submission'. Every act of obedience by which man submits to his Lord and obeys His order is *islām*, whereas *īmān* is only one of the basic elements of *islām*. So all *īmān* is *islām*, but not all *islām* is *īmān*.[13]

This is the standard interpretation of the theory of the five Pillars, and the only possible one, it would seem. The diagram given above clearly shows *īmān* as but a part (*baʿḍ*) of *islām*. And, in fact, this is the view generally held by the Orthodox. Ashʿarī, for instance,[14] gives as one of the articles of faith peculiar to the People of Truth and Sunnah: 'We profess that *islām* is wider than *īmān*, so that not all *islām* is *īmān*,' i.e. *islām* comprises a number of other things in addition to *īmān*.

To formulate it in a slightly different way, the dictum is tantamount to saying that every Muslim is necessarily a Believer (because the concept of Muslim itself comprises that of *īmān*; nobody can be a Muslim without 'believing') but not every Believer is a Muslim (because a Believer who only believes not fulfilling properly his ritual duties does not deserve the title 'Muslim'.) Thus formulated, this position reveals itself as exactly the opposite of the thesis maintained by Ibn Taymiyyah, which we have examined above. He holds that such an interpretation makes the concept of *islām* not only wider and more comprehensive but, as a matter of fact, also higher in rank (*afḍal*) than *īmān*.

---

13. *Kitāb al-Tamhīd*, ed. Richard McCarthy, Beirut, 1957, p. 347. Bāqillānī was a great Ashʿarite theologian (d. 1013).

14. *Kitāb al-Ibānah*, Haydarabad, 2ed., 1948, p. 7.

This, he says, is absurd.[15]

For Ibn Taymiyyah, a Believer who only believes with the heart and does not do 'good works' is a contradiction in terms. Far from being a part of *islām*, *īmān* is a higher and more comprehensive concept than the latter. *Islām*, in the sense of acts of obedience is included within the concept of *īmān*. *Islām*, in other words, is a part of *īmān*. In his *Kitāb al-Īmān* there is a short but interesting chapter in which he discusses and criticizes Bāqillānī's position, which he traces back to the Murji'ites, the Jahmites in particular. The following is an abbreviated translation of the chapter.[16] At the outset he quotes the words of Bāqillānī which we have given above, and says:

> This, besides being an absurd theory, contradicts the teaching of the Koran and Sunnah, and is a contradiction in itself. It makes *īmān* one of the constituent parts of *islām*, all acts of obedience (*ṭā'āt*) being *islām*, and *īmān* being regarded here as consisting only in the mental act of 'assent' *taṣdīq*. The Murji'ites certainly say that *īmān* comprises *islām*, and yet, on the other hand, they limit the meaning of *īmān* to 'assent' by the heart and the tongue, while the Jahmites make it still narrower and say that it is 'assent' by the heart only. If this were right, then 'witnessing', Worship, *zakāt*, or for that matter any other thing would be excluded from *īmān*. This contradicts the words both of God and the Apostle.
>
> The reason why I say this is a contradiction in itself is as follows. If *īmān* were, as they assert, a part of *islām*, it would mean that he who has actualized *īmān* has actualized only a part of *islām*, not the whole of *islām* which is obligatory. Such a man would not be a Muslim for he has not actualized the whole of *islām*, just as, in their theory, nobody can be a Believer unless he has actualized the whole of *īmān*.
>
> Their theory implies that *islām* is divisible into as many parts as there are acts of obedience. Thus the *shahādah* of the Unity of God would be by itself an *islām*, and the *shahādah* of the Apostleship of Muḥammad would by itself be an *islām*. Likewise, Worship by itself would be an *islām*, *zakāt* by itself would be an *islām*. Nay, each coin which you give to the poor would be an *islām*, each prostration you perform in prayer would be an *islām*, each day of your fasting would be an *islām*, and so on and so forth indefinitely.

15. *Op. cit.* p. 324.
16. *Op. cit.* pp. 129–133.

Furthermore, if a Muslim cannot be a Muslim unless he does all the things which these people call *islām*, it necessarily follows that the Fāsiqs (those who have committed a grave sin) are not Muslims although they are still Believers. Thus they regard the Believers having—in their view—a perfect *īmān* as non-Muslims. This is even worse than the thesis of the Karrāmites.[17] Nay, if we are to regard as *islām* all acts of obedience, whether obligatory or supererogatory, he who neglects even non-obligatory duties cannot be a Muslim, for the supererogatory acts are also obedience to God. Such an attitude is contradictory to the often-quoted verse (XLVII, 14) in which *islām* is distinguished from *īmān*, and the Bedouins whose faith is only superficial are excluded from the name of *īmān*, but not from that of *islām*. (In other words, they are acknowledged as Muslims, but not as Believers.) This proves that excluding the Fāsiqs from the name of *islām*, as these people do, is a far more serious mistake than excluding them from the name of *īmān*. For in both the Koran and the Sunnah, the name of *īmān* stands higher than *islām*.

If those who take up this position protest and say: 'No, (what we mean to say is that) anyone who does an act of obedience is entitled to be called Muslim', then we may point out to them that it would follow necessarily from such a thesis that a man who does one single act of obedience out of all the possible ones *is* a Muslim, even if he does not confess the Unity of God and the Apostleship of Muḥammad. These people say: 'Every Believer is a Muslim, but not every Muslim is a Believer'. There is a contradiction between (the latter half of) this dictum and their understanding of *islām*. For a Muslim, i.e. a man of *islām*, is in their understanding the same as (one who is) obedient to God. But how can a man be 'obedient' if he lacks 'belief'? It is unthinkable that anybody should do anything pertaining to *islām* without being at the same time a believer, even if it be the lowest kind of obedience. We must conclude, therefore, that every Muslim is a Believer, whether by *islām* is meant the whole of acts of obedience or one single act of obedience. When they say: 'Every Believer is a Muslim', they mean by *īmān* only the act of assenting (*taṣdīq*) with the heart. But from this it follows, as we saw above, the most evidently absurd conclusion that a man may be a Muslim even if he does not confess openly the Unity of God and the Apostleship of Muḥammad, and even if he does not fulfil at all any duty which he has been commanded to fulfil. Even the

17. The Karramites or *al-Karrāmiyyah* will be dealt with later.

Jews and the Christians know very well that nobody can be a Muslim without *shahādah* or something equivalent to it.

Now (since *īmān*, according to their own definition, is the mental act of assenting only,) the term Believer (*mu'min*, i.e. man of *īmān*) in their dictum 'every Believer is a Muslim' does not mean a man who has openly confessed the belief in the Unity of God and the Apostleship of Muḥammad, nor even a man who has done anything of the five Pillars. It can only mean a man who has done one single act of obedience (i.e. assent), which is merely an inner kind of obedience. Such a man, however, is not even a Muslim as understood by the Koran and the Sunnah, nor by our authorities, whether of the earlier or the latter period.

They refer to the Koranic verse XLVII, 14 in which the Bedouins are described as men of superficial *islām* who confess the belief in the Unity of God and the Apostleship of Muḥammad as a matter of formality, whether truthful or not. And yet, they go on to point out, God recognizes in them *islām*, and denies only *īmān*. And those who do not know the truth of the matter[18] tend (to be deceived by this and) think that such must have been the view of our earlier authorities based on the Koran and the Sunnah, namely that 'every Believer is a Muslim, but not every Muslim is a Believer'.

In reality, however, the difference between the thesis of these people and the view of the earlier authorities is even greater than that between the latter and the thesis of the Muʿtazilites concerning *islām* and *īmān*. In fact, the Muʿtazilite thesis on this point is far nearer (to the view of the earlier authorities) than the thesis maintained by the Jahmites.[19] Only the Muʿtazilites' assertion that the People of Qiblah[20] will be made to remain in Hell for ever is farther away from the saying of the earlier authorities than even the Jahmites' view. So that those of the later theologians who support the Jahmite view on the problem of belief give us the impression that they are supporting thereby the authentic opinion of the earlier authorities on this and other related problems. This, however, is only a matter of verbal congruence. In reality, their view is most radically different from that of the earlier authorities. Of all the theories

18. This will be made clear in section II of the present chapter.

19. On the Jahmite position, see Chap. V.

20. I.e. the grave sinners among them. Reference is to the intransigent Muʿtazilite theory of *waʿīd*.

> that have been put forward in Islam, nothing indeed is more remote from the Ancients' view than that of the Jahmites.
> As to the thesis maintained by the Muʿtazilites, the Khārijites and the Karrāmites concerning the concepts of *islām* and *īmān*, we should say that it is nearer to the view of the earlier authorities than that of the Jahmites. Only, as we have said before, the Muʿtazilites and the Khārijites maintain that the sinners will be in Hell eternally. This is more remote from the view of the Ancients than any other theory proposed.
> Thus the Muʿtazilites and the Khārijites are closer to the Ancients in their theory of 'names' but farther away from them in their theory of 'judgments'.[21] The Jahmites, on the other hand, are closer (to the Ancients) in regard to 'judgments', in their view that the grave sinners among the Muslims will not remain in Hell eternally, but in regard to their understanding of the real nature of the 'names', *islām* and *īmān*, they are far more removed from the real teaching of the Koran and the Sunnah than all others. The Jahmite view contradicts Reason, Revelation, and the Arabic language to such a degree that there can be nothing similar to it in this respect in any other school.

Ibn Taymiyyah has much more to say about the relation between *īmān* and *islām*. But before we proceed further, I would like to introduce into our discussion at this point another view which is opposed to both Ibn Taymiyyah and those whom he criticizes. Up till now the difference between the two concepts, *īmān* and *islām*, has been the center of interest. The major question, as we have seen, has been: Which of the two is the wider concept connotatively? Does *īmān* comprise in itself the concept of *islām* (Ibn Taymiyyah), or does *islām* include *īmān* (Ashʿarī,[22] Bāqillānī)? The former view is based on the Ḥadīth

---

21. 'Names' (*asmā'*, sg. *ism*) are major theological concepts like *īmān*, *islām*, *kufr*, *mu'min*, *muslim*, *kāfir*, while 'judgments' (*aḥkām*, sg. *ḥukm*) are various problems raised by the 'names', e.g. whether *īmān* increases and decreases, whether a Fāsiq will be made to remain in Hell eternally, etc. Here Ibn Taymiyyah says that the Muʿtazilites are closer to the Ancients than the Jahmites in their application of the terms 'Muslim' and 'Believer', but far removed from them regarding the 'judgments' connected with these 'names'.

22. Ashʿarī in the *Ibānah* p. 7, where he describes the general tenets of the Orthodox, clearly states that 'the concept of *islām* is wider than that of *īmān* (*al-islām awsaʿ min al-īmān*)'. But in the *Maqālāt* p. 293, where also he gives the common tenets of the Orthodox, he simply says that the two are different.

of Gabriel, and the latter on the doctrine of five Pillars. But Muslim theology produced in the course of its history another opinion opposed to both of them. This third thesis emphasizes the similarity between the two concepts rather than the difference, and asserts that they are in the last analysis one and the same thing, the difference being merely a matter of different names. In the following section we shall first examine this last position, and then go on to observe how Ibn Taymiyyah analyses and criticizes it.

II Is *īmān* identical with *islām*?

Are *īmān* and *islām* but two names for one and the same thing? Are they identical with each other in every respect? The terse phrase '*īmān* and *islām* are one'[23] given by the Māturīdite theologian Nasafī seems to suggest that. What the Ashʿarite commentator Taftāzānī says about this phrase, however, makes it clear that the underlying idea is not as simple as it appears at first sight, as we shall see presently. Why two different names if they were completely identical?

The easiest way of solving this difficulty would be to say that the two *qua* concepts—or, as a matter of language—are different things, but *practically* they come to the same thing. In other words, they are not exactly the same thing, but they are so inseparable from each other, i.e. they from such a solid unity, that neither of them can exist without the other. Let us now examine a typical instance of this kind of handling the problem. It is a passage from the Fiqh Akbar II (as Wensinck calls it) ascribed to Abu Ḥanīfah and representing the Hanafite school of theology at about the time of Ashʿarī.[24] The explanatory remarks of the Hanafite commentator Abū al-Muntahá al-Maghnīsāwī are given in parentheses.

> The *īmān* consists in 'confession' *iqrār* (by the tongue) and 'assent' *taṣdīq* (i.e. acceptance with the heart of what a reporter reports)[25] .... All Believers

---

23. *al-īmān wa-al-islām wāḥid*, Najm al-Dīn al-Nasafī, *al-ʿAqāʾid al-Nasafiyyah* with Taftāzānī's commentary, Cairo, 2 ed., 1939.

24. Cf. Wensinck, *op. cit.* p. 246.

25. As we shall see later, the first place given to 'verbal confession' in the definition of 'belief' is quite typical of the Hanafite-Māturīdite school. The real significance of the elements, *iqrār*, *taṣdīq* (and *aʿmāl*) in this kind of context will be made clear in the following chapters.

are equal in *īmān* and *tawḥīd* (i.e. an absolute denial of anything being associated with God). They differ in rank only in regard to 'works' *a'māl* (i.e. the acts of obedience, internal as well as external. This shows clearly that a 'good work' does not constitute part of *īmān*, for acts allow of 'more or less'. Some people, for example, pray all the five daily prayers, whereas some others pray only some of the prescribed prayers. And yet even the prayers of this latter type are quite authentic, not invalid. ... Judge by this standard all other 'works', whether obligatory or supererogatory. The *īmān* is not like that, for the *īmān* of one who believes only in some parts of what one has to believe in is not an authentic *īmān*; it is invalid. Such an *īmān* may be compared to the fasting of a man who begins to fast but breaks it soon after within the same day.) The *islām* consists in complete surrendering and obedience to the commands of God (i.e. being content with the judgments of God regarding what one should do and what one should not do. It is to accept with absolute docility and without any objection at all whatever God has called a 'duty' as a duty and whatever He has called 'forbidden' as forbidden.) So, as a matter of language, there is a distinction between *īmān* and *islām* (because *īmān* linguistically means 'assent' *taṣdīq* while *islām* means 'total surrendering' *taslīm*. 'Assent' has a special locus, which is the 'heart', and the 'tongue' is nothing but its 'interpreter'. The 'surrendering', on the contrary, is not limited to a specified locus; it covers the 'heart', the 'tongue' and 'the bodily members'. That *islām* is linguistically wider than *īmān* is proved by the fact that the Munāfiqs are, from the point of view of language, included in the category of Muslims even though they are certainly not Believers according to the ordinary usage of language nor according to the Divine Law).

However, there can be no *īmān* (in the sense in which the Divine Law defines it) unless there be *islām*, (because *īmān* consists, as we have said above, in the verbal confession of, and inner assent to, the essential divine nature of God as well as His attributes and names. This implies that he who has acknowledged and believed has thereby 'surrendered' himself totally to God and accepted all the commands and judgments of God as truly obligatory duties). And there can be no *islām*, unless accompanied by *īmān* (because, since *islām* is humble submission to whatever God commands, it cannot possibly be realized except after 'assent' and 'confession'. So it is unthinkable according to the Divine Law that there be a Believer who is not a Muslim, or a Muslim who is not a Believer. And this is meant by the theologians when they speak of the synonymity of the two names *īmān* and *islām*, and of their basic oneness). They

> are, so to speak, back and belly (i.e. they are inseparable from each other). And the word Religion (*dīn*) covers both *īmān* and *islām* together with all the Divine Laws (i.e. the word *dīn* is sometimes used to mean *īmān*, sometimes *islām*. It is also used to mean sometimes the Law of Muḥammad, sometimes the Law of Moses, sometimes the Law of Jesus, or the Laws brought by other Apostles).[26]

The central point of this argument for the synonymity of *īmān* and *islām* is that *īmān* contains in its semantic structure an important element of 'submission' or 'yielding'. He who 'believes' in the sense in which the Divine Law understands it has implicitly 'submitted' to Divine commandments. In this manner, *īmān* is identified with *islām*.

Exactly the same argument is used by Taftāzānī in his commentary on the Creed of Nasafi.[27] Here the common element connecting *īmān* and *islām* is expressed by the word *idhʿān* which means 'submission' 'obedience'. Like Abū al-Muntahá, he begins by defining *īmān* linguistically as *taṣdīq*. Now *taṣdīq*, he says, has as a technical term in logic the meaning of 'judgment' as opposed to 'conception' *taṣawwur*.[28] But even at this logical level *taṣdīq* contains an element of *idhʿān*, that is, 'submitting' and 'acknowledging.'

> The real nature of *taṣdīq* does not consist merely in the occurrence of a truth-relation in the mind vis-à-vis a piece of information or the informant without its being accompanied by a submissive acceptance. On the contrary *taṣdīq* is *idhʿān* and the willing acceptance of the information to such a degree that it may properly be called *taslīm*, or 'complete surrender'.

It would have been much more simple if Taftāzānī made a clear-cut distinction between *taṣdīq* as a technical term in logic in the sense of 'judgment', affirmative and negative, and *taṣdīq* as a technical term in theology where the concept of *idhʿān* is an essential element. However this may be, his main inten-

---

26. *Kitāb Sharḥ al-Fiqh al-Akbar*, Haydarabad, 2 ed., 1948, pp. 57–61.

27. *Op. cit.* pp. 432–433.

28. Cf. Fakhr al-Dīn al-Rāzī, *Muḥaṣṣal afkār al-Mutaqaddimīn wa-al-Muta'akhkhirīn*, Cairo, 1323 A.H., pp. 2–3: 'When we comprehend something, we may either consider it in itself without passing any judgment upon it, whether affirmative or negative, e.g. the concept of 'man' in itself—and this is *taṣawwur*—or we may pass a judgment upon it, either affirmative or negative. This last is what we call *taṣdīq*'.

tion is unmistakably clear. By pointing out that *taṣdīq* (*īmān*) contains in itself *idhʿān* as an essential constituent, he wants to make it a connecting link between *īmān* and *islām*. This is quite easy because:

> *islām* itself means 'submissiveness' and 'obedience' in the sense of the acceptance of the judgments (of others) and *idhʿān*. But this is nothing other than the real meaning or *taṣdīq* as we have seen above. ... Generally speaking, the Divine Law does not allow us to judge anybody by saying 'He is a Believer, but not a Muslim', or 'He is a Muslim, but not a Believer'. And this is in short exactly what we mean when we say that the two are identical. The identity should not be taken in the sense of a conceptual identity (i.e. they are, as concepts, different from each other). But they are not different in the sense that one can exist separated from the other. ... There can be no *īmān* independently of *islām*.[29]

Ibn Ḥazm is one of the great thinkers in Islam who defend the thesis of the basic identity of *īmān* and *islām*. However, he takes in his argument quite a different way from the variety which we have been studying. His argument is, as always, based on his original linguistic or semantic theory. Briefly stated, it amounts to this. Every Arabic word has its normal, standard meaning. God, however, has transferred (*naqala*) some of them in His Arabic Revelation to special non-normal meanings defined only by Himself. In other terms, some of the Arabic words used in Revelation have acquired a God-defined technical meaning. Applying this principle to *īmān* and *islām*, he says that the two words, as ordinary and normal Arabic words, mean quite different things, but that these words on the level of divinely instituted technical terminology mean exactly the same thing.

> Thus the word *īmān* originally means in Arabic *taṣdīq*. But God in His Revelation has used it in such a way that it means the whole of the acts of obedience and the avoidance of the acts of disobedience, by which, whether positive or negative, man seeks the countenance of God (i.e. *īmān* means the doing of the acts of obedience and the not-doing of the acts of disobedience, with the clear intention of serving God).
> The original meaning of the word *islām* in Arabic, on the other hand, is *tabar-*

29. Taftāzānī, *op. cit.* pp. 450–453.

> *ru'* or 'being acquitted', i.e. 'getting rid of responsibility and handing it over to somebody else entirely'. Thus you say, 'I have handed over (*aslamtu*) such-and-such a matter to such-and-such a person' when you have transferred a matter completely to another person. The original meaning in which a Muslim was called *muslim* (lit. he who has done *islām*) is that 'he got rid of (*tabarra'a*)' everything and handed it over altogether to God. But God, in the next stage, has transposed again the name of *islām* from this original meaning to all acts of obedience. Furthermore, the *tabarru'* of everything to God coincides exactly with the meaning of *taṣdīq*, for nobody can hand over everything to God unless he trusts Him and believes in Him. In this way, when the word *islām* is used in the sense in which it is opposed to *kufr* and opposed to *fisq* (i.e. when it is used as a divinely instituted technical term), it is exactly the same thing as *īmān*.
>
> This, of course, should not be taken to mean that the word *islām* in the Koran is always used in this technical sense. Even in the Koran it happens that *islām* is used in the ordinary, non-technical sense of *istislām* 'submission', that is, a man's submitting himself to the Islamic religion simply and solely because of the fear of life, without inner belief in it. In such a case *islām* is not by any means synonymous with *īmān*. The word used in reference to some Bedouins in XLIX, 14 must be understood in this sense.
>
> Thus it stands patent that the words *islām* and *īmān* (as technical terms) have been transposed (by God Himself) from their proper places in the Arabic language to certain specified meanings which the Arabs had never known before God sent down Revelation upon His Apostle, telling him that he who acted in accordance with these (specified meanings) was alone entitled to the names of *īmān* and *islām* and to be called a Believer-Muslim, whereas he who did not do so could be called neither a Believer nor a Muslim, however much he believed in all other things and however sincerely he handed over all other things to God.[30]

Against the view which thus identifies in one way or another *īmān* with *islām*, Ibn Taymiyyah raises a strong objection. As in the case of Ibn Ḥazm, his theory is based on an original theory of language. But there is a fundamental difference between the two semantic theories.

30. *Fiṣal* IV, pp. 225–227.

He begins by rejecting the commonly-held rigid view of the semantic function of the linguistic signs, according to which a word keeps its definite range of basic meaning whenever and in whatever conditions it is used. And he replaces it with a more subtle, flexible view of language. The concrete result of this is his distinction between the absolute (*muṭlaq*) usage of a word and the conditioned (*muqayyad*) usage. I shall illustrate this distinction first.

Suppose a word, say *A*, comprises in its connotation five basic elements, say *a*, *b*, *c*, *d*, *e*. When this word is used in an 'absolute' way, it must naturally mean *a*, *b*, *c*, *d*, and *e*. But it often happens that the words are used in a 'conditioned' way. This occurs when, for instance, we pick up *a* and *d* out of the five, and say [*A* and *a* and *d*]. In such a case *a* and *d* have been made explicit for some reason or other, given, so to speak, an independent existence, and put side by side with *A* as if they were something different from it. Here we have apparently a combination of three different concepts, although, in reality, the concept of *A* includes within itself the remaining two concepts so that the formula should be [*A* (*a*, *d*)] instead of [*A* and *a* and *d*].

By way of illustration, Ibn Taymiyyah analyses the meaning structure of some of the key-terms in the Koran. The pair *maʿrūf* (good)-*munkar* (bad) provides a telling example. When used in the 'absolute' way, the word *maʿrūf* means everything (morally) good, and the word *munkar* everything (morally) bad. They are used in this way in VII, 157, which reads: '(The Apostle) enjoins upon them (i.e. his followers) *maʿrūf* and forbids them *munkar*'.[31] In this and similar verses, the meaning of *maʿrūf* and *munkar* is general; that is, everything which is at all capable of being described as morally good (*khayr*) is implied by *maʿrūf*, and, likewise, every evil (*sharr*) imaginable is implied by *munkar*. In terms of the symbolic notation introduced above we might say that the occurrence of *A* suggests automatically and implicitly the occurrence of *a-b-c-d-e*.

Quite different from this is the use of the same word in IV, 114, where we find the formula [*A* (*a*, *d*)] actualized. The verse reads: 'Much of their secret conversation is of no value except (in case) somebody enjoins almsgiving (*ṣadaqah*) and *maʿrūf* and making peace (*iṣlāḥ*) among the people'. Here, as we see, almsgiving and peace-making are treated as two independent conceptual units separate from 'doing good'. Properly speaking however, 'doing good'

31. Similarly III, 110, IX, 71.

ma'rūf comprises within itself these two elements among many others. To put it in another way, the usage of the word *ma'rūf* here is 'conditioned'. In a similar manner, the usage of the word *munkar* in XXIX, 45, is 'conditioned', where we read: 'Verily Worship (*ṣalāt*) prevents lewdness (*faḥshā'*) and *munkar*'. In this verse *faḥshā'* is regarded as something different and separate from *munkar*, whereas in the verse quoted above, '(the Apostle) forbids them *munkar*', *faḥshā'* is naturally contained in, and implied by, *munkar*.[32]

Exactly the same is true of the Koranic usage of the word *īmān*. Sometimes it is used 'absolutely', sometimes it is used 'conditionally'. And we have to be very careful when reading the Koran to distinguish between the two cases, for the majority of errors and misunderstandings concerning the meaning of *īmān* and the relation of the latter to *islām* are nothing but the result of inattentiveness to this basic semantic fact. The word *īmān* (under its various forms) is one of those that occur most frequently in the Koran, and consequently is also one of those that are most frequently on the lips of the people.

The 'absolute' use of *īmān* is in itself relatively easy to handle. But the 'conditioned' one may prove very misleading unless we be on our guard. For sometimes the usage of the word *īmān* is 'conditioned' by a particular concept (formula: *A* and *b*), some other time we find it used with another of the possible concepts (formula: *A* and *c*). And this naturally is likely to lead to confusion. Somebody, for instance, may have noticed the word *īmān* used in the Koran in the form of *A*-and-*b*. He may take it as the standard usage of the word, and form his own conception of *īmān* on the basis of this particular combination. This of course leads to a specialization of the meaning of *īmān*. And henceforward he will be understanding the word in that particular sense whenever it is used, regardless of whether it is 'conditioned' this way or that, or even whether it is 'conditioned' at all or 'absolute'.[33]

To put it in more concrete terms in particular reference to the topic of the present chapter, what Ibn Taymiyyah wants to emphasize is that when the word *īmān* is used in a combination like [*īmān* and *islām* and *ṣāliḥāt* (good works)], for instance, it should not be understood in the form of [*A* and *B* and *C*]. Rather, it should be understood in the form of [*A* (*b* and *c*)], *b* and *c* being regarded here as two of the many constituent elements of *A*, made explicit for a particular

32. *Īmān*, p. 135.
33. *Ibid.* pp. 304–305.

reason. The meaning structure of *īmān* in such a case is naturally different from the meaning structure of the same word when it is used unconditionally.

What, then, is *īmān* according to Ibn Taymiyyah? What is *islām*? And how are the two related with each other? The very basis and the starting-point of his argument lies in the understanding of the concept of *īmān* when the word is used, 'absolutely'.

> The word *īmān*, used 'absolutely' in both the Koran and the Sunnah, means the same thing as the word *birr*[34] and the word *taqwá*[35] and the word *dīn*.[36] The Prophet himself explained *īmān* in this way in the Ḥadīth: '*īmān* consists of seventy odd branches, the highest of all being the confession of the Unity of God, and the lowest, removing anything which might be harmful to others from the road'. This Ḥadīth suggests that everything that pleases God comes under the name of *īmān*. Likewise the words *birr*, *taqwá*, and *dīn* (or *dīn al-Islām* 'religion of Islam'), when they are used 'absolutely'.
>
> As regards *birr*, for instance, it is related that the verse: 'The *birr* does not mean that you turn your faces (to the East and the West) etc.'[37] was revealed when the people asked about the meaning of *īmān*. What God mentions in this verse as the meaning of *birr* is nothing other than *īmān*, *taqwá*, and the good works through which men approach toward God.
>
> There is also a Ḥadīth in which the Prophet himself explains the meaning of the word *birr* by equating it with *īmān*. 'One day a man came to Abū Dharr and asked him about the meaning of *īmān*. Abū Dharr[38] (instead of giving him a direct answer) recited the verse: "The *birr* does not mean that you turn your faces etc.", to the end of it. The man said, "I did not ask you about *birr*". Then Abū Dharr replied, "Once a man went to the Prophet and asked him exactly the same question as you have. The Prophet in reply recited the same verse which I have just recited to you, Then the man made exactly the same remark as you, and refused obstinately to be content with this answer. There-

34. generally translated as 'piety'.

35. generally translated as 'fear of God'.

36. generally translated as 'religion'.

37. Koran, II, 117.

38. one of the famous Companions of the Prophet. On the very interesting character of this man see, for example, Wensinck, *Muslim Creed*, p. 46.

upon the Prophet told him: The Believer (lit. man of *īmān*) is one who, when he has done something good, is delighted and hopes for a reward, but, when he has done something bad, feels sorry and fears the chastisement for it.'"[39]

Ibn Taymiyyah goes on to show that the same relation holds between *birr* and *taqwá*. In the verse: 'O you who believe …, help each other unto *birr* and *taqwá*' (V, 2), the two concepts are distinguished from each other. In other words, each of them, in this particular place, is used in a narrowly specified sense. We notice this because we see them used in a 'conditioned' way (*taqyīd*), being 'yoked together' (*iqtirān*). Furthermore, the beginning of the verse ('O you who believe!') makes it clear beyond any doubt that the whole thing concerns the key-concept of 'belief'. But in some other places, the word *taqwá* is used 'absolutely'. And in such a case *taqwá* is completely synonymous with *birr*, as is shown by the verse: 'Those, indeed, are the God-fearing (*muttaqūna* pl. of *muttaqī* meaning roughly "a man of *taqwá*")'. It is significant that these words are the concluding sentence of the whole verse (II, 177) beginning with 'The *birr* does not mean that you turn your faces to the East and the West'. In other words, those who are characterized by *birr* and those who are characterized by *taqwá* are simply equated with each other.

All this, Ibn Taymiyyah concludes, goes to show that *īmān*, *birr*, and *taqwá* are one and the same thing when these words are used 'absolutely'. The Believers (*mu'minūn*) are the same as the God-fearing (*muttaqūn*), and the latter, in turn, are the same as the Pious (*abrār*).[40]

Now *īmān*, taken 'absolutely', is a very wide and comprehensive concept. And it is clear that there can be no *īmān* in this 'absolute' sense where there is no 'good work'. The Koran itself attests to it.[41] The very verse, to which reference has been made and which gives a perfect verbal definition of the concept of *birr* (= *īmān*), enumerates as the essential conditions of *birr*: (1) belief in God, the Last Day, the angels, the Book and the Prophets, (2) giving one's wealth to kinsfolk, orphans, the needy, the wayfarer, and those who ask, (3) setting slaves free, (4) observing worship in due form, (5) paying the *zakāt*, (6) keeping one's treaty, (7) being patient in misfortune and adversity.

39. *Īmān*, p. 149.
40. *Ibid.* pp. 152–153.
41. *Ibid.* pp. 150–152.

Of all the seven items enumerated, only the first one concerns the psychological aspect of *īmān*, i.e. *īmān* as an inner state of the Believer. Only here is *īmān* synonymous with *taṣdīq*. All the rest, from (2) to (7), concern the various concrete manifestations of the inner state. Evidently the Koran considers them all as integral parts of *īmān* together with (1).

Ibn Taymiyyah recognized the supreme importance of the 'heart' *qalb* in the constitution of *īmān*. 'The heart is the very root (*aṣl*)'.[42] But we must observe, he goes on to argue, that the heart has not only the intellectual function of 'knowing' (as the definition *īmān* = *taṣdīq* tends to suggest), but also it has its own 'works' *aʿmāl*, such as the love of God and His Apostle, the fear of God, the love of what God and His Apostle love, the disliking of what God and His Apostle dislike, complete reliance upon God, etc. All these acts of the heart have also been enjoined by God upon all Believers. And such a heart, once realized, must of necessity exercise a decisive influence on the whole body, control and govern it, and manifest itself in good bodily works. And this, Ibn Taymiyyah says, is the meaning of the Ḥadīth: 'Lo, there is in the body a morsel of flesh (*muḍghah*). When it is in good order the whole body is in good order, but when it is corrupted the whole body becomes corrupted accordingly. Lo, that thing is the heart!'

The gist of the whole argument is, as we have already seen, that the word *īmān*, when used 'absolutely', includes in its meaning 'works'. Exception has often been taken to such a view on the ground that the Koran constantly uses the phrase 'those who believe and do good works' (*alladhīna āmanū wa-ʿamilū al-ṣāliḥāt*). Why did God distinguish at all 'belief' and 'work', if the latter were implied by the former? For Ibn Taymiyyah, the answer is easily found. The problem is solved immediately if we understand the above phrase not in the form of [*A* and *B*], but in that of [*A* (*b*)].

The real significance of the problem, however, can only be seen when we consider it against the background of the Murji'ite conception of *īmān*, for the argument, properly speaking, is directed against the Murji'ites who assert that *īmān* is *īmān* by itself, and that the concept of 'work' is essentially external and irrelevant to it. So the discussion of this problem belongs to a later context. We shall come back to Ibn Taymiyyah's attitude toward the Murji'ite position in

42. *Ibid.* pp. 155–156.

chapter VI. Let us now concentrate upon his view on the relation between *īmān* and *islām*.

The Ḥadīth of Gabriel which, as we remember, served as the starting-point for Ibn Taymiyyah's argument, distinguished *īmān* from *islām* in this way: *īmān* is that one believes in God, His Angels, His Books, His Apostles, the Last Day, and the predestination, whether of good or bad', while *islām* is 'the verbal confession of the Unity of God and the Apostleship of Muḥammad, the worship, the *zakāt*, the pilgrimage, and the fast of Ramaḍān. In short, *īmān* is inner belief while *islām* is external work. This, says Ibn Taymiyyah, gives the meaning of *īmān* and *islām* when these words are used together in a coordinate relationship, that is, in the form of [*A* and *B*]. And since this is the answer given by the Apostle himself, we have no other answer to offer concerning what these words mean when used in such a form.[43]

So the real problem here is rather: What do *īmān* and *islām* mean, and what is the conceptual relation between them, when they are used as independent concepts? To this question Ibn Taymiyyah gives the following answer.

> *Islām* is nothing other than *dīn*.[44] And *dīn* is the nominal form of the verb *dāna* meaning 'humble submission'. And the *dīn* of *islām* in which God found satisfaction and with which He sent His Apostles is nothing other than 'total surrender' *istislām* to God alone. Thus its root is in the human heart, and it is submissiveness to God alone coupled with worshipping Him alone. So he who worships Him, but worships some other god with Him, is not a Muslim (lit. man of *islām*). Nor is he a Muslim who does not worship Him, being too haughty to do so. ... Thus *islām* is basically a kind of 'work'; it is both the work of the heart and the work of the body.[45]
>
> *Islām*, in short, is that you worship God, and God alone, without associating

43. *Ibid.* pp. 217–218.

44. This proposition is based on the Koran. 'Verily the *dīn* (generally translated as "religion") in the sight of God is *islām*' (III, 19); 'Whosoever seeks as *dīn* anything other than *islām*, it will not be accepted from him, and he will be among the losers in the Hereafter' (III, 85); 'Who is better in *dīn* than he who has surrendered (*aslama*, verbal form corresponding to *islām*) his face (i.e. his whole being) to God?' (IV, 125), etc.

45. *Īmān*, p. 221. The definition of *islām* is given on p. 223: it is 'total surrender' *istislām* to God by the heart together with external works.

> anything with Him, in an attitude of sincere submissiveness. And this is the *dīn* of God, other than which He never accepts from anybody. And since He has sent to us His Apostles, we cannot serve Him except by doing what the Apostles have commanded us to do; anything other than this is simply 'disobedience'. Besides, He has put an end to the series of Apostles with Muḥammad. So nobody can be a Muslim unless he witness that there is no god but God and that Muḥammad is His servant and His Apostle. With these words (of *shahādah*) anybody can enter into *islām*. So he who asserts that *islām* is 'saying' (verbal confession) is right if he means thereby this fact. However, (this is not all) for it is necessary for a Muslim to do all the 'external works' which the Apostle has commanded. And he who neglects to do any part of them has made his *islām* defective to that extent. … Whoever does the 'external works' with sincerity will surely be rewarded for it, but only on condition that he acknowledges with his heart the Unity of God and the Apostleship of Muḥammad. Such a man has in himself *īmān* to the extent that he gives this kind of mental assent. This does not imply, however, that this assent requires the existence in the man of an absolute certainty (*yaqīn*) which leaves no place for doubt, nor does it require that the man be characterized by all the distinguishing traits that are peculiar to a true man of *īmān*.
> Many of the Muslims are by nature like that inwardly as well as outwardly. In other words, they are born with the kind of *islām* here described with the limited amount of *īmān* which necessarily accompanies it, without, however, attaining to the degree of (*īmān* as an) absolute certainty.[46]

In Ibn Taymiyyah's view, this description holds true of the Bedouins to whom reference is made in XLIX, 14 of the Koran. They are recognized as Muslims, but not as Believers, because they do not fulfil the conditions of the perfect *īmān*. Some think that the belief of those Bedouins is simply that of the Hypocrites (*munāfiqūn*). But this is wrong. Surely, the *īmān* in its 'absolute' sense cannot be attributed to them, but they are nonetheless real Muslims, not Hypocrites. Their *islām*, although defective, will be rewarded in the Hereafter. Further, they have enough *īmān* to be worthy of reward.[47]

> (More generally) the same applies to most of the new converts to Islam. Nay, even to most of the (Muslims) who do not know yet the real depth of *īmān*.

46. *Ibid.* pp. 227–228.
47. *Ibid.* pp. 201–205, 211–212, 237–238.

> Take, for example, the case of a man who was converted to Islam after fighting—the Kāfirs, we must remember, at first fought stubbornly against Islam, then accepted it—or a man who became a Muslim after being taken prisoner, or again a man who heard about Islam, came, and accepted it. Such a man is a Muslim in the sense that he obeys readily the orders of the Apostle, but there has not yet penetrated deep into his heart the knowledge of the real *īmān*. This last state is achieved only when the man has at his disposal the means thereto, i.e. a (perfect) understanding of the Koran, direct and intimate contact with people of real *īmān*, imitating what proceeds from them in both saying and doing, or a special personal guidance bestowed upon him by God Himself. …
> Thus many of the Muslims of whom we are talking now, whenever they hear words of criticism, are very likely to be driven back to doubt and uncertainty and to begin to hesitate to fight in the way of God. Such people (cannot be regarded as Believers in the full sense of the word) for they do not certainly fall under the category of those who are described by the divine words in the following manner: 'The Believers are those only who, once they believe in God and His Apostle, never doubt afterward, but fight in the way of God with their wealth and their lives' (XLIX, 15)
> However, they are not Hypocrites (Munāfiqs) either, who harbor *kufr* in the depth of their hearts. A man of this type is neither a Believer (man of *īmān*) in the real sense of the word, nor a Hypocrite, nor again a grave sinner. On the contrary, he performs the external acts of obedience. However, he does not satisfy the full and essential requirements of *īmān*. He has a certain amount of *īmān*, which, however is not sufficient to make him entitled to be called a real man of *īmān*. But he will be rewarded for what he does of the acts of obedience.[48]

The foregoing explanation of the concept of *islām* has, I think, already made fairly clear what Ibn Taymiyyah wants us to understand by *īmān*. The main point he makes is that *īmān* is a higher concept than *islām* and comprises the latter within it. This we have seen in the first section of the present chapter. Here is what he says about it.

48. *Ibid.* pp. 204–205.

> The original meaning of *īmān* is assent (*taṣdīq*), acknowledging (*iqrār*) and knowledge (*maʿrifah*). It is, in this sense, a kind of inner act of the heart (*ʿamal al-qalb*). The real basis of it is 'assent', and 'act' is something that follows it. This is why the Prophet explained *īmān* as being essentially believing by the heart and the submissiveness of the heart, i.e. 'belief in God, His Angels, His Books and His Apostles', while he explained *islām* as a particular kind of 'submission' *istislām*, i.e. the performance of the five basic duties. … In other words, *īmān* is higher than *islām*. And this is expressed by his words: *islām* is external, whereas *īmān* is in the heart,' The meaning of all this is as follows. The external acts are visible to others, but what is in the heart is an inner state (and is invisible), like assent, knowledge, the love of God, hope etc. However, the inner states must of necessity manifest themselves externally, and these necessary manifestations (*lawāzim*) point to the inner states. An external manifestation cannot possibly point to a certain inner state unless there is a necessary connection between them. (This implies that *islām* as external acts must be understood only as the necessary and inevitable manifestations of *īmān*.)[49] The kind of *īmān* which characterizes a Believer (man of *īmān*) in the true sense of the word comprises a concrete knowledge of all the details of what is to be believed; it comprises also a sense of satisfied security and an absolute certainty. … And the absolute certainty and the firmness that are in the hearts of those who are characterized by this type of *īmān*, and the inseparability of *taṣdīq* from their hearts, are such that they are not possessed by men of *islām*. Men of this kind of *īmān* are the true Believers. Thus it comes about that every Believer is necessarily a Muslim, because *īmān* requires necessarily 'good works', but not every Muslim is a Believer taken in the sense of a man of 'absolute' *īmān*. And this because the total surrender (*istislām*) to God and acting in accordance with it (i.e. *islām*) do not require such a particular (i.e. such a high degree of) *īmān*. The difference between *īmān* and *islām* is capable of being felt by everybody in himself and observed in other people.[50]

The second point to note about the basic difference between *īmān* and *islām*, according to Ibn Taymiyyah, is that the promise of Paradise is connected exclusively with the name of *īmān*, while the word *islām*, when used 'absolutely',

49. *Ibid.* pp. 221–222.
50. *Ibid.* p. 228.

has no connection at all in the Koran with man's entering Paradise. This does not mean of course that the Koran belittles *islām*. On the contrary, the Koran repeatedly emphasizes its importance, affirming that *islām* is the only religion that satisfies God, and that He will never accept any other thing from anybody.[51] And yet, in spite of that, He has never said, 'Verily the Garden is there prepared for the Muslims' or 'God promises the Garden to the Muslims.' Such a promise is given only to 'those who believe'. 'God promises to the Believers, both men and women, Gardens underneath which rivers flow' (IX, 72), where the concept of *īmān* appears in its 'absolute' form. Or, 'Give glad tidings unto those who believe and do good works, that they will enter Gardens underneath which rivers flow' (II, 25), where the concept of *īmān* appears in a 'conditioned' form, that is, 'yoked' with that of good works (i.e. *islām*). Similar examples abound in the Koran. In any case, *islām* alone is never associated with the Garden. Even when *īmān* and *islām* are yoked together in contexts of this sort, it is *īmān*, and not *islām*, that is thought to be deserving the reward of Paradise, for, as we have seen before, the combination is to be understood in the form of [*A* (*b*)], not in that of [*A* and *B*] which places an equal amount of emphasis on both elements.[52]

The next point to note is that *īmān*, according to Ibn Taymiyyah, must not be represented as a fixed and immovable entity, because the Believer is constantly exposed to temptation.

> Even a real Believer may from time to time be assailed by this or that trait of Hypocrisy (*nifāq*). Then, after a while, God will turn toward him (and he will return to his perfect *īmān*). Very often there occurs in his heart something that necessitates an act of *nifāq*, but God repels it from his heart.
> The Believer, in general, is constantly tried by the 'whisperings' of Satan and the 'whisperings' of *kufr* which 'make his heart straitened'. Some of the Companions of the Prophet once confessed to him saying, 'O Apostle of God, we feel sometimes in ourselves something (which is so horrible that) we would rather fall down from the heaven to the earth than talk about it.' The Prophet replied to this, 'that is a pure and unmixed kind of *īmān*!'
> The *īmān* is pure and unmixed because of the feeling of horror and abhorrence of it (i.e. whispering of Satan) and their trying to keep it away from

51. For example, III, 85, X, 71, 72, II, 130, 132, etc.
52. *Ibid.* pp. 218–219, 295–298.

their hearts. … It is as pure and unmixed as pure milk. And it is pure because they abhorred the whisperings of Satan and defended themselves from them so that their belief was kept intact.[53] The *īmān* begins by being a small white spot in the heart. Then as the man grows in *īmān*, the heart goes on growing white until at last, when the *īmān* reaches its perfection, the whole heart turns pure white. Similarly the hypocrisy begins by being a small black spot in the heart. And as the man increases in hypocrisy, the heart, too, goes on increasing in blackness until at last, when the hypocrisy reaches its perfection, the whole heart turns black.[54] … (This suggests that *īmān* and *nifāq* may very well co-exist in one and the same heart.) Many sayings have been handed down to us, affirming that the heart sometimes contains *īmān* and *nifāq* at the same time. And both the Koran and the Sunnah clearly testify to the truth of this view. In fact, the Prophet often referred to the 'branches' (*shuʿab*, pl. of *shuʿbah*) or 'portions' of belief and hypocrisy. 'He who has in himself a portion of these qualities (i.e. telling lies, breaking promises, etc.) has a portion of *nifāq* until he abandons it'.[55] In such a case this one portion of *nifāq* may be co-existing within the heart of the man with many portions of *īmān*. And this explains why the Prophet said, 'He who has in his heart even the measure of a tiny grain of *īmān* will be allowed to go out of the Fire.' In other words, if a man has the smallest imaginable amount of *īmān* he will not be made to stay in the Fire forever. In case he has a great amount of *nifāq*, he will be punished in the Fire exactly according to that amount, and then will be allowed to go out of the Fire. …

Thus we can safely say that the interpretation given by some of the earliest authorities of the word *aslama* (verbal form of *islām*)[56] is correct, namely that it means *istaslama*, i.e. surrendering for fear of the sword. Also correct is the opinion that even this kind of *islām* is *islām*. For what is meant thereby is nothing but a (formal) entrance into Islam. And the formal and external *islām* of this sort may even comprise the Hypocrites not to speak of those in whose

53. *Ibid.* p. 238.

54. As is evident, this is an answer given to the question raised by the Murji'ites as to whether '*īmān* increases and decreases.' The problem itself in its original form will be discussed in the next chapter.

55. Cf. Bukhārī, *Īmān*, No. 32, 33. Instead of *shu'bah*, the word *khaṣlah* is used here.

56. Reference is to the Bedouins in the Koran, of whom mention has been made above.

hearts there coexist *īmān* and *nifāq*, although the pure Hypocrites whose hearts are totally black will (in the Hereafter) be put into the lowest region of the Fire.

This is why the Companions of the Prophet were so much afraid of *nifāq* with respect to themselves, though they were not at all afraid of the occurrence of *takdhīb* (which means 'giving the lie', as we saw in Chapter II) to God and His Apostles. They were not afraid of *takdhīb* because every true Believer is absolutely sure that he will never give the lie to God and the Apostle.

This is what justifies a Believer's declaring, 'I am really a Believer (man of *īmān*)'.[57] By saying so he only indicates that he knows most definitely his own *taṣdīq*. Only *īmān* does not consist in *taṣdīq* alone; it also includes, as we saw above, various acts of the heart (like fear of God, love of God etc.) and the latter in turn requires external acts.[58] …

It is certain, for example, that the adulterer, when he commits adultery, does so simply because there is love in his heart for that act. If there is fear of God, or love of God, firmly rooted in his heart and if it overcomes his carnal lust he would not commit adultery. … So he who is truly and sincerely devoted to God will never commit adultery. Man commits adultery solely because such fear or love is missing in him. It is this aspect of *īmān* that is problematic. His *taṣdīq* itself remains untouched.

This is why it is said of such a man that he is a Muslim, but not a Believer (in the full sense of the word), for a Muslim deserving a reward must necessarily be a man of *taṣdīq*—otherwise he would be a man of *nifāq*—and yet not everyone who is a man of *taṣdīq* is necessarily a man who fulfils all the requirements of the true *īmān*. … He may believe (*taṣdīq*) what the Apostle has told him, but he may, in spite of that, be inclined toward making a show before people and may find his wealth and family dearer to his heart than God, the Apostle, and the fighting in the way of God.

A man can be a Believer in the full sense of the word only when he finds God and His Apostle dearer to him than all others. The true Believer is he who never wavers, who fights willingly for the cause of God with his wealth and life. Anybody who lacks these properties of the true *īmān* is one of whom the

57. I.e. without there being necessity for adding *in shā'a Allāh* 'if God wills'. This problem will be dealt with later in a special chapter.

58. In other words, the core itself of *taṣdīq* may remain intact, but the surrounding parts may very well change at any moment.

> Apostle denied the name of *īmān* even if he has *taṣdīq*, and even if *taṣdīq* is part of *īmān*. … The mere *taṣdīq* which is not accompanied by the love of God and the fear of God is in no way the true *īmān*. It is like the *taṣdīq* of Pharaoh, the Jews, and Iblīs. And it was for this reason that the earlier authorities did not approve of the theological position of the Jahmites who declared *īmān* to be 'knowledge' *maʿrifah* alone.[59]

The last sentence of the long passage just quoted would seem to give us a good excuse for leaving Ibn Taymiyyah for a while and turning to an examination of the Murjiʾites. The Jahmites are generally classified by the Muslim heresiographers as one of the most important Murjiʾitesects.

59. *Ibid.* pp. 257–260.

CHAPTER V

THE ESSENTIAL STRUCTURE OF THE CONCEPT OF BELIEF

I The Murji'ites and the problem of *īmān*

Reference has already been made in an earlier chapter to the Murji'ites in connection with the problem of the grave sinner. Against the Khārijites, who exercised *takfīr* indiscriminately, the Murji'ites took up the attitude of non-commitment, i.e. of 'suspending the judgment' on the question of whether a particular individual was a Believer-Muslim or a Kāfir. Historically this was the original meaning of the word *irjā'* 'suspending, or postponing judgment', from which was derived their very name Murji'ite, that is, people of *irjā'*. In this form, the concept of *irjā'* was certainly more of a political nature than purely theological.

But we have seen also how this concept developed in the course of time into a theological one. At this second stage *irjā'* no longer meant 'suspending or postponing judgment' implying the attitude of political neutrality; it meant putting 'work' behind 'belief', that is, regarding 'work' *'amal* (pl. *a'māl*) as of secondary significance in relation to *īmān*, which alone is of essential importance. It is this aspect of the Murji'ites that we are concerned with in the present chapter. But we must remember that the problem of the relation between *īmān* and *'amal* was not the only concern of the Murji'ite theologians. It was but a part of a wider question: What is *īmān*?

It is indeed the most remarkable contribution of the Murji'ites toward the development of Muslim theology that they raised in a straightforward and crucial form the question of the essential structure of *īmān*. This was noticed and acknowledged by Muslim thinkers themselves, although most of them were more concerned with attacking vehemently the Murjiʾites for having belittled the significance of 'good work' and even excluded it completely from the conceptual field of *īmān*. This last point is largely true, as we shall see. But still the fact remains that the Murjiʾites were the first of the Muslims to take up seriously the problem of the inner structure of *īmān* as a theological concept.

It is very significant in this respect that Ashʿarī begins the chapter on the doctrines of the Murjiʾites in his *Maqālāt al-Islāmiyyīn* with the question:[1] What is *īmān* (*al-īmān mā hū*)? This exactly was the starting point and the center of all Murjiʾite thinking when it reached the second, i.e. theoretical and purely theological, stage. Before we go on to analyze the Murjiʾite concept of *īmān*, it is advisable that we try to have a bird's-eye view of different opinions put forward by the leading thinkers of this school. What follows is a summary of Ashʿarī's chapter just mentioned, with running commentary here and there. Ashʿarī divides the whole of the Murjiʾites into twelve groups, basing his divisions on the various types of responses to the problem of *īmān*.

[I] Jahm b. Ṣafwān and his followers called *Jahmiyyah* or the Jahmites[2]

(1) *Īmān* in God consists solely in knowing (*maʿrifah*) God and His Apostles and all that has come from God.

(2) Anything other than this kind of 'knowledge' is not *īmān*. So, for example, verbal confession (*iqrār*) by the tongue, humble submissiveness (*khuḍūʿ*)[3] in the heart, love of God and His Apostle, respect (*taʿẓīm*) for them, fear (*khawf*) of them, external works, etc. are completely excluded from *īmān*.

(3) *Kufr* means ignorance (*jahl*) of God.

(The above are the doctrines of Jahm himself. The following three points are ascribed to his followers).

(4) If a man has acquired the 'knowledge', then even if he denies by the tongue, the verbal denial does not make him a Kāfir.

(5) *Īmān* is indivisible into parts, and (consequently) the Believers cannot excel one another in regard to *īmān*.

1. *Maqālāt*, p. 132.

2. *Maqālāt*, p. 132.

3. Compare with this Ibn Taymiyyah's view discussed in the last part of the preceding chapter. For Ibn Taymiyyah, there can be no *īmān* where there is no 'submissiveness' of the heart.

(6) Both *īmān* and *kufr* have their seat in the heart, not in any other part of the body.

[II] Ṣāliḥī (Abū al-Ḥusayn) and his followers (*Ṣāliḥiyyah*)[4]

(1) *Īmān* is absolutely nothing other than 'knowledge' *maʿrifah*, and *kufr* is absolutely nothing other than 'ignorance' *jahl.*

(2) 'Knowledge' here means love of God and submissiveness to God.

(3) Belief in God in itself does not include belief in the Apostle. So theoretically it is quite possible that a man believes in God without believing in the Apostle. Practically, however, no one can believe in God without believing at the same time in the Apostle, because the Apostle has said: 'He who does not believe in me does not believe in God either'.

(4) Worship (*ṣalāt*) is not a means of serving God. There is no service to God but *īmān* in God, which is 'knowledge'.

(5) *Īmān* neither increases nor decreases; it is a single unit. And so is *kufr*.

(6) The saying of a man who says 'God is one of the three' (i.e. the profession of belief in the Trinity) does not constitute in itself *kufr*, but such a saying can come out only from a Kāfir.[5]

[III] Yūnus and his followers (*Yūnusiyyah*)[6]

(1) *Īmān* is the knowledge (*maʿrifah*) of God, submissiveness to Him, abandoning all haughtiness (*istikbār*) to Him, and loving Him.

(2) When a man gathers in himself all these qualities together, he is a Believer (man of *īmān*). Iblīs (i.e. Satan) knew God,[7] but he became a Kāfir because of

4. *Maqālāt*, pp. 132–133.

5. This seemingly strange statement is in reality nothing but a direct consequence of the thesis that *īmān* and *kufr* are exclusively a matter of 'knowledge' and 'ignorance' respectively. Whatever one says does not essentially affect *īmān* and *kufr*, because it is totally external to the heart. Thus Ṣāliḥī excludes from *īmān* the concept of 'verbal confession' *iqrār*. Ibn Ḥazm (*op. cit.* IV, p. 216), ascribing this theory to the Jahmites and the Ashʿarites (!), says that, according to them, denial of God, vilification of God, and denial of the Apostle do not constitute *kufr*, as long as these are a 'matter of the tongue', but they constitute a decisive evidence that there is *kufr* in the heart of one who says such things.

6. *Op. cit.* p. 133.

7. I.e. Iblīs had 'knowledge', one of the basic constituent elements of *īmān*.

his overbearing haughtiness to God.

(The next statement, Ashʿarī says, was the opinion of some of the followers of Yūnus, but Yūnus himself did not support it. Baghdādī, however, ascribes it to Yūnus.[8])

(3) Nobody can be a Believer unless he gathers all the above-mentioned qualities in himself, but the abandoning of even one of them is enough to make a man a Kāfir.

[IV] Abū Shimr and his followers (*Shimriyyah*)[9]

(1) *Īmān* is the knowledge of God, submissiveness to Him, loving Him with the heart, together with the verbal confession (*iqrār*) that He is One and that there is nothing like unto Him.[10]

(2) The above holds true so long as there is no witness of the Prophets concerning God. When, however, Prophets have been sent and their testimony established, *īmān* is believing in them and acknowledging them verbally. In the latter situation the knowledge of what has come down to us from God (i.e. directly, without the mediation of a Prophet) does not constitute part of *īmān*.

(3) No single quality of all the qualities (mentioned under 1) can be called by itself *īmān*, nor even a 'part of *īmān*'. Only when all of them are gathered together, is the whole thing called *īmān*.

(4) But the abandoning of these qualities, whether all of them or even a single one, constitutes *kufr*.

(5) *Īmān* is indivisible, and it is capable neither of increase nor of decrease.

(Ashʿarī adds one more item to the foregoing, saying that it is based On what Muḥammad b. Shabīb and ʿAbbād b. Sulaymān have related as Abū Shimr's personal opinion. It emphasizes especially Abū Shimr's relation with the Qadarite-Muʿtazilite movement. In fact Abū Shimr was one of the representative thinkers of what is generally known as *Murji'ah-Qadariyyah*).

(6) *Īmān* is knowledge of God and the verbal confession of it and of whatever

8. *Farq*, p. 191.

9. *Maqālāt*, pp. 134–135. It is noteworthy that Ashʿarī explains this fourth category as 'the followers of Abū Shimr *and* Yūnus'.

10. As we see, (1) of Abū Shimr is almost the same as (1) of Yūnus except for the fact that the former emphasizes that knowledge of God does not constitute *īmān* unless coupled with the confession of the Unity of God.

has come down from God, together with knowledge of Divine justice (*'adl*), that is to say, the knowledge of everything that affirms the 'justice' of God and everything that denies the existence of anything 'eternal' other than God,[11] whether the knowledge be based directly on the Scripture or derived from it by reasoning. All this is *īmān*, and the knowledge of it is *īmān*. He who doubts it is a Kāfir and the doubter of the doubter is also a Kāfir.[12]

[V] Abū Thawbān and his followers (*Thawbāniyyah*)[13]

(1) *Īmān* is the verbal confession of God and His Apostles[14] and of everything the doing of which is recognized by Reason[15] as obligatory. Everything the doing of which is not recognized by Reason to be obligatory does not form part of *īmān*.

(2) *Īmān* can increase but not decrease.

[VI] Najjār and his followers (*Najjāriyyah*)[16]

---

11. As is easy to see, this is nothing but the affirmation of the two basic tenets of the Mu'tazilites, 'justice' *'adl*, i.e. admitting the existence of free will in man, and 'Unity' *tawḥīd*, i.e. a denial of the existence of eternal attributes in God.

12. On page 477, Ash'arī gives again the Qadarite definition of *īmān* by Abū Shimr in almost the same terms.

13. *Maqālāt*, p. 135.

14. Baghdādī gives in his *Farq* (p. 192) practically the same definition of *īmān* by Abū Thawbān, but adds 'knowledge' and says: *Īmān* is the verbal confession and the knowledge of God and His Apostles, etc.

15. The original sentence in Ash'arī is a little confusing. Following faithfully the punctuation given in the text (*Maqālāt* ed. Ritter, p. 135) Professor Tritton (*Muslim Theology*, London, 1947), for instance, translates the passages as follows: 'Faith is confession of God and the apostles. Those acts, which reason declares to be necessary, and those, which reason says need not be done, are not part of faith.' This, however, would completely obscure the point which Abū Thawbān wanted to make. This will be clear immediately if one compares Ash'arī's description with what other writers, like Shahrastānī, and Baghdādī, report on Abū Thawbān's position. Particularly illuminating is what Maqrīzī writes about it: 'He asserts that *īmān* is 'knowledge' and 'verbal confession', and also that *īmān* is doing what Reason considers obligatory. Thus he bases the obligatory nature of *īmān* on Reason and thinks that Reason can decide before the Divine Law decides upon it'. (*Khiṭaṭ*, II, p. 350)

16. *Maqālāt*, pp. 135–136.

(1) *Īmān* consists of three things: Firstly, knowledge of God and His Apostles and of the religious duties (*farā'iḍ*) upon which there is an unanimous agreement among the Muslims; secondly, submissiveness to Him in all these matters, and thirdly, verbal confession.[17]
(2) One who is ignorant of any of the above-mentioned things when there is an undeniable evidence in proof of them, is a Kāfir. Also guilty of *kufr* is one who knows them and yet does not confess verbally.
(3) No single one of the above can by itself be called *īmān*. (Only when all of them are actualized together, do they constitute *īmān*).
(4) When all these *īmān*-making qualities are actualized together, each single quality constitutes an act of obedience (*ṭā'ah*). But the same quality, when actualized in isolation without the rest of them being done, does not constitute obedience. The knowledge of God, for example, does not constitute obedience if it stands isolated from the verbal confession. The reason for this is that God has commanded us to 'believe' as a single matter, and whoever does not obey God's command is not 'obedient' to Him.
(5) The neglect of any one single article is an act of 'disobedience', but nobody becomes a Kāfir by neglecting one single article (i.e. it is a sin, but not *kufr*). The name of *īmān* is not removed from a Believer except by his committing *kufr*.
(6) There is a difference of degrees among the people in regard to their *īmān*, for some of them may very well be superior to others in the degree of the knowledge of God, and show more of *taṣdīq* than others.

[VII] Ghaylān and his followers (*Ghaylāniyyah*)[18]
(1) *Īmān* consists of four things: the 'secondary knowledge' of God, love of God, submissiveness to Him, and the verbal confession of belief both in what the Apostle has brought and what has come from God.
(2) The 'primary' knowledge is a 'natural compulsion' *iḍṭirār* (i.e. 'inborn', being a direct act of God), and therefore is outside of *īmān*.[19]

---

17. Baghdādī in his *Uṣūl al-Dīn* gives an extremely brief formulation of the position taken by the Najjāriyyah on this problem. He writes (p. 249): *Īmān* consists of three things, knowledge (*ma'rifah*), verbal confession (*iqrār*), and submissiveness (*khuḍū'*).

18. *Maqālāt*, pp. 136–137.

19. Ghaylān's distinction between the 'primary' and the 'secondary' knowledge is extremely interesting. It will be discussed in the next chapter.

(According to Zurqān, one of the followers of the famous Muʿtazilite Naẓẓām, Ghaylān formulated his position here described as (1) and (2) in the following way. *Īmān* linguistically means *taṣdīq* 'assent'. And 'assent' is nothing but 'verbal confession'. Therefore, *īmān* is nothing other than 'confession by the tongue', whereas 'knowledge' *maʿrifah* of God, being a direct act of God, cannot be part of *īmān*.)[20]

(3) One single element of *īmān*, when isolated from others, cannot be called *īmān*, nor even 'part of *īmān*'. The Ghaylāniyyah on this point are completely at one with the Shimriyyah.

(4) The knowledge (*ʿilm*) that the things are created in time and absolutely under the Divine control is 'inborn' (*ḍarūrī*), while the knowledge (*ʿilm*) that He who has created them in time and exercises an absolute control upon them is (one) and not two, let alone more than two, is something acquired (*iktisāb*). Likewise the knowledge about the Prophet and about what has come from God must be regarded as 'acquired'. And this latter type of knowledge constitutes *īmān*, when what has come from God is scripturally grounded according to the Consensus of the Muslims. Nothing pertaining to the secondary level of pure philosophical theology (*dīn*)[21] is to be regarded as *īmān*.

(5) *Īmān* is indivisible and, therefore, capable neither of increase nor of decrease.

[VIII] Ibn Shabīb and his followers[22]

(1) *Īmān* is the verbal confession (*iqrār*) of God and the knowledge (*maʿrifah*) that He is One and nothing is like unto Him.

(2) *Īmān* is also the verbal confession and knowledge of the Prophets and the Apostles, and of all that they have brought down from God, and which has been accepted by the Muslims and handed down to us from the Apostle of God (Muḥammad), such as ritual worship, fasting etc., about which there is no dis-

---

20. *Maqālāt*, p. 137.

21. For this usage of the word *dīn* see *Maqālāt* p. 137, II. 10–11 (see below, [VIII], 2). It seems to mean in this context roughly a rational and free personal discussion of philosophical problems as contrasted to knowledge based directly on Revelation and the Prophet's teaching.

22. *Maqālāt*, pp. 137–138. Muḥammad b. Shabīb was a representative Murjiʾite thinker of a Qadarite type.

agreement and dispute among the Muslims.

As regards matters pertaining properly to philosophical theology,[23] such as the divergence of opinions on the (nature of) 'things', for example, he who opposes the truth is not a Kāfir, for it is merely a matter of personal conviction and secondary rational thinking and such a man does not in any way oppose the Apostle of God regarding what he has brought from God nor the Muslims regarding what they have received from their Prophet and definitely accepted.

(3) *Īmān* is also submissiveness to God and abandoning haughtiness. Iblīs knew God and confessed his belief in Him, and yet he became a Kāfir simply because of his haughtiness toward Him.

(4) *Īmān* is divisible, and there can be various degrees among the people in regard to *īmān*. Only when a man keeps all the elements of *īmān* is he a Believer. For, although a single element may very well be an act of 'obedience' *ṭāʿah* and 'part' *baʿḍ* of *īmān*, the man who keeps it intact can be a Kāfir by abandoning some (other) 'part' of *īmān*. For example, even if a man knows that God is One and that there is nothing like Him, and acknowledges openly what he knows to be true, his denial of the Prophets makes him a Kāfir by this every rejection of the Prophets. In so far as he knows God he has an element of *īmān*, for that is what God has commanded him to do, and yet he is a Kāfir by abandoning another important element of *īmān*; he has obeyed God's command only partially.

[IX] Abū Ḥanīfah and his followers[24]

(1) *Īmān* is knowledge of God and the verbal confession (of belief in) God, and knowledge of the Apostle and the verbal confession of all that has come from God (through him), (accepting it) as a whole, without any interpretation (*tafsīr*).

> (The expression 'as a whole, without any interpretation' has a very special meaning in the case of Abū Ḥanīfah, as the famous anecdote concerning a conversation between him and ʿUmar b. Abī ʿUthmān al-Shimmazī indicates. The anecdote suggests that 'interpretation' in this context means 'particularization'.
>
> When God has forbidden the Muslims to eat pork, for example, the words

23. *dīn*; see above, note 21.
24. *Maqālāt*, pp. 138–139.

must be taken 'as a whole', i.e. on the abstract level of thinking which is concerned only with Universals, not with Particulars. The prohibition, in other words, does not 'mean' this or that particular pig.
In the same way, when we are told that God has imposed upon us as a religious duty the pilgrimage to the Kaʿba, we have to accept it only on this abstract level. We do not have to know whether by Kaʿba is meant this particular Kaʿba in Mekka or some other one. We shall come back to this intellectualist tendency of Abū Ḥanīfah in section II of the present chapter.)

(2) *Īmān* is indivisible.[25]
(3) *Īmān* neither increases nor decreases. And there can be no difference of degrees among the people in regard to *īmān*.

(The article (3) is the direct theoretical consequence of the typically Murji'ite thesis that 'good works' do not constitute an essential element of *īmān*. Ashʿarī's formulation does not make this point explicit. Ibn Ḥazm in his formulation of Abū Ḥanīfah's position puts a special emphasis on this very point: *īmān* is knowing with the heart and confessing by the tongue. So he who knows the religion with his heart and verbally acknowledges it is a Muslim of perfect *īmān* and perfect *islām*. Good works are not to be called *īmān*, for they are but practical rules of conduct derived from *īmān*.' (*Fiṣal* IV, p. 188; see also II, p. 111)

(4) Nothing pertaining to pure philosophical theology is to be regarded as *īmān*[26]

[X] Tūmanī (Abū Muʿādh) and his followers (*Tūmaniyyah*)[27]
(1) *Īmān* is that which protects (man) from (falling into) *kufr*.
(2) It is a name for a number of constituent elements. If a man neglects them, or even one of them, he is a Kāfir. Thus the whole of those elements, the neglect

---

25. As an illustration of Abū Ḥanīfah's unshaken conviction of the indivisibility of *īmān*, Wensinck (*op. cit.* p. 140) gives a very interesting story. In Abū Ḥanīfah's view, *īmān* is a whole entity and there can be no 'parts' discernible in it. This naturally leads to the thesis that no Muslim can turn into a Kāfir on account of grave sins he has committed, a thesis which is diametrically opposed to the Khārijite position.

26. See above, Ghaylān (3). Ashʿarī notes that this is Abū Ḥanīfah's personal view, suggesting that it is not a thesis generally shared by his followers.

27. *Maqālāt*, pp. 139–140.

of which, or the neglect of even one of which, makes a man a Kāfir, is *īmān*. No single element is to be regarded as *īmān*, not even as a 'part' of *īmān*.
(3) He who does an act of disobedience which happens to be a religious duty must be described in a verbal (not nominal) form, namely that 'he commits a sin' *fasaqa*. He should not be described (in the nominal form which suggests stability and a constant nature) as a Fāsiq, i.e. 'a sinner'. Generally speaking, grave sins do not drive the man out of the domain of *īmān*, unless the act done be an act of *kufr*.
(4) If a man neglects religious duties like worship, fasting and pilgrimage with a clear consciousness of denial, opposition and disdain, he is a Kāfir because of this consciousness. If, on the contrary, he neglects them with no such intention, but merely because he happens to be too busy at the moment either with business or pleasure, then he is not a Kāfir as long as he has the intention of fulfilling the duty some day or sometime later. In such a case he only 'commits a sin.'

[XI] Bishr al-Marīsī and his follower (*Marīsiyyah*)[28]
(1) *Īmān* is 'assent' *taṣdīq* and nothing else, for, linguistically, *īmān* does mean *taṣdīq*. So anything other than *taṣdīq* cannot be *īmān*. But *taṣdīq* here (should not be taken exclusively in the sense of 'assent by the heart'); it is 'assent' by both the heart and the tongue.

[XII] Ibn Karrām and his followers (*Karrāmiyyah*)[29]
(1) *Īmān* is a verbal confession, that is, an acknowledgment by the tongue alone, not by heart. 'Knowledge' (*maʿrifah*) by the heart, or for that matter anything other than 'assent by the tongue', must be excluded from *īmān*.
(2) *Kufr* is a denial of God by the tongue.
(3) Therefore, the Munāfiqs (Hypocrites) of the period of the Apostle of God (who are described in the Koran as people who say by the tongue 'We believe', and yet do not believe by the heart) were Believers in the real sense of the world.

(Ashʿarī in this chapter does not assign a separate section to Ghassān of Kūfah and his followers. Only at the end of the section dealing with Abū Ḥanīfah, he

28. *Maqālāt*, p. 140.
29. *Maqālāt*, p. 141.

gives one of the main tenets of Ghassān as something common to him and to some of the followers of Abū Ḥanīfah. But certainly Ghassān is a big figure in the Murji'ite movement, important enough to be given an independent section. So I give here as XIII his main tenets concerning the concept of *īmān*, according to Baghdādī.)[30]

[XIII] Ghassān and his followers (*Ghassāniyyah*)
(1) *Īmān* is the confession of God, love (*maḥabbah*) for God, reverence (*taʿẓīm*) toward Him and abandoning haughtiness (*istikbār*) before Him.
(2) *Īmān* can increase, but cannot decrease.
(3) Each single element of *īmān* is a 'part' of *īmān*.

Having finished a broad survey of the main subdivisions of the Murji'ites in regard to their views on the essential nature of *īmān*, let us now set out to analyze their thought more systematically in order to see how *īmān* establishes itself as a conceptual entity in the minds of the Murji'ite thinkers, a conceptual entity endowed with a definite structure. This aspect of the Murji'ite thought is very important historically because, as we shall see in the following chapters, almost all the major theological directions connected with the concept of *īmān* will subsequently be determined by the problems raised by the Murji'ites.

II The essential structure of *īmān*

In approaching this problem, we shall do well to recall at the outset what was said before regarding the main points of reference in the understanding of the concept of *īmān* in general.

'Verbal confession' and 'external work' are made here two additional reference points to the main structure consisting of 'subject', 'object', and 'inner belief', in order to make the diagram particularly suitable to the Murji'ite thesis. But the tripartite main body will suit for a conceptual analysis of anything corresponding to the Arabic *īmān*. In other words, the concept of 'belief' or 'faith' is always capable of being approached profitably from the three points of view

30. *Farq*, p. 191.

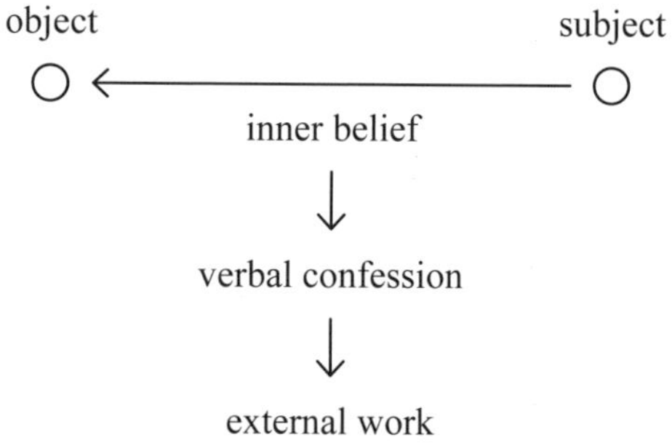

here suggested. First, the 'subject' of belief, i.e. he who believes, or Believer. We may note that it was historically the Khārijites who put particular stress on the 'subject' of belief in this sense. At any rate their primary concern was the question: 'Who is the Believer (*mu'min*)?' This problem, as we have seen in the first chapter, was approached by them negatively. That is to say, they began by asking 'Who is the Kāfir?', and by way of elimination, i.e. by eliminating from the Muslim community all the Kāfirs they tried to establish the identity of the believers. And this because they were primarily interested in the problem of the ideal formation of the Muslim community (*ummah*).

The second pole of the conceptual structure of *īmān* is the 'object' of Belief. The Koran and the Ḥadīth put very strong emphasis on this aspect of the phenomenon. The problem here is: 'What are the objects in which to believe?' The standard answer to this question is: 'God, His angels, His book, meeting with Him, the final resurrection', which is found in the above-mentioned Ḥadīth of Gabriel. In this famous Ḥadīth, we must note, *īmān* is defined in terms of its objects. Of course, the answer may take many other forms. Indeed, the Koran pays attention to all the remaining four aspects distinguished above as well. In this respect we would probably be closer to the real picture when we say that both the Khārijites and the Murji'ites did not pay much attention to the second point of reference, being occupied as they were with some important problems arising from the rest.[31]

---

31. The Khārijites with the first reference point, and the Murji'ites primarily with the third and secondarily with the fourth and the fifth. However, it is not true either to say that the Murji'ites did not elaborate at all the problem of the 'object' of *īmān*. We shall come to this point presently.

However this may be, the third reference point, i.e. the act of believing itself, was very much developed and elaborated theoretically by the Murjiʾites. The central problem in their theological thinking was: 'How is *īmān* structured?' 'What is the real nature of *īmān*?' The fourth and fifth reference points, i.e. 'verbal confession' and 'work', were, so to speak, the natural outgrowth of the discussion among them of the most basic problem 'What is *īmān*?'

It is worthy of note that all the post-Murjiʾite discussions on the essence of *īmān* almost invariably follow the pattern originally devised by the Murjiʾites. In fact, the classical form in which Muslim theologians discuss the nature of *īmān* is based on the recognition of three major factors in the concept of *īmān*. These are:

(1) *taṣdīq* (*bi-al-qalb*), assent or avowal by the heart.
(2) *iqrār* (*bi-al-lisān*), verbal acknowledgment or confession by word in mouth.
(3) *ʿamal* (*al-ṭāʿāt*), acts of obedience or (good) works.

The first one, *taṣdīq*, concerns the inner structure of the act of believing itself, and corresponds to the third reference point in the above-given diagram. This, in other words, represents the Murjiʾite interpretation of the mental act of *īmān*. To be more exact, however, we should say that, instead of understanding *īmān* in terms of *taṣdīq* as almost all the later theologians do, the Murjiʾites themselves preferred rather to understand it in terms of 'knowledge' *maʿrifah*.

The second factor, *iqrār*, is an explicit verbal acknowledgment of the fact that one has in his mind *taṣdīq* or *maʿrifah*. It is a verbal expression of inner *īmān*, while the third, *ʿamal* (pl. *aʿmāl*) is an outward, bodily expression of the same inner *īmān*.

It is remarkable that the Murjiʾites raised the problems of (1) and (2) positively, that is, by stressing the importance of these two factors, while they raised the problem of (3) negatively, i.e. by denying the essential importance of it in the concept of *īmān*. The Murjiʾites, except the extremists among them with whom we shall deal in the following chapters, did not deny absolutely the value of *ʿamal*. But, at least, they did not consider it one of the 'pillars' (*arkān*, sg. *rukn*) of *īmān*; they rather regarded it as of secondary importance. Hence the name of *irjāʾ*, as we saw above, meaning literally the 'postponement' of *ʿamal*. In modern terminology we might say that the Murjiʾite position is, ethically, a motivation theory. They put emphasis on the motive—*niyyah* in Arabic, which plays an exceedingly important role in the Ḥadīth—rather than on the action itself. In any case this negative attitude of the Murjiʾites toward *ʿamal* evoked strong protests in the Muslim community; hot disputes ensued, and thus *ʿamal* soon ended by becoming a key-concept of Islamic theology.

Before we go on to examine the important theoretical problems connected with each one of the three major factors of *īmān*, let us go back to the main tenets of the Murji'ites which we have given in the first section and consider their thought more analytically.

The first point to note is the preponderance given to 'knowledge' *maʿrifah* in the definition of *īmān*. Ṣāliḥī's concise dictum:[32] '*Īmān* is the knowledge of God only' is representative of this attitude, but the equation (*īmān* = *maʿrifah*) itself is common to almost all the Murji'ites and is, indeed, most typical of their thought concerning *īmān*. Ibn Karrām[33] is the most conspicuous exception.

This explicit emphasis on 'knowledge' as the very essence of *īmān* was but a direct manifestation of a basic tendency of the Murji'ites, another manifestation of which, as we have just observed, was the motivation theory in ethics. In other words, the Murji'ites were not content with regarding *īmān* as something external, but wanted to emphasize that it is something lying deep in the human heart, a spiritual event occurring in the very depth of the mind.

There was a man in the Murji'ite school who pushed this tendency still further, that is, who wanted to make 'knowledge' of God something even deeper. That man was Ghaylān.[34] The true 'knowledge' of God, he asserted, is something innate, inborn in the human mind. It is a direct working of God, and man is not capable of doing anything about it. It is something 'necessary' *ḍarūrī*,[35] a natural 'compulsion' *iḍṭirār*. This kind of deep, inborn 'knowledge' of God Ghaylān calls 'primary knowledge' *al-maʿrifah al-ūlá*, and he denies the name of *īmān* to it. What we call *īmān* is nothing but the 'secondary knowledge', i.e. a knowledge of God that is 'acquired' by man.

According to Baghdādī, this attitude led him to an extraordinary conclusion shared only by Ibn Karrām and usually identified as the typically Karrāmite position, namely that *īmān* is merely a matter of 'verbal confession'. Ashʿarī, however, is probably nearer to the truth when he says that for Ghaylān *īmān*

32. See above [II], (1)
33. See above [XII], (1)
34. See above [VII], (1), (2), (4)
35. Baghdādī, *Farq*, p. 194

consists of the 'secondary knowledge' coupled with 'verbal confession', for, otherwise, there would have been no point in Ghaylān's calling the deeper kind of knowledge 'primary'.

Even though other Murjiʾites did not go to such an extreme thesis as Ghaylān, still they, in general, had a very marked tendency to regard *īmān* as something deep, something that touches the very core of the human heart. This is shown by their predilection for words standing for emotional —existential, we might say—attitudes in their definition of *īmān*, like 'love' of God and 'submissiveness' to Him. It is remarkable in this respect that Ṣāliḥī,[36] who begins by saying that '*īmān* is absolutely nothing other than "knowledge" *maʿrifah*', goes on to say that 'by "knowledge" is meant love of God and submissiveness to Him'. Others simply put 'love', 'submissiveness' and 'abandoning haughtiness' side by side with 'knowledge' in their definition of *īmān*, e.g. Yūnus, Abū Shimr, Ibn Shabīb, Ghassān. The most notable exception is Jahm,[37] who deliberately and explicitly excludes all emotional attitudes together with external works from *īmān*.

The second feature of the Murjiʾite theories of *īmān* that must be pointed out is the importance given to 'verbal acknowledgment' or 'confession by word of mouth' *iqrār bi-al-lisān*, which is the second major factor of *īmān* as distinguished above. Many of the Murjiʾites combine 'knowledge' and 'confession' in their definition of *īmān*. This is exemplified by Abū Shimr,[38] who not only defined *īmān* as 'knowledge' and 'confession' together, but, according to Baghdādī,[39] asserted that 'knowledge' cannot be *īmān* unless it is accompanied by 'confession'.

Equally interesting is Bishr al-Marīsī's position that *īmān* is nothing but 'assent' *taṣdīq*, but *taṣdīq* should not be taken solely in the sense of 'assent by the heart'; it includes also 'assent by the tongue'.

However, by far the most important of all in this respect is the position taken by Ibn Karrām, to which reference has been made above in connection with Ghaylān. In emphasizing the importance of 'verbal confession', he went to the

36. See above [II], (1), (2)
37. See above [I], (2)
38. See above [IV], (1)
39. *Farq*, p. 193, *al-maʿrifah lā takūnu īmān illā maʿa al-iqrār*

extreme. He declared openly that *īmān* is 'verbal confession' alone, nothing else, and that 'knowledge' by the heart has nothing at all to do with *īmān*.[40]

This naturally aroused widespread indignation in the Muslim community, and Ibn Karrām and his followers became a target of all manner of abuse and vehement attack. The Karrāmite thesis was felt to be scandalous and even blasphemous because, besides being in itself expressive of an attitude which slighted *īmān*, it would lead to the most surprising conclusion that all the Hypocrites are real Believers, a conclusion to which Ibn Karrām himself was actually led.[41] The popular sentiment against the Karrāmites found its expression in the form of a Ḥadīth: The Prophet once said, 'Cursed are the Murji'ites by the mouth of seventy prophets!' Someone asked him, 'Who are the Murji'ites O Apostle of God?' To this the Prophet replied, 'They are those who assert that *īmān* is nothing but speech (*kalām*)'.[42]

It is worthy of note that in this Ḥadīth, the Murji'ites are simply identified with the Karrāmites. In other words, the Karrāmite thesis is here taken as the extreme form of Murji'ism. As we shall see later, the enemies of the Murji'ites often had recourse to this identification in attacking them. They attacked the Murji'ites by attacking the Karrāmites, tacitly taking it for granted that the latter were representative of the former. This evidently made the attack extremely easy, but of course by doing this the critics were not doing justice to the schools of the Murji'ism other than the Karrāmites.

In the third place, we must observe that some of the Murji'ites paid attention to the second reference point of *īmān* as distinguished above, that is, the 'object' of belief, although their attention was, as I have pointed out before, mostly drawn toward the problem of the act of belief itself. Most Murji'ites define *īmān* as 'knowledge'. But 'knowledge' of what? That is the question.

God forms incontestably the first object of 'knowledge'. Then comes in the second place the Apostle (or Apostles). About this second object, however, we witness a considerable divergence of opinion among the Murji'ites. Some of them simply put the Apostle side by side with God as objects of 'knowledge'.[43] Others show some hesitation and admit the Apostle as the second object of

40. See above [XII], (1)
41. [XII], (2)
42. quoted by Baghdādī, *Farq*, p. 190.
43. for example Jahm [I]

'knowledge' with some reservation.[44] It is worth noting in this connection that Yūnus, according to Baghdādī,[45] includes knowledge of the Apostles in the definition of *īmān* under a certain condition. Namely, when the Apostles have been sent and their evidence established, then acknowledging them and knowing what they have brought constitute part of *īmān*. But even then, he adds, what is required is a general knowledge of what has come from them; a concrete knowledge of the details does not constitute *īmān*, nor even a part of *īmān*. Almost the same thing is ascribed by Ashʿarī[46] to 'the followers of Abū Shimr and Yūnus'. But in Ashʿarī's description the position taken by Abū Shimr (or Yūnus, or both) is more radical and thoroughgoing. For it is asserted that when the Prophets' evidence has been established, *īmān* consists in acknowledging them by the heart and by the tongue, and the knowledge that has come down from God without a prophetic intermediary no longer constitutes part of *īmān*.

Some Murji'ites went beyond God and the Apostle in assigning to the 'knowledge' in question its proper objects. Ibn Shabīb,[47] for instance, emphasized Consensus or *ijmāʿ*. For him, the first object of 'knowledge' is God, the second His Apostles, and the third object is constituted by all that has been revealed by God and then unanimously accepted by the community, like worship, *zakāt*, fasting and pilgrimage.

In place of Consensus, Abū Thawbān emphasizes the authority of Reason.[48] After God and the Apostle, he recognizes as the third necessary object of 'knowledge' everything the doing of which is deemed obligatory by Reason. Consequently, everything the doing of which is not rationally obligatory does not form part of *īmān*.

We find these two authorities, Consensus (*ījmāʿ*) and Reason (*ʿaql*), combined by Abū Shimr. According to Baghdādī,[49] he counted as the objects of

---

44. The most conspicuous example of this is Ṣāliḥī [II], (3)

45. *Farq*, p. 191.

46. See above [IV], (2), and note 9. Baghdādī ascribes this thesis only to Yūnus. He does not mention anything of the sort in regard to Abū Shimr.

47. See above [VIII], (2)

48. See above [V], (1)

49. *Farq*, p. 193. Also see above [IV] (6). Ashʿarī here writes merely: '*īmān* is knowledge of God … and of whatever has come down from God, together with knowledge of Divine justice'. The important implication of these words is made much more explicit by Baghdādī.

'knowledge', (1) God, (2) whatever has come down from God and upon which the Muslim community is unanimously agreed like worship, *zakāt*, fasting, pilgrimage, the prohibition against the meat of animals not slaughtered in accordance with the Law, etc., and (3) that which can be known by Reason, meaning thereby specifically, (a) the 'justice' *ʿadl* of God as understood in the Qadarite sense, and (b) the 'unity' *tawḥīd* of God as understood in the Muʿtazilite sense, i.e. negation of God's eternal attributes, and (c) the non-existence of any 'similarity' *tashbīh* whatsoever between God and the creatures.

In the fourth place, I would like to point out, as one of the characteristic features of the Murjiʾite theory of *īmān*, the concept of divisibility (*tabaʿʿuḍ*). The question is whether *īmān* is an indivisible unity or a compound of several 'elements' (*khiṣāl*, sg. *khaṣlah*). This was a typically Murjiʾite problem, and it not only occupied an important place in the Murjiʾite thinking, but it promoted remarkably the development of an analytical way of thinking among the people. The people began to talk about the 'branches' (*shuʿab*, sg. *shuʿbah*) of *īmān*, and to ask themselves, 'Of how many branches does *īmān* consist?' To this question a Ḥadīth gives the following answer. *Īmān* is composed of sixty odd branches, the moral scruple (*ḥayāʾ*) being one of them'.[50]

By analogy, the Ḥadīth discusses the concept of 'hypocrisy' *nifāq* in terms of its constituent elements (*khiṣāl*). For instance, '(*Nifāq* consists of four elements.) Whoever possesses these four in himself is a downright Hypocrite. He who possesses one of these elements has in himself an element (*khaṣlah*) of hypocrisy until he abandons it. (The four elements are as follows:) (1) When a man, being entrusted with something, betrays it; (2) when he speaks, he lies; (3) having made a compact with someone, deceives; (4) when engaged in a dispute, has recourse to dishonest ways.'[51]

However this may be, it is clear that the divisibility and indivisibility of *īmān* was a very serious question for the Murjiʾites. Most of them took the position that *īmān* consists of several parts, and is therefore divisible. Ibn Shabīb, Yūnus, Tūmanī, and Ghassān were representative of this position.

For those who thus admitted the compound nature of *īmān*, the next im-

50. Bukhārī, *Īmān*, No. 8.

51. *Ibid.* No. 33. Note the characteristically Murjiʾite mode of thinking: he who has a *khaṣlah* of them, has in himself a portion of *nifāq*.

portant question was whether every single element was to be considered a part (*baʿḍ*) of *īmān* or not. Ghassān said, 'Yes, every single element (*khaṣlah*) is a part of *īmān.*' Ibn Shabīb went a step further and asserted, 'since every element is a part of *īmān*, whoever abandons one is a Kāfir because he thereby abandons part of *īmān.*' To this he added, 'no single part of *īmān*, however, makes a man a Believer; only when he adheres to all the elements together is he a Believer'.

Some of the Murjiʾites refused to regard a single isolated element as a part of *īmān*, not to speak of regarding it as *īmān* itself. Yūnus and Tūmanī represent this thesis.

Against all those people who asserted the divisibility of *īmān* into constituent parts, there were some who categorically denied this and took up the position that *īmān* was a single unit (*khaṣlah wāḥidah*), and essentially indivisible just as *kufr* was a single unit and indivisible. Ṣāliḥī was a typical representative of this position. So too was Jahm.

Closely connected with the problem of the divisibility of *īmān* was that of 'increase and decrease' of *īmān*. This is also a typically Murjiʾite approach. It is but natural that Ṣāliḥī, who, as we have just seen, denies the divisibility of *īmān*, denies also the possibility of its increasing and decreasing. And since there is no increase and decrease, there can be no different degrees among men as regards their *īmān*. People, in other words, cannot excel one another in *īmān*. Such was also the position taken by Abū Shimr, Jahm, Ghaylān, and Abū Ḥanīfah.

As to those who admitted the divisibility of *īmān* into parts, some admitted only the possibility of increase, but not of decrease (Najjār, Ghassān). It is remarkable that, the Murjiʾites, generally speaking, were definitely inclined toward the denial of the increase and decrease of *īmān*. And the proposition: '*īmān* neither increases nor decreases' is usually mentioned as one of the characteristic features of the Murjiʾite conception of *īmān*. The question seems to have aroused much discussion in the Muslim community. It attracted the keenest attention of those who were engaged in collecting and studying Ḥadīths. Bukhārī, for instance, makes this problem the very first section of his 'Book of *īmān*'. There he takes up a definite position against the Murjiʾite tendency and declares that '*īmān* does increase and decrease'.

It is important to observe that the Murjiʾite attitude toward the problem of the increase and decrease of *īmān* was not only connected with the concept of indivisibility of *īmān*, as we have seen in the foregoing, but even more immediately with the question of the low evaluation of 'work' in the structure of *īmān*. This last point may be isolated as the fifth characteristic feature of the Murji'ite conception of *īmān*.

It has been often pointed out that the very name of *Murji'ah* owes its origin to the fact the thinkers of this school 'put external work behind inner belief'. We would be doing gross injustice to the Murji'ites, however, if we thought that they simply dismissed 'work' *'amal* as of no value at all for *īmān*. We have remarked above in discussing the proper 'object' of *īmān* in the Murji'ite conception, that some of the leading thinkers, like Ibn Shabīb, Abū Thawbān and Abū Shimr, did attach great importance to the acts of obedience including the so-called five Pillars of Islam. However, the point is that, even in the thought of those Murji'ites who admit the 'work', the knowledge (*ma'rifah*) by the heart of the acts of obedience is all that is primarily required. *Īmān* is basically a matter of knowledge, not of practice. Whether a Muslim really *does* good works or not is of secondary significance. Here the intellectualist inclination of the Murji'ites is revealed in a most interesting way. They are interested in discussing the nature of *īmān* solely as a matter of conceptual analysis. And on this level of analysis the 'knowledge' of the obligatory works may be included in the concept of *īmān*, but not 'doing' itself, for the latter belongs to an entirely different level, that of practice. Their dictum that the (concept of) *īmān* does not comprehend *a'māl* 'works' must be understood in this way. But for those who are opposed to them, the Murji'ite concept of the Believer who has the knowledge of God, the Apostle, and all works that are obligatory either by Reason or by Consensus, and yet does not carry these works into practice, is simply absurd and inadmissible. In this sense the critics of the Murji'ites are justified in blaming the latter for relegating 'work' to the place of non-essentials.

The most important theoretical consequence of the thesis that the concept of *īmān* does not comprise 'work' is that *īmān* remains essentially unaffected by sins, even by grave sins. In terms of the 'subject' of *īmān*, this is the same as saying that a Believer does not turn into a Kāfir on account of sin. He who has committed a grave sin is a Believer-Sinner, or simply Fāsiq. This position brings into the semantic field of *ummah* or the Muslim community a remarkable change in the distribution of concepts.

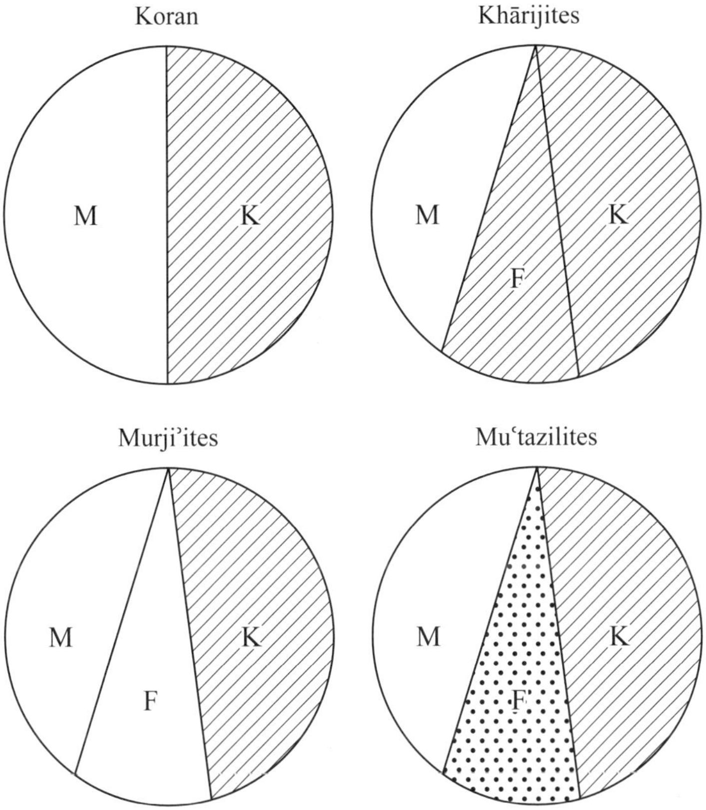

M *Muʾmin* (Believer) K *Kāfir* (Infidel) F *Fāsiq* (Sinner)

As this diagram shows, the Koranic conception is based on simple dichotomy. The Khārijites made *F* part of *K*, thus making the region of *M*, i.e. the Muslim community, as narrow as possible. The Murjiʾites, on the contrary, considered *F* part of *M*, while the Muʿtazilites, as we saw earlier, made *F* an independent section standing between *M* and *F*.

We have now finished a general survey of the Murjiʾite standpoint regarding the concept of *īmān*. As has been indicated above, the Murjiʾites raised several fundamental problems and left them for those who followed them. These problems may be classified under three heads: (1) those that concern the identification *īmān* = *taṣdīq* = *maʿrifah*, (2) those that concern the place of *iqrār* ʻverbal acknowledgment' or 'confession' in the conceptual structure of *īmān*, and (3) those that concern *ʿamal* 'work'. In what follows we shall devote a separate chapter to each one of these three major problems.

CHAPTER VI

BELIEF AND KNOWLEDGE

I The predominance given to 'knowledge' in the definition of *īmān*

The most conspicuous feature shared by the leading Murji'ite thinkers is, as we have seen in the preceding chapter, the predominance given to 'knowledge' *maʿrifah* in their definition of *īmān*. It is easy to push this position to a perilous extreme, as many of the later critics of Murji'ism actually did. In that extreme form, the Murji'ite thesis would be nothing other than extolling 'knowledge' as the sole determining factor of *īmān* and assigning no value at all to 'verbal confession' and external 'work'. Malaṭī, for example, describes the typical Murji'ite position in the following way:[1]

> Some of the Murji'ites assert: *Īmān* is exclusively 'knowledge' by the heart. It includes neither an activity of the tongue nor any bodily action. So that he who knows by his heart that He is unique there being no other thing like Him, is a (true) Believer whether he prays toward the East or the West, and even if he wears a girdle[2] round his waist. They declare that imposing upon such a man an open confession by the tongue would simply mean imposing upon him a bodily action. Some of them went even to the length of asserting that the ritual worship (*ṣalāt*) is a sign of the weakness of *īmān*, and that he who participates in worship weakens thereby his *īmān*.

After saying these words which depict the Murji'ites in a very disfavorable light, Malaṭī starts to criticize them relentlessly. And, needless to say, it is an extremely easy task for him. To those who have an objective knowledge of the

1. *Op. cit.* pp. 142–143.
2. *zunnār* a girdle worn by the Christians, Jews, and Magians, as a sign of a *dhimmī*.

real Murjiʾite theory of *īmān*, however, Malaṭī's criticism would give the impression of a man fighting against a phantom which he himself has conjured up. Still, it is of some interest to us, because it gives us an idea of the way the orthodox community of the later ages pictured the 'hideous heresy' *shanāʿah* of the Murjiʾites. We shall meet with the same kind of attitude on the part of the Orthodox toward Murjiʾism when we examine in the next chapter the Karrāmite position which was taken as the representative thesis of the Murjiʾites. Be this as it may, here is Malaṭī's comment on the Murjiʾite thesis as he has presented it:

> (1) How is it permissible at all that a Believer pray toward the East and the West indifferently? God Himself says (II, 144) 'We see thee (Muḥammad) turning thy face to this or that point in the heavens. Now We shall give thee a definite direction in prayer which will satisfy thee. Turn thy face toward the place of Worship in Mecca. And ye (Believers) turn your faces toward it wheresoever ye may be'. And the Prophet once wrote to the people of Yemen: 'Whoever does the same ritual worship as ours and turns his face toward the same direction as ours ..., verily he is a Muslim with all the duties and rights that belong to a Muslim'.
> (2) How is it imaginable that a Believer should wear a *dhimmī* girdle on his waist when we have the Prophet's own words against it: 'he who resembles (even in outward attire) (non-Muslim) people is one of them'?
> (3) How can 'knowledge' with the heart suffice without 'verbal confession'? God Himself says (IV, 59) 'O ye Believers, obey God, and obey the Apostle and those of you who possess authority'. This kind of 'obedience' can never occur except by 'saying' and 'doing'.

To equate Belief and Knowledge completely and to assert that *īmān* is nothing but *maʿrifah* would be no doubt a pure intellectualist-rationalist attitude.[3] But we know already from what we have seen in the foregoing chapter that it is wrong to picture the leading Murjiʾite thinkers as pure rationalists of this type. We have seen how they recognize the importance of 'verbal confession', and

3. unless we take the word 'knowledge' *maʿrifah* in the Sufi sense of a 'personal and intuitive knowledge' of God. In the Murjiʾite context the 'knowledge' ordinarily means to know God as He describes Himself in the Koran. See the interesting remark made by Professor Henri Laoust on the meaning of *maʿrifah* as a technical term in Hanbalism, in his *La profession de foi d'Ibn Baṭṭa*, Damas, 1958, p. 3, note (1).

put it on a par with 'knowledge' in their definition of *īmān*. The only conspicuous exceptions in this respect are Jahm and Ibn Karrām. The former, explicitly excludes 'verbal confession', while the latter definitely excludes everything other than 'verbal confession' from *īmān*.

Furthermore, things like 'love of God', 'fear of God', 'abandoning human pride and haughtiness', and 'submissiveness' are frequently mentioned by the Murji'ites as essential elements of *īmān* besides 'knowledge' and 'confession'. All these words standing for emotional states point to a deeply pious mind which, even when it is working on the intellectual level of thinking and theorizing, cannot afford to neglect the more subjective side of religious feeling and emotion that is involved in the act of *īmān*.

And yet, with this reservation, we must admit also the existence of a predominantly intellectualist-rationalist tendency in the Murji'ites. It is interesting to note in this connection that, according to Ashʿarī,[4] the Murji'ites as a whole were divided into two opposing camps in regard to the question of whether a true *īmān* is possible or not without being based on reasoning (*naẓar*). 'One party asserts that any conviction of the Unicity of God that has been obtained without reasoning does not constitute *īmān*, while the other takes the position that the conviction of the Unicity of God which is not based on reasoning is *īmān*'. As we shall see later in the present chapter, this question, once raised in this particular form, leads to the more crucial one of whether the common people, who by nature are incapable of the strictly logical way of thinking, can be real Believers or not.

The intellectualism of the Murji'ites is represented by Abū Ḥanīfah and his school, which develops later into Māturīdism in Transoxiana. The famous anecdote, to which reference has been made earlier, discloses the intellectualist inclination of Abū Ḥanīfah himself. The anecdote as related by Ashʿarī runs as follows:[5]

> According to Abū 'Uthmān al-Ādamī, Abū Ḥanīfah and 'Umar b. Abī 'Uthmān al-Shimmazī met once in Mecca. 'Umar asked him, 'Tell me, what do you think of a man who asserts that God has forbidden the eating of pork, and yet he is not sure whether this prohibition of the eating of pork applies to this particular pig (which is concretely before his eyes at this moment)'? He an-

4. *Maqālāt*, p. 144.
5. *Ibid.* pp. 138–139.

> swered, 'Such a man is a Believer'.
> Thereupon ʿUmar asked him, 'Suppose this man asserts furthermore that God has made the pilgrimage to Mecca a religious duty, but that he is not sure whether what is meant is this (Kaʿba in Mecca or) some other Kaʿba in some other place.' He answered, 'Such a man is a Believer.'
> Then (ʿUmar) asked him, 'What if the man asserts furthermore, "I know the fact that God has sent Muḥammad as His Apostle. But who knows? It may well be that (the Apostle meant by God) happens to be this black African slave"?' He answered, 'Such a man is a Believer'.

The genuineness of this anecdote has been often doubted, rightly to my mind. At least there is something artificial about the whole event here narrated. We have to keep in mind, on the other hand, that the story was very well-known and widely circulated among the Muslims. Even if it were a forgery entirely, i.e. a story forged by those who did not like Abū Ḥanīfah's method and foisted it upon him, yet it would have been completely pointless to forge such an anecdote even to ridicule him, if there had not been something in Abū Ḥanīfah himself that would have justified the criticism. In this sense, the anecdote, whether genuine or forged, must be interpreted as an illustration of one of the most salient features of Abū Ḥanīfah's way of thinking.

What, then, is the most salient feature revealed by this anecdote? I would be inclined to think that it discloses Abū Ḥanīfah's rationalist or intellectualist position. The point may be made clear by observing a basic fact about two different ways of 'knowing' things. Generally speaking, knowledge of a thing may be obtained on two different levels of thinking: (1) the level of Universals, which produces the essentialist type of knowledge, and (2) the level of Particulars, i.e. concrete individual things, which produces the existentialist type of knowledge. On the first level, the knowledge we obtain is of an analytic nature. Instead of 'knowing' (directly) a person A, for example, we 'know (something) about' him. In other words, we know *that* A is such-and-such. But we do not know him, on this level, as a matter of personal, intimate and absolutely unique relationship with him. The knowledge on the first level gains in precision and articulation but loses in depth.

The true depth of knowledge can be reached only on the second level of knowing things. On this level our knowledge of A is a personal knowledge obtained from our close personal association with him. The highest ideal of this type of knowledge is that of a true lover knowing his beloved in the most intimate way. This is the reason why the Mystics like to use erotic terms, the so-called 'language of love' in describing their experience. For the Mystics are the people who aspire to know God and claim to know God on this level.

In fact, the basic distinction comes out very clearly when God forms the object of these two types of knowledge. On the second level we 'know the One God (*Allāh al-aḥad*)'. And this is possible only by personal union with the One God. On the first level, we 'know the Unity of God (*waḥdāniyyah Allāh*)', that is, as the Murjiʾite Ibn Shabīb says, we know *that* God is One (*anna Allāh wāḥid*). And the immediate, intuitive and profoundly personal knowledge of the One God is of a completely different nature from the knowledge *that* God is One.

Usually the former, i.e. mystical, type of knowledge is called in Arabic *maʿrifah*, while the latter, i.e. analytic, type of knowledge is called *ʿilm*. It is remarkable that the Murjiʾites in general preferred to use the word *maʿrifah* in their definition of *īmān*, giving it the meaning of *ʿilm* as here explained. It is of course dangerous to push this sort of analysis too far, because the Murjiʾites were not systematic philosophers. But we may safely say that their understanding of 'knowledge' was of an essentialist type, that is, a kind of knowledge usually obtainable through the activity of Reason.

That it was so is shown by the striking contrast offered by the case of Ghaylān. As we have seen in the preceding chapter,[6] Ghaylān revolted, so to speak, against this general tendency among the Murjiʾite thinkers toward equating *īmān* and *maʿrifah*, the latter being understood in the sense of *ʿilm*. This type of knowledge is surely solid and of universal validity, but it is after all formal and superficial. And this is particularly clear in matters pertaining to religion and God. Ghaylān wanted to make the 'knowledge of God' *maʿrifah Allāh* something deeper. Thus he distinguished between 'primary knowledge' and 'secondary knowledge' of God. The former is an intuitive and immediate understanding of God; this kind of knowledge is ineffable, and is above *īmān* understood in the sense of *maʿrifah* (=*ʿilm*). *Īmān* can only be the 'secondary knowledge' which is a conceptual knowledge *about* God and is capable of being formulated verbally. This interpretation makes the above-quoted remark of Zurqān understandable. Ghaylān equated *īmān* and 'verbal confession' and

6. Cf. Chap. V, I, VII (1) and (2)

asserted that *īmān* was nothing but 'verbal confession'.

Now, to come back to our main topic, the essentialist type of knowledge is characterized by its being obtainable through the activity of Reason on the level of Universals. And it remains on that level; theoretically it cannot come down to the level of Particulars. It cannot grasp concrete individual things in their individuality. In order to know a thing in its concrete individuality, one has to know it immediately, i.e. by immediate personal contact. 'Knowing A', to use the formula introduced above, is the only possible way of obtaining knowledge of this kind. 'Knowing that A is such-and-such' gives only a knowledge on the level of Universals.

The anecdote about Abū Ḥanīfah reflects, I suppose, the teaching of this remarkable thinker on this particular point, that is, the theoretical distinction between the two basic types of knowledge. When we are told that God has forbidden us to eat pork, we understand the words and accept them as a matter of objective knowledge. And that is *īmān*. At this level we know only that *khinzīr* 'pig' is prohibited, *khinzīr* being a Universal. We do not know yet whether the prohibition applies to this or that particular, individual *khinzīr*.

All this may sound absurd or appear to be a piece of sheer sophistry, because the anecdote pushes the matter to the extreme. But the underlying intention is quite a serious one. Whether the story is an invention or narrates an event that really took place, it reflects in any case an important aspect of Abū Ḥanīfah's teaching. We must remark that Abū Ḥanīfah in this anecdote goes to the extreme in order to show as clearly and definitely as possible that, *as long as he is a dialectician*, he cannot tolerate the confusion between the two levels of meaning. And by putting the matter in this paradoxical form the anecdote declares categorically that 'knowledge', according to Abū Ḥanīfah, must remain on the level of Universals. It is, in short, a declaration of Abū Ḥanīfah's thoroughgoing intellectualism. He was an able dialectician among many other things, and as a dialectician he took up definitely the attitude of rationalism.

Be this as it may, it is a very significant fact that the Murji'ites attached great importance to 'knowledge'. And it raised among the Muslim thinkers a number of interesting questions. The most important of them will be dealt with in what follows.

II Reason and Revelation

One would naturally expect to see the Muʿtazilites coming forth at this juncture as true representatives of the rationalist theory of *īmān* = 'knowledge', for the Muʿtazilites were unquestionably the most radical rationalists Islam ever produced. The expectation of this sort is soon defeated. We must keep in mind that the theory of *īmān* was not among the fundamentals of the Muʿtazilites. They had other important problems with which to be occupied like the negation of the eternal Divine attributes and the affirmation of human freedom and responsibility and they did not develop any highly elaborated theories on the nature of *īmān*.

When we examine what Ashʿarī presents as the representative opinions of the Muʿtazilites on this problem,[7] we notice immediately that their concern lay elsewhere. All these opinions have this in common that they invariably emphasize the importance of 'work' in *īmān*. So much so that we even get the impression that in their minds *īmān* was almost completely identified with 'work'.[8] This emphasis on 'work' in the Muʿtazilite understanding of *īmān* is not hard to explain, because the concept of 'work' had a direct and central hearing on the problem of 'promise and threat' *al-waʿd wa-al-waʿīd* which was one of the five fundamentals of Muʿtazilism.

And yet it is also clear that they had their own peculiar conception of *īmān* as essentially identified with 'knowledge'. And here they proved to be perfect rationalists. The basic question was: With what does man know God? The answer they gave was quite simple: with Reason (*ʿaql*). And *ʿaql* in their conception is something common to all men and equal in all men. The Kāfirs and the Believers have exactly the same kind of Reason. As far as Reason is concerned there can be no difference even between a Prophet and an ordinary man.

And by 'knowledge by Reason' they meant knowledge acquired by reason-

7. *Maqālāt*, pp. 267–269.

8. Abū al-Hudhayl's definition, for example runs: '*īmān* is the whole of the acts of obedience, both essential and supererogatory' (p. 266). That of ʿAbbād b. Sulaymān is: '*īmān* is the whole of the essential duties that God has commanded man to fulfil and the supererogatory duties that He has encouraged man to fulfil' (p. 278). That of Naẓẓām: '*Īmān* is avoidance of grave sins' (p. 278).

ing and deduction (*istidlāl*), knowledge based on logical argument. It was, as Wensinck says, 'rational insight in religion'.[9] The rational nature of *īmān* in the Muʿtazilite conception is made incontestably clear by the grave consequence they drew from it, namely the rejection of *īmān* based on the authority of others. The problem of *īmān bi-al-taqlīd*, or belief on authority and by hearsay, will form the special subject of the next section. Suffice it for the moment to observe that if the Muʿtazilites denied the validity of the naive belief of the common folk who had nothing at all to do with dialectics and philosophical thinking, it was because this kind of belief was not based on logical argumentation. And this alone would shed light on the rationalist concept of *īmān* as 'knowledge' among the Muʿtazilites. Even Revelation was in their eyes a kind of 'knowledge' which, lacking naturally a rational basis, should be substantiated by the working of human reason. If the early Muʿtazilite thinkers did not develop this point into a coherent theory, they disclosed their conviction amply by the way they argued on almost every important question.

A far more consistent rationalistic theory of *īmān* was elaborated by the Māturīdites, the followers of Abū Ḥanīfah in Transoxiana. Particularly interesting is their view on the problem of the relation between Reason and Revelation in regard to the concept of *īmān*, the problem that arises when one defines *īmān* by 'knowledge', understanding the latter as an activity of Reason. The pivotal point of the Māturīdite thesis lies in the question of what makes knowledge of God obligatory. Is it Reason? Or is it the Divine Law?

Here the obligatory nature of the knowledge of God (*maʿrifah Allāh*) is taken for granted, *maʿrifah* being in this context synonymous with *īmān*. The real question which is being considered is whether knowledge of God becomes incumbent upon man as soon as he acquires a mature capacity for reasoning; or whether it becomes incumbent upon him only after an Apostle has been sent to his community to inform it of all that is necessary for man to know. The Māturīdites in general choose the first alternative, and the Ashʿarites the second, and they are sharply opposed to each other in this respect.[10]

The Ashʿarite position is described by the author of *al-Rawḍah al-Bahiyyah*

9. *Op. cit.* p. 135.

10. except in the case of the school of Bukhārā from among the followers of Māturīdī. We shall touch upon this point presently.

in the following way:[11]

> As regards the obligatory nature of the knowledge of God, there is no dispute at all between the two schools. The only difference is that Ashʿarī says: it is made obligatory by Revelation or the Divine Law (*sharʿ*), whereas Māturīdī says: by Reason (*ʿaql*). Its obligatoriness, according to Ashʿarī, is based solely on the evidence of Divine words. It is obligatory because Revelation has made clear that *kufr* and *shirk* are blamable, and that they will surely be punished with the Fire, while 'those who know' *ʿārifūn* (pl. of *ʿārif* derived from the same root as *maʿrifah*) will be rewarded with the Garden and Divine appreciation.
>
> The obligatory nature of the knowledge of God, Ashʿarī goes on to assert, has nothing to do with Reason. The view that Reason makes anything obligatory is based on the principle[12] that the good and the bad are determined by the judgment of Reason (and not by God). Reason, however, has no power over the five legal categories. …
>
> If *īmān*[13] were obligatory by Reason, then it would be obligatory even before God's sending an Apostle, because Reason precedes the sending of Apostles. And if it were obligatory before the coming of an Apostle, those who neglect (to know God) before the advent of an Apostle would deserve Divine punishment. But this conclusion is belied by what God says (XVII, 15) 'We never punish until We have sent an Apostle'. If God does not punish anybody before the sending of an Apostle, the thesis that Reason makes the 'knowledge' (= *īmān*) obligatory must necessarily be denied. In other words, the obligation to know God comes from the Divine Law alone.

To this Ashʿarite position the Māturīdite position is diametrically opposed. The obligatory nature of the knowledge of God is based on Reason. That is to say, man *must* know God with his Reason even when there has been no Revelation. Evidently, Reason (*ʿaql*) is the most important key-word here. We must begin by explaining the Māturīdite conception of Reason. The following is what the Ḥanafite-Māturīdite theologian Bayāḍī says about it:[14]

---

11. pp. 34–35.

12. The principle which is peculiar to, and characteristic of, the Muʿtazilites.

13. Note that the words *īmān* and *maʿrifah* are used indifferently in this passage; they are synonymous with each other.

14. *Op. cit.* pp. 77–78.

> Reason (or Intellect) is the epistemological principle of the soul which can be looked at from two different points of view, namely, (1) its *intentio* (*tawajjuh* i.e. its propensity toward grasping its objects), and (2) its power (*quwwah*). In its first aspect, it is a substance by which are grasped through sense perception, the sensible objects that are immediately present and the objects that are not immediately present, through indirect means like proofs and reasoning. In its second aspect, it is a kind of light, the activity of which begins at the lowest stage of the senses, and by which the object grasped is presented clearly illumined to the mind.
>
> The philosophers divide *ʿaql* into four kinds: (1) material (*hayūlānī*), (2) *in habitu* (*bi-al-malakah*), (3) *in actu* (*bi-al-fiʿl*), and (4) acquired (*mustafād*). By the first is meant the state of the soul when it is actually void of the knowledge in spite of the fact that it has a capacity for knowing things. The second refers to the state of the soul when only the immediately evident propositions (*ḍarūriyyāt*) are present in it. The third refers to the state when the soul has in potency theoretical propositions (*naẓariyyāt*, i.e. the knowledge of things that are not immediately evident but require a process of reflective thinking before becoming present to the soul). At this stage the soul is supposed to be merely *intending* to grasp these objects. The fourth refers to the state of the soul when the theoretical propositions are no longer in potency, but are actually present in it.
>
> This fourfold division of Reason by the Philosophers is entirely groundless. The only true theory of Reason is the following. Man has from the very beginning a potentiality for developing Reason and propensity toward grasping what is there to be grasped intellectually. This potentiality or preparedness is called Reason in potency (*ʿaql bi-al-quwwah*) or inborn Reason (*ʿaql gharīzī*). Then this Reason develops little by little by the creative activity of God until it reaches perfection. Reason thus perfected is called 'acquired Reason' (*ʿaql mustafād*).

Now we are in a better position to understand the Māturīdite position on the problem of the basic relation between Reason and Revelation, or *ʿaql* and *sharʿ*, in regard to *īmān* as understood in the sense of 'knowledge'. The key-text is provided by Abū Ḥanīfah's words as they have been handed down by Abū Yūsuf: 'Even if God had not sent to mankind a single Apostle, men would still have been required to have a knowledge (*maʿrifah*) of Him by Reason.'

The following is the interpretation of this key-text by Bayāḍī.[15] Abū Ḥanīfah's original text is reproduced here intercepted by Bayāḍī's explanatory remarks in parentheses.

> Even if God had not sent to mankind a single Apostle (who would explain for them all that would be obligatory upon them), men would still have been required to have a knowledge of Him[16] (i.e. the knowledge of His existence in the first place, and then all that follows from it such as His Unicity, His Knowledge, His Power, His Speech, His Will, and that He is the one who has produced the world), by their Reason (i.e. the 'acquired Reason' as defined above, which is the very thing on which is imposed the duty of reflection and reasoning during the period of probation).[17]

To this we may add some important remarks based on what Bayāḍī and Abū ʿUdhbah write about the Māturīdite theory of Reason.

(1) Reason is nothing but an 'instrument' *ālah* in the hand of man by which he comes to know the things about God that he has to know. It is the instrument of knowledge, and properly speaking he does not need the Divine Law for that purpose.

Is the Māturīdite position, then, exactly the same as that of the Muʿtazilites who are also notorious for accrediting Reason with an authority which surpasses even the authority of the Scripture? There is a very subtle but fundamental difference between the two, at least from the point of view of the Māturīdites. Referring to this very point, Abū ʿUdhbah, the author of *al-Rawḍah al-Bahiyyah* gives the following explanation:[18]

> The difference between the Māturīdites and the Muʿtazilites (may God make them perish!) consists in this, namely that the latter consider Reason self-sufficient in making the 'knowledge' necessary, while for the former Reason is nothing but an instrument by which the 'knowledge' is made necessary, the one who really makes it necessary being God Himself. In other words, He (makes the 'knowledge' necessary) by using the human Reason as a means.

15. *Ibid.* p. 75.

16. Note that the 'knowledge' which is being spoken of is the essentialist type of knowledge as I have explained above in connection with Abū Ḥanīfah's rationalism. In other words, it is a knowledge *about* God, i.e. a knowledge *that* God exists, is One, etc.

17. See below, additional remark (3)

18. pp. 36–37.

> This comes from the fact that God does not make any duty really necessary without there being (on the part of man) Reason. The existence of Reason is the basic condition. The same is true of the function of the Apostle. The Apostle does not make anything necessary; he only makes what is necessary known to men. Here again the real imposer of the duties is God Himself. Only He imposes them upon men through the intermediary of an Apostle.
>
> The whole process may be compared to the working of a lamp. A lamp is a light because of which the eye sees things when it looks at them; the lamp makes the vision necessary.
>
> We must understand in this sense the words of Abū Ḥanīfah: 'Even if God had not sent to mankind a single Apostle, men would still have been obliged to have a knowledge of Him by their Reason'. This makes it clear that the particle *bi* meaning 'by' or 'with' in the phrase (used by Abū Ḥanīfah in this sentence) *bi-ʿuqūli-him* (lit. 'by or with their reasons') is a *bi* of causality (*sababiyyah*).[19] And the sentence must be understood to mean: the knowledge of God is obligatory upon men *because* of their Reason, the one who really makes it obligatory being God (and not Reason).

The difference as well as the close similarity between Muʿtazilism and Māturīdism are disclosed clearly by the position each of them takes concerning the problem of whether or not children before puberty and people to whom no prophetic message has reached are to be held responsible for lack of 'knowledge' and *īmān*.

Abū ʿUdhbah observes that the difference between the Ashʿarites and the Māturīdites in this respect is far greater than that between the latter and the Muʿtazilites. Indeed, he says, the Māturīdites and the Muʿtazilites agree with each other on several essential points because of their common emphasis on the role of Reason.

> Suppose there is a man who has been born on a high mountain-top, has grown up there, and has had no chance to (hear about the Apostle and consequently has not) believed in God. If he dies in that state, will he or will he not be punished (in the Hereafter) because he has not believed?
>
> The Ashʿarite answer is: No, he will not be punished because in his lifetime

19. Strictly speaking Abū ʿUdhbah should have said *āliyyah* 'instrumentality' instead of *sababiyyah*.

> the condition necessitating belief in God has been missing, and that condition is Revelation.
> The Māturīdites, on the other hand, assert: Yes, he will be punished because there has been the condition necessitating *īmān*, and that condition is Reason. We get just the same answer from the Muʿtazilites.[20]

The problem of the *īmān* of children makes clear to us how the Māturīdites and the Muʿtazilites agree with, and differ from, each other in a very subtle way. Indeed, we may regard it as an illustration of the treatment of the principle of Reason by the two schools, which we have just learnt from Abū ʿUdhbah. Here is what he writes about this problem:

> According to the Muʿtazilites, whoever has Reason has no excuse for not having the 'knowledge' required, whether he be a small child or a grown-up. For (his Reason) makes it incumbent upon him to seek the truth. So a child having Reason must necessarily have *īmān* because he *has* Reason. If he dies without believing he will be punished.
> According to the Māturīdites, nothing is incumbent upon a child before puberty, because his case falls under the Apostle's words: 'The Pen has been removed from three things. One of them is the child before he reaches his puberty'. Thus such a child will be excused, in the view of the Māturīdites, if he dies without belief.
> There is, however, Māturīdī's statement that 'knowledge' of God is incumbent upon a child equipped with Reason. If we follow this interpretation, there is no difference at all between Māturīdism and Muʿtazilism as far as the factual application of the principle is concerned. But (even in this case) there *is* a difference between them regarding the principle itself in that Reason alone has the power to necessitate the 'knowledge' according to the Muʿtazilites, whereas according to the Māturīdites Reason has no such independent power.[21]

(2) The emphasis put by the Māturīdites on Reason, however, should not be taken to mean that in the view of the Māturīdites the Divine Law is of no use once we have Reason. Bayāḍī[22] draws attention to the hypothetical structure of

20. *Op. cit.* p. 39.
21. *Ibid.* p. 37.
22. *Op. cit.* p. 77.

the Abū Ḥanīfah's sentence (Even if God had not sent an Apostle. …). The sentence structure clearly indicates that exactly the contrary situation is the reality. That is, the Apostles have been sent by God as a matter of actual fact. What, then, is the significance of God's sending the Apostles?

Reason is capable of comprehending its objects only grossly in a broad and general way. The Apostles are sent to make concrete and particular what Reason has already grasped in a general way; they disclose the special details of it. Thus the necessity of 'knowledge' is placed on a more solid basis by the sending of the Apostles.

(3) The question raised in (2) is indeed a very delicate point. And historically it contributed greatly toward the splitting of the followers of Māturīdī into the school of Bukhārā and the school of Samarqand. On the whole, the Samarqand school remained more faithful to the intellectualism of Abū Ḥanīfah.

Concerning the problem which occupies our attention now, the Bukhārā school took the same position as the Ashʿarites. The gist of their contention was: there can be no obligation at all before God's sending an Apostle and before the prophetic call reaches the ears of the people. In such a state, therefore, neither *kufr* is forbidden nor is *īmān* obligatory. The most important proof-text for the Ashʿarites is the above-quoted verse (XVII, 15): 'We never punish until We have sent an Apostle'. This verse evidently denies the occurrence of Divine punishment before the coming of the Law.

The theologians of the Samarqand school, however, do not accept such an interpretation of the verse. They assert that the above argument may be valid against Muʿtazilism, but not against the Māturīdism of Samarqand. For the 'punishment' *ʿadhāb* here spoken of is the heaviest punishment of 'extirpation' *isti'ṣāl*. And this is proved by the verse which immediately follows the one just quoted: 'When We want to destroy a town, first We give a command to those of its inhabitants who live at ease so that they commit sins therein so that it deserve (Our decisive) Word (of doom), then only do We destroy it with a complete destruction.' (XVII, 16)

In the light of this verse, the preceding one can only mean that God never has recourse to the final and heaviest punishment of complete annihilation of a whole community before He sends warnings to its people through an Apostle. Thus the verse does not deny the possibility of God's sending a lesser punishment upon the individuals who have neglected to fulfil what is obligatory (i.e.

by Reason) even before the sending of an Apostle. In other words, the negation of punishment in verse 15 ('We never punish ...') is not the negation of the occurrence of punishment, but it is simply intended to mean that the heaviest kind of punishment in a pre-Apostolic period does not befit His wisdom and mercy. And the conclusion is that he who does not 'know' what he can know by his Reason without the aid of the Divine Law may very well be punished by God.[23]

In a similar fashion, the following statement of Abū Ḥanīfah (handed down by Abū Yūsuf) is understood quite differently by the people of Bukhārā and the people of Samarqand: 'And there can be no excuse for anybody for not knowing (what he is to know) about his own Creator by what he sees of the creation of the heaven and the earth and the creation of himself and others.' The Bukhārā school asserts that this becomes effective only after the advent of an Apostle, whereas the Samarqand school does not admit such a condition. According to the latter school, the right interpretation of this statement is as follows:

Every person endowed with Reason, when he observes the creation of the heaven and the earth and the creation of himself and others, must necessarily come to know the existence of the Creator after passing through a process of reasoning.[24] The phrase 'after passing through a process (or period) of reasoning'[25] expresses a conception which is very typical of Māturīdism. The conception is based on XXXV, 37 of the Koran which reads: 'Have We not granted you a life long enough for anybody capable of reflection to reflect therein?'

> The particle *mā* (here translated 'long enough') indicates the period of reflection and reasoning.[26] This indefinite expression is used to show that there is no definitely fixed length of time which would be common to all men. The length of time required is determined by God in each case, because the degree of Reason differs from man to man.[27]

Thus the verse just quoted (XXXV, 37) purports to give a stern rebuke to

23. Bayāḍī, pp. 79–80. To Sūrah IV, 165 is applied a similar interpretation.

24. *Ibid.* pp. 82–83.

25. *baʿda muḍīyy muddah al-istidlāl*

26. The point is that God shows 'signs' *āyāt* to man, and he is supposed to reflect upon them and infer from them by exercising his Reason the existence of God. For more details, see my *God and Man in the Koran*, p. 133 *sqq*.

27. Bayāḍī, p. 77.

> the Kāfirs who have neglected to exercise reflection (*naẓar*) and reasoning (*istidlāl*) in order to know the existence of the Creator the most Exalted, and His being qualified by all the attributes of Perfection. The Kāfirs are rebuked so severely because God has granted them a period of time long enough to enable them to exercise reasoning by the power of their Reason.[28]

(4) As the preceding discussion clearly suggests, the most important of all duties (*wājibāt*) is in Māturīdism the duty of reflection and reasoning for obtaining 'knowledge' of God. This is the basis, and all others are simply dependent upon it. Concerning this point Bayāḍī writes as follows:[29]

> In the view of Abū Ḥanīfah, all the religious duties depend upon the primary duty of knowing God through reasoning. He takes the position that the first and absolute duty is to reflect upon the created things and to infer from them the existence of One who has created them.
>
> Thus the first of all duties of every legally capable Muslim is that kind of thinking and reasoning that would lead to 'knowledge' of God, His attributes, His Unicity, His Justice and His Wisdom. In the second place is the duty of the kind of thinking and reasoning that would lead to the recognition of the possibility of (God's) sending Apostles and imposing the duties upon His servants.
>
> Then, in the third place is that kind of reasoning that would lead to the affirmation of the fact of Apostleship by the evidence of the miracles (performed by the Apostles), and the affirmation of the commandments and duties.
>
> Then, in the fourth place is the kind of reasoning that would lead to the concrete knowledge of the main tenets of the Divine Law.
>
> And finally comes the duty of acting in accordance with what is required of him by the Law.

By this Bayāḍī declares the priority of Reason (*ʿaql*) to the Divine Law. Of course, for him too the Divine Law (*sharʿ*) is of great importance, as we have seen in (2). But what he wants to emphasize is that *sharʿ* can be active and effective only when man, through the exercise of his Reason, has already acquired knowledge of God, belief in God, and the conviction of the truthfulness

28. *Ibid.* p. 83.
29. *Ibid.* p. 84.

and absolute reliability of the Prophet. In other words, *sharʿ* depends upon *ʿaql* in that the former needs for its activity a field already prepared beforehand by the latter.[30] Bayāḍī bases this statement on Abū Ḥanīfah's words of which I give here an English translation, putting Bayāḍī's comments in parentheses.[31]

> If 'knowledge' of God (i.e. the knowledge of the necessary existence of God, His Unicity, and His attributes, both those which pertain to His essence and those that express His actions, the latter including the sending of the Apostle and the creation of miracles through him) were to come from (the teaching of) the Apostle (i.e. by the Divine Law which he has brought, and if, in this way, everything depended upon him), then the special favor conferred upon mankind in 'knowledge' of God would have to be attributed to the Apostle, and not to God (whereas in reality it *is* a favor granted by God, and by God alone, by His establishing Reason in man and thus making reasoning possible for him). The truth is that God first grants the favor to the Apostle in causing him to know his Lord (either by making reasoning possible as in the case of Ibrāhīm, or by instructing him by means of inspiration and by an act of special consideration as in the case of some Apostles). Thus the favor in this case comes solely from God (and God alone, even if it is actualized by the intermediary of Apostles). The favor is conferred upon mankind by God's making them understand (by endowing them with Reason and rendering reasoning possible) that they should assent to (the truth brought by) the Apostle.

(5) There remain two more small points to be mentioned in this particular context. The one is quite simple. It concerns the nature or degree of the obligation to 'know'. According to Bayāḍī, 'the kind of knowledge (of God) which is based on a broad general reasoning,[32] and which raises the man who thinks and reasons above the lowest level of a blind submission to authority, is a duty imposed upon every individual Muslim. It is, in other words, *farḍ ʿayn*, not *farḍ kifāyah*.[33]

---

30. *Ibid.* p. 99.
31. *Ibid.* p. 102.
32. As remarked in the foregoing, the detailed knowledge of concrete facts is not obtainable by the exercise of Reason alone; it is given only by an Apostle.
33. Bayāḍī, p. 76.

The second problem concerns the way in which reasoning leads to 'knowledge'. How does a correct reasoning produce a right 'knowledge'? To this question the Muʿtazilites answer, 'by generation (*tawlīd*)'. The Philosophers' answer is different from this. They say that it is 'by logical necessity (*ījāb*)'.

Contrary to these two typical answers, the Māturīdites assert, the occurrence of 'knowledge' after a process of right reasoning is due to a divinely-instituted custom (*ʿādah ilāhiyyah*). The connection of 'knowledge' and reasoning is essentially a matter of custom established by God; it is neither a logical relation nor a matter of a natural production.[34]

III Belief on the authority of others (*īmān bi-al-taqlīd*)

The foregoing has made it clear that both the Muʿtazilites and the Māturīdites emphasized greatly the importance of logical thinking or reasoning (*istidlāl*) for *īmān*. If, as they claim, *īmān* is essentially reducible to 'knowledge', and if the right kind of knowledge is one that is based on logical proof, then it is clear that the true *īmān* must be an *īmān* based on reasoning.

This understanding of *īmān* was pregnant from the very beginning with a very grave consequence. For it inevitably questioned the value of an *īmān* based merely on the authority of others (*al-īmān bi-al-taqlīd*) rather than on reasoning and logical proof. The question was of grave concern to the community because by far the greatest majority of Muslims, that is, the common people, who were not trained at all in reasoning and the art of dialectics, would not, according to this theory, deserve the qualification of Believer (*mu'min*, 'a man of *īmān*'). The thesis in this latter form is known as *al-qawl bi-kufr al-ʿāmmah*, i.e. the thesis which condemns the common people as Kāfirs. The thesis, besides being completely absurd to common sense, was likely to lead to the still more astonishing conclusion that only a professional Mutakallim (dialectician) could be a true Believer, because he was the only one who could base his *īmān* on a solid logical demonstration. Of course this was mainly a mere matter of implication. But the implication was there, and the danger was felt.

Contrary to our expectation, the Māturīdites with all their emphasis on the

34. *Ibid.* p. 84.

importance of reasoning, did not go to the extreme of maintaining the thesis of *kufr al-ʿāmmah*. They did not reject '*īmān* on authority' as valueless or wrong. Strangely enough, it was Ashʿarī and the Ashʿarites who were generally blamed for upholding *kufr al-ʿāmmah*.

This thesis is often attributed to the Muʿtazilites and called a Muʿtazilite thesis. But this is not wholly correct. The Muʿtazilites, to begin with, took the position of *manzilah bayna al-manzilatayn*, as we have already seen, in the question of *takfīr*. This would imply that even if the *īmān* on authority was to be rejected entirely, the man who believed on authority was a Fāsiq (sinner), and neither a Kāfir nor a Believer. Besides, to be very exact, not all the leading Muʿtazilites were agreed that true 'knowledge' could only be gained by reasoning. Some of them did assert that 'knowledge' of God, His Books, and His Apostles was something to be acquired (*iktisāb*) through reflection and reasoning. In the view of these people, the man who neglected to exercise reasoning would naturally be a Fāsiq.[35] But for others of the Muʿtazilites, 'knowledge' was not an acquirement; but it was something inborn and of immediate evidence (*ḍarūrī*), something that did not require a process of logical thinking.[36]

Some of them did not altogether reject an *īmān* based on authority. No less a great exponent of Muʿtazilism than Jāḥiz, for example, taught, according to Shahrastānī: 'Of all those who belong formally to the religion of Islam, there are some who are convinced that God is not a body, nor a form, nor visible to the eye, and that He is just and does not do any injustice, and does not will the

---

35. The Shīʾite-Muʿtazilite Ibn Abī al-Ḥadīd (d. 1257) in his commentary on *Nahj al-Balāghah* (*Sharḥ*, Beirut, 1957, vol I, p. 34) explaining the dictum attributed to ʿAlī, *Awwal al-dīn maʿrifatu-hu* 'The first stage of religion is knowledge of God', writes as follows: This indicates that *taqlīd* is invalid, and that the very first of all religious duties is 'knowledge'. Somebody may raise an objection to this and ask, 'But you assert in scholastic theology that the first duty is reasoning with the aim of obtaining knowledge of God, and sometimes you assert that the very intention of reasoning is the first duty. Is it possible to reconcile this assertion with the dictum of ʿAlī?' To this we reply 'Reasoning and the intention of reasoning are obligatory merely accidentally, not essentially, because both are means of gaining knowledge; what is really obligatory is knowledge itself. The commander of the Faithful (ʿAlī) meant to say that the first duty of religion by essence is knowledge of God. Thus understood, there is no contradiction between his statement and the view of the theologians.'

36. Baghdādī, *Uṣūl al-Dīn*, p. 255.

act of disobedience (on the part of man). These people, if in addition to this conviction do confess it verbally, are Muslims in the true sense of the word. … But even those who have never reasoned about these matters, but simply believe that God is their Lord and that Muḥammad is the Apostle of God, are to be regarded as Believers. They should not be blamed (for neglecting reasoning), nor are they required to do more than that'.[37]

But the attribution of the rejection of *al-īmān bi-al-taqlīd* to Ashʿarī and his followers raises a more serious and delicate problem. The question to solve is whether Ashʿarī himself upheld such a view or not.

'Ashʿarī himself', Wensinck writes, 'did not wholly share the Muʿtazilite view.' But he did share it to a considerable extent for, according to Baghdādī, he taught: 'He who believes the truth on the authority of others (*taqlīdan*) is neither a Mushrik (polytheist or idolater) nor a Kāfir.' Is such a man a Believer? To this crucial question Ashʿarī replied, 'I do not call him a Believer unconditionally.'[38] Some more details will be given in the next chapter regarding Ashʿarī's conception of *īmān*. For the moment we are more interested to know what the Muslim critics of Ashʿarism said about this point. We find the Ashʿarites vehemently attacked for maintaining *kufr al-ʿāmmah*.

First, let us examine a typically Māturīdite argument against Ashʿarism. The Māturīdite commentator on the *Fiqh Akbar* I, whoever he was,[39] tries to combine non-rejection of the *īmān* on authority with recognition of the priority of reasoning. The starting-point of the argument is furnished by Abū Ḥanīfah's statement which is often quoted in support of the thesis that 'work' *ʿamal* is not included as an essential constituent in *īmān*: Suppose there is a man living in the farthest limit of the country of the Turks. He acknowledges Islam in a broad and general sense. But he does not know anything of the religious duties, the articles of creed, and of the Book (because he has not had access to these things), nor does he acknowledge any of them (because he does not understand them with his Reason). But he acknowledges God and *īmān* (in its most elementary form). Such a man *is* a Believer (who will be rewarded for his *īmān*, and forgiven

37. Shahrastānī, *Milal*, I, p. 101.

38. *Op. cit.* p. 137.

39. As I mentioned earlier, the commentary is attributed to Abū Manṣūr al-Māturīdī himself.

his neglect of 'work')'.[40] This statement is interpreted by the commentator of the *Fiqh Akbar* I in the following way:[41]

> The statement implies that the *īmān* on authority is acceptable, even if this kind of *īmān* has not yet reached the (higher form) of *islām*. This is the opposite of the position taken by the Muʿtazilites and the Ashʿarites, who do not admit the *īmān* on authority and declare that the common people are Kāfirs. This thesis of *kufr al-ʿāmmah* is inadmissible because it makes meaningless God's wisdom in His sending the Apostles and Prophets. Those who have been entrusted with Apostleship and Prophethood have been commanded first of all to propose Islam to the unbelievers. So if Islam obtained by proposal (on the part of an Apostle) and uncritical acceptance (on the part of the community) were not right, then the Divine wisdom in sending the Apostles would entirely be lost.
>
> However (this does not mean that the two kinds of *īmān* are exactly of the same value); the degree of reasoning (*istidlāl*) is a thousand times higher than that of uncritical acceptance (*taqlīd*). And the more man exercises reasoning and deduction the more illumined is his *īmān*. The famous Ḥadīth about the *īmān* of Abū Bakr must be understood in this sense. The Prophet in the Ḥadīth declares that if one weighs the *īmān* of Abū Bakr against the *īmān* of the whole of mankind, the scale of the former will surely outweigh the latter. The *īmān* of Abū Bakr outweighs because of its brighter illumination. The difference should not be understood (as is usually done) in terms of 'increase and decrease' (i.e. the greater or lesser quality of *īmān*).[42]

The conception, of *īmān* in terms of 'light' (*nūr*) furnishes Ghazālī, too, with a basis on which to criticize the thesis of *kufr al-ʿāmmah*.[43] In scholastic theology, Ghazālī is an Ashʿarite, but he launches a determined attack against this the-

40. The words of Abū Ḥanīfah are given here as they are quoted by Bayāḍī (*op. cit.* pp. 74–75). The explanatory remarks that are put in parentheses belong to Bayāḍī.

41. p. 8.

42. This is addressed against the Murjiʾite theory of *īmān*. The conception of *īmān* in terms of 'light' and 'brightness', evidently of a Sufi origin, is characteristic of Māturīdism. We shall come back to this point in the next section.

43. *Fayṣal al-Tafriqah*, pp. 202–204.

sis, without, however, attributing it to Ashʿarism.[44] He attributes it very vaguely to 'a certain group of theologians', evidently meaning the Muʿtazilites. These theologians, he says, condemn the unsophisticated, naive Muslims as Kāfirs, claiming that he who does not know scholastic theology (*kalām*) as they do, and does not know the details of the Divine Law through the logical proofs which they have established, is a Kāfir.

Such a view, Ghazālī says, makes the infinitely wide scope of Divine mercy extremely narrow, and leads to an absurd consequence that only the professional theologians will merit the reward of the Garden.

Ghazālī goes on to point out that scholastic theology has almost nothing to do with the birth of *īmān* in man's mind. *Īmān* is not of such a nature that it could be obtained by the activities of Reason, like establishing abstract proofs, making systematic classifications, hairsplitting argumentation, etc.

> Nay, *īmān* is a kind of illuminating 'light' *nūr* which God Himself throws into the hearts of His servants as a free and gracious gift. Sometimes it comes in the form of a firm and irresistible conviction welling up from the innermost soul, which is completely ineffable. Sometimes, it occurs as the result of one's observing a certain trait in a pious man; one feels, while one sits and talks with the man, a flash of light suddenly coming from him and striking one. Sometimes, again, it is caused by some personal circumstance. Once a Bedouin who had been offering resistance to the Prophet with bitter enmity came to him. When his eyes fell upon the brilliant face of the Prophet and saw a scintillating light of Prophethood coming forth from it, he said, 'By God, this is not the face of a liar!' And he asked the Prophet to tell him about Islam, and became a Muslim.[45]

---

44. There are some who even flatly deny that Ashʿarī ever taught such a thing. Abū ʿUdhbah, for example, in his *al-Rawḍah al-Bahiyyah* (p. 23) quotes Abū al-Qāsim al-Qushayrī asserting that 'the thesis of *takfīr ʿawāmm* (*ʿawāmm* pl. of *ʿāmmah*) is an invention foisted by the Karrāmites upon Ashʿarī.' Abū ʿUdhbah says (p. 22): it is undeniable that Ashʿarī required reasoning (*istidlāl*) as a condition of true *īmān*. But that was only an easy and popular type of *istidlāl* exemplified by the words of an uneducated Bedouin in Ḥadīth saying that the splendor of the heaven and earth proves the existence of One who has created them, just as the form of excrement shows the kind of camel that has passed the place. This type of *istidlāl*, Abū ʿUdhbah says, is completely different from the kind of logical *istidlāl* required by the Muʿtazilites.

45. *Op. cit.* p. 262.

The naive Believers of this kind, Ghazālī continues, were taught the formula of the confession of faith (*shahādah*), instructed about things like ritual worship and *zakāt*, and then, ordinarily, were sent back to their places to resume their professions.

Of course it is undeniable that in a certain type of men, the logical proofs provided by scholastic theology do act as a cause of *īmān*. But it is not the only cause. Besides, such cases are very rare. In the majority of cases, theological arguments give us the impression that they are something invented deliberately to confuse the common people who are without high education. Rather than causing *īmān* in the hearts of men, the discussions of the professional theologians tend to produce bigotry in the hearts and, consequently, even stronger aversion to *īmān*.

From these observations Ghazālī draws the following conclusion which is of great interest as a short formulation of the Ghazalian theory of *īmān*.[46]

> The indubitable truth is that anybody who accepts the Prophet's teaching and the content of the Koran with a determined faith is a Believer, even if he does not know the logical proof of it. On the contrary, *īmān* obtained from a scholastic argument is extremely weak and is ready to break down at any moment because of some slight difficulty in thinking.
>
> Nay, the deep-rooted *īmān* is the *īmān* of the common people, which either has been planted firmly in their hearts in childhood by authentic teaching, or has been acquired after maturity through certain personal experiences that are ineffable.
>
> And this type of *īmān* grows and becomes perfected by constant acts of devotion and inner piety. When, as the result of a long experience of devotion and constant exercise of *dhikr* of God, man finally reaches *taqwá* (pious belief based on the fear of God) in the deepest sense of the word, and a perfect clearing of the innermost heart from all the impurities of the present world, then an overwhelming light of 'knowledge' *maʿrifah*[47] is disclosed to him. When this moment comes, those things which he accepted at first as a matter of blind submission to authority turn, as it were, into objects of personal

46. *Ibid.* p. 204.

47. Note that here Ghazālī uses the word *maʿrifah* in the Sufi sense of an immediate and most intimate personal knowledge, which is completely different from the ordinary activity of Reason.

> observation and experience. And this is the real 'knowledge' which becomes obtainable only after the knot of formal beliefs is untied and 'the heart is expanded'[48] by the light of God.

More theoretical and thoroughgoing than Ghazālī's is the criticism by Ibn Ḥazm who ascribes the thesis of *kufr al-ʿāmmah* to Muḥammad b. Jarīr al-Ṭabarī and all the Ashʿarites except al-Samnānī.[49]

His formulation of the problem is this: Can anybody who has been converted to Islam without reasoning be a Believer? Or is it the case that no one can be a Believer-Muslim without reasoning? Ṭabarī, according to Ibn Ḥazm, says that one must begin training the boys and girls at the age of seven in the art of logical reasoning, for any boy or girl who, in puberty, does not yet by reasoning know God with all His names and attributes is a downright Kāfir whose life and possessions are not to be safeguarded by the Law. This is of course the reverse side of the view that the *īmān* based on *taqlīd*, i.e. blindly following the authority of others, is of no value and validity.

Ibn Ḥazm presents the main points of the anti-*taqlīd* argument and then refutes them one by one.[50]

(1) That *taqlīd* is blamable is known from the Koran itself (II, 165, XXXIII, 67, XLIII, 22, etc.) in which God reprimands severely those 'who follow blindly the footsteps of their fathers and forefathers or their leaders in religion. If *taqlīd* is thus an evil, then we have to conclude that *istidlāl* (reasoning) is the only right way, because the contrary of *taqlīd* is *istidlāl* and there is no third term between the two.

(2) Any thesis that is not based upon, and supported by, a logical proof is merely a 'claim' *daʿwah*. A claim is in itself indifferent to truth and falsity. So there is no guarantee of veracity to a thesis which is not based on a logical proof. Therefore such a thing cannot produce *īmān* in the hearts of men.

(3) Anything that is not 'knowledge' *ʿilm* is nothing but 'doubt' and 'conjecture'. 'Knowledge' means that man becomes convinced (*iʿtiqād*) of a thing as it really is, either through immediate sense perception (*ḍarūrah*) or logical reasoning. Now if we apply this to the question of distinguishing right religions

48. *inshirāḥ al-ṣadr*, reference to VI, 126.

49. *Fiṣal* v, p. 35.

50. *Ibid.* pp. 35–40.

from wrong ones, we notice at once that the rightness of a right religion cannot be known by immediate sense perception, so that we must conclude that it can be known only by reasoning. As long as a man does not exercise his Reason about the truthfulness of a religion, he is not a 'knower' of that religion; and as long as he is not a 'knower', he is simply a 'doubter' and an 'erring' man.

(4) According to Ḥadīth, each human soul is questioned in the grave by an angel. The angel, pointing to Muḥammad, asks the soul, 'What do you say about this man?' Thereupon those who were Believers on the earth reply, 'He is Muḥammad, Apostle of God!' But those who were Hypocrites and Doubters reply, 'I am not sure. I happened to hear people saying something and I just began to say the same thing (by imitation)'.

Against these four points made by the anti-*taqlīd* school, Ibn Ḥazm argues in the following way.

(1) The basic dichotomy on which their first point stands, i.e. the dichotomy into *taqlīd* and *istidlāl* which does not allow of a third term between them, is nothing but sophistry. It is sophistry because the word *taqlīd* in this argument is used in an improper way, having been removed from its place arbitrarily and surreptitiously.

> The real meaning of *taqlīd* (in the sense of 'blind submission to authority') is that a man accepts and acknowledges an opinion of somebody other than the Apostle of God, somebody whom we are not commanded by God to follow and whose opinion we are not commanded to accept. More positively still, *taqlīd* is to follow somebody whom God has forbidden us to follow. Thus when a man follows someone who is not the Apostle of God and adopts his opinion just because it is the opinion of that particular man, and is convinced that if that 'someone' did not uphold that thesis he himself would not uphold it either, then and then only is he a *muqallid* (a man of *taqlīd*). Such a man disobeys God and His Apostle, is unjust and sinful, regardless of whether the particular thesis he maintains in this way happens to agree or disagree with what God and His Apostle have said. He is a sinner (*fāsiq*) because he follows the footsteps of one whom he has not been commanded to follow, and because he does something which is different from what God has commanded him to do.[51]

51. *Ibid.* pp. 36–37.

It is in this sense that the Koran rebukes those who 'follow blindly the opinion of their forefathers.' Following the Apostle of God is totally different from this in nature. It is, properly speaking, not *taqlīd* at all.

> When a man, in contrast to the above case, accepts and upholds the opinion of the Apostle of God, what he does is not *taqlīd*; it is *īmān* itself, it is 'assent' *taṣdīq*, following the truth, obedience to God, and fulfilling the duty, because God has commanded us to obey His Apostle, has made it our duty to follow him and give assent to whatever he says, and has warned us against disobeying his command, and has threatened us, saying that if we should disobey him we would be punished most severely.[52]

(2) The second point is the thesis that logical proof is the only criterion of truth and falsity and that, therefore, without proof there can be no true *īmān*. Ibn Ḥazm says that this is a good example of the mistake of turning a particular case into something of general and universal validity. He shows this by dividing men in general into two types.

> To the first category, which is only an insignificant minority, belongs a man in whose soul there is a natural impulse which presses him toward demonstration (*burhān*). The soul of such a man can never be at ease in assenting to what the Apostle of God has brought until he hears its logical proof. It is incumbent upon a man of this type to seek the proofs, for if he dies in doubt or in denial before he has a chance to hear the proofs and has his soul eased, he dies as a Kāfir and must remain forever in the Fire.
>
> If we judge it to be incumbent upon a man of this type to seek demonstration, it is only because he has the religious duty to seek the salvation of his soul from *kufr*.
>
> The second category is constituted by the common people, men and women, merchants, artisans, farmers, as well as men of pious devotion, Traditionists, and those of the great Masters who disdain scholasticism and dialectics.
>
> To this group belongs a man whose soul is steady and calm in assenting to what the Apostle of God has brought, whose heart is quite as ease in *īmān*, and who feels no impulse in his soul to seek demonstration, as the result of God's special favor and help by which He has made the way easy for him

52. *Ibid.* p. 36.

> toward the good and virtue. A man of this type does not need demonstration, nor does he have to take the trouble to reason.
> God Himself calls (XLIX, 7–8) by the name of 'rightly guided' *rāshidūn* those people 'to whose hearts He has endeared *īmān*, and has made *kufr* and disobedience hateful by an act of bounty and grace.' And this is what we call the creation of *īmān* by God in the heart and on the tongue. This is an act of pure grace on the part of God. And He has not even mentioned 'reasoning' *istidlāl* in respect to it. A man of this type is far from being a *muqallid* (man of blind submission) to his fathers and teachers.[53]

(3) The definition of 'knowledge' by the anti-*taqlīd* people is completely wrong. They define 'knowledge' as man's being convinced of a thing as it really is, either through immediate sense perception or logical reasoning. Ibn Ḥazm thinks that the last part of this definition, namely the phrase 'either through immediate sense perception or logical reasoning', is a wrong and unnecessary addition. It is against the Koran, the Sunnah, and the Consensus. Moreover, it is supported neither by the ordinary usage of Arabic nor by natural Reason.

> 'Knowledge' must be defined simply as man's being convinced of a thing as it really is. So everybody who is convinced of anything as it really is, and is not assailed by a doubt is a 'knower' of that thing. It does not matter essentially whether the conviction has been arrived at by the immediate evidence of sense, or by intellectual intuition, or by an apodictic demonstration, or lastly by the grace of God and His creating in his soul that very conviction.[54]

(4) As to the Ḥadīth about the angel's questioning people in the graves, Ibn Ḥazm asserts that, instead of being an argument in favor of the anti-*taqlīd* school, it is an argument against it. He who replies to the angel's question by saying, 'He is Muḥammad, Apostle of God' is called in this Ḥadīth a Believer. The Prophet does not call him a *mustadill*, i.e. a 'reasoner'. This implies that a Believer, whatever the origin and source of his *īmān*, is assured of salvation. We must remark furthermore, Ibn Ḥazm goes on to say, that the Prophet does not call a Doubter or a Hypocrite *ghayr-mustadill*, i.e. a 'non-reasoner'. The answer given by a man of this type, 'I happened to hear people saying something

53. *Ibid.* p. 38.
54. *Ibid.* p. 40.

and I just began to say the same thing (by imitation)', is quite characteristic of the *taqlīd* in the proper sense of the word as explained in (1). In other words, this is exactly the typical act of a man who accepts and acknowledges an opinion of somebody other than the Apostle of God. This kind of real *taqlīd* is something to be definitely rejected. But the *taqlīd* of which the anti-*taqlīd* people speak is not *taqlīd* at all. Thus the Ḥadīth is in reality an evidence against them, not for them.[55]

To the preceding four points Ibn Ḥazm adds one more criticism in which he discloses, as he says, the most horrible aspect of Ashʿarism concerning the present problem. He repeats the same accusation in almost exactly the same terms in two different places of his *Fiṣal*,[56] showing the great importance he attached to this point.

It is quite easy to see how he came to ascribe this 'horrible thesis' to the Ashʿarites. The emphasis put on the indispensability of logical demonstration for true *īmān* implies naturally that there can be no *īmān* before demonstration. Now this thesis, if pushed to its logical limit, could be interpreted to mean that as long as man does not establish his belief on a logical proof, he is not by any means a Believer but he is rather a Doubter (*shākk*). Since, however, no one would try to prove rationally anything unless he is in doubt and uncertainty about it, the above thesis would imply that no one would be a real Believer unless he has experienced doubt about God and His Apostle.

This conclusion is simply attributed by Ibn Ḥazm to Ashʿarism. The Ashʿarites, according to him, are impudent enough to assert that nobody can have the right sort of *islām* (and *īmān*) until he becomes first a Doubter and a non-Believer after the age of maturity.

> By God, we have never heard of anybody more profoundly Kāfir than these people who assert that nobody can be a Muslim unless he entertains a doubt about God and about the truth of Prophethood, about whether the Apostle of God is truthful or a liar! … Their argument is that there can be no *īmān* in the true sense of the word except through *kufr*, nor can there be any true 'assent' *taṣdīq* except through denial; that one can attain God's satisfaction only by doubting Him; that he who has come to believe firmly with his heart

55. *Ibid.* p. 40.
56. V, pp. 41–44 and IV, pp. 216–217.

> and to confess with the tongue that God is his Lord, there being no other god than God, and that Muḥammad is the Apostle of God, and that the religion of Islam is the religion of God, there being no other religion, is a Kāfir and a Mushrik.[57]

These people, Ibn Ḥazm points out, say that 'doubt' is indispensable to the existence of real *īmān*; if so, what will become of those who entertain doubt and then cannot resolve it however much they try?[58]

> What a shamelessness, what a foolishness! They do not even fix the period during which one should be in search of a logical proof. According to this theory (may God curse it, those who uphold it and those who invite others to it!), miserable indeed will be the destiny of a man who accepts this advice from these people (which is nothing but an advice of the cursed Satan!) and really entertains doubt about God and Prophethood, and engages himself in a fruitless search for demonstration for days and months and years[59] until he dies. Where will be his final abode? His destination will surely be the Fire in which, by God, he will stay forever and ever!
>
> Thus we know for certain that those who uphold such a thesis are nothing but conspirators against Islam who are trying to lay snares for its people and to invite them to *kufr*.[60]

Furthermore, Ibn Ḥazm continues his criticism, if the demonstration in question is to be absolutely flawless, as it really should be, then the majority of men would have no access to *īmān*. If, on the other hand, they say that the demonstration may not be so rigorous, then what is the use of a demonstration which is easily refutable?[61]

Besides, they must be reminded of the fact that their opponents in theology too have done reasoning as much as they have. Their opponents have done reasoning but that reasoning has been wrong, they claim. Well, in that case, their opponents, even though they have done reasoning, are in the last analysis just the same as those who have never done reasoning. Reasoning (*istidlāl*), in short, does not guarantee the soundness of *īmān*.

---

57. *Ibid.* V, p. 41, IV, p. 216.
58. *Ibid.* V, p. 41.
59. reading *sanawāt* for *sā'āt*
60. *Op. cit.* IV, p. 217.
61. *Ibid.* V, p. 42.

From this Ibn Ḥazm concludes:

> He who reasons often falls into a mistake. Of course it often happens also that a man who reasons reaches truth, but that is the result of God's special care (and not because of his reasoning). Likewise, he who does not reason often falls into a mistake. It often happens also that such a man reaches truth by God's help. Indeed, 'for each person is the way made easy toward that for which he has been created.'
> Thus he who happens to have reached (i.e. without reasoning) a true thesis, for which others have established a right logical proof, is in the right; he is an upholder of the truth regardless of whether he has passed through the process of reasoning or not. And he for whom 'the way has been made easy' toward a wrong view, which others have proved to be wrong by logical demonstration, is an upholder of a wrong thesis, a man who has committed a mistake, or even a Kāfir, regardless of whether he has reasoned or not.
> I conclude: anybody who is convinced of (the truth of) Islam in his heart, and expresses his conviction by his tongue is a Believer in the full sense of the word, a member of the people of the Garden. It does not matter at all whether his conviction has originated in mere acceptance (of a given teaching) or in the education he has received in childhood, or in demonstration.[62]

IV The locus of *īmān*

The special emphasis on the first of the three major elements of *īmān*,[63] whether it is conceived of as 'knowledge' or 'assent', produced another interesting conception among the Māturīdites. The key-term of this conception is *maḥall* or *mawdiʿ* meaning literally a place, i.e. the 'locus' of *īmān*. And the 'heart' *qalb* is especially assigned to *īmān* as its proper locus.

This of course should not be taken to mean that the idea is peculiar to the Māturīdites. In fact all theologians, of whatever school and sect, when they speak of 'knowledge' or 'assent' as an element of *īmān*, almost invariably add the phrase *bi-al-qalb* 'with the heart'. However the emphasis is undoubtedly on 'knowledge' or 'assent'. The 'heart' is not represented in a clear conscious way

62. *Ibid.* p. 44.
63. 'knowledge' or 'assent', 'verbal acknowledgment', and 'work'.

as the particular 'place' in which the phenomenon of 'assent' takes place. The interesting point is that the Māturīdites, obviously under the influence of Mysticism, developed a special theory of 'locus' and gave it a systematic coherence.

The idea can be traced back to Māturīdī himself. In his *Kitab al-Tawḥīd* he repeatedly emphasizes the 'heart' as being the 'locus' of *īmān*, and declares: 'It is definite that the heart *is* the locus (*mawḍiʿ*) of *īmān*.[64] In origin, I think, the idea was suggested by the bitter controversy evoked among the Muslim thinkers by the Karrāmite thesis that *īmān* is nothing but a confession by the tongue. As we have seen above and shall see more in detail in chapter VIII, the Karrāmites held that the moment one *says* 'I believe', he is a real Believer by that very declaration; absolutely nothing more is required of him.

It is quite understandable that the objection to this Karrāmite theory of *īmān* was almost universal. It was not by any means peculiar to Māturīdī and his followers. One of the famous Ashʿarite theoreticians, Baghdādī, for example, raises the same objection to the Karrāmites in exactly the same form. There are many Koranic verses, he says, which go to prove definitely that 'the root (*aṣl*) of *īmān* is in the heart (*qalb*), contrary to what the Karrāmites assert.'[65] This is clearly a statement that the 'heart' is the locus of *īmān*.

The same seems to be true of Māturīdī, for he begins by saying, 'there are people who claim that *īmān* is confession (*iqrār*) by the tongue alone, and that there is in the heart nothing'. Against this he takes the position that 'the most appropriate place for *īmān*, according to both Revelation and Reason, is the heart (i.e. not the tongue)'.[66] He also adduces several Koranic verses in support of this thesis and concludes that however much man manifests his belief by the tongue, it is of no avail if his heart (*qalb*) contradicts what he says.

Māturīdī points out that the Ḥadīth which tells us that the Prophet was 'commanded to fight the Kāfirs relentlessly until they witness with the tongue' does not tell us in reality that the verbal attestation itself is the *īmān*, i.e. the *īmān*

---

64. Abū Manṣūr al-Māturīdī, *Kitab al-Tawḥīd*, Cambridge University Library, MS. Add. 3651, fol. 387.

65. *Uṣūl*, pp. 250–251. The Koranic verses adduced are XL, 14. and V, 41. He also adduces a Ḥadīth in which the prophet says: *īmān* does not consist in outward show or mere wishful thinking, but it is something grave that has established itself firmly in the heart, and corroborated by works.

66. *Tawḥīd*. fol. 384–385.

with the heart. It only tells us that the verbal confession is an outward sign of *īmān*, and that anybody who does it may be treated as a Muslim in a formal and external sense, for nobody is able to go inside the heart of another man.

So we see that in this respect Māturīdī's position was not essentially different from others. It was originally a theoretical protest against the Karrāmite theory of *īmān*. But he was inclined to emphasize the concept of 'locus' in his criticism of the Karrāmites. And this led to an interesting theory of *loci*, which assigns a particular 'locus' to each of the major functions of the religious mind.

The following system is reproduced from the commentary of the *Fiqh Akbar* I[67] which is, as mentioned earlier, attributed to Māturīdī. It is interesting to note that in this commentary the Māturīdite author, whoever he may be, declares that the system is that of Māturīdī himself and that it is the only right way of distinguishing between *īmān* and *islām*. In any event, that the system which we are going to examine here was something commonly accepted among the Māturīdites is shown by the fact that exactly the same thing (with less details) is given in a short Māturīdite Creed[68] which is also (spuriously) attributed to Māturīdī himself.

The system is constituted by four kinds of the 'knowledge' *maʿrifah* of God, arranged in the form of successive stages according to the degree of interiority of the 'locus' where each one of them occurs.

(1) The most exterior kind of 'knowledge' is *islām*, by which is meant 'the knowledge about God without any theoretical specification. Its locus is the 'bosom' *ṣadr*.[69]

(2) The second stage is 'knowledge of God in regard to His divine nature (*ulūhiyyah*)'. And its locus is the 'heart' *qalb* which is within the 'bosom'. In other words, this kind of 'knowledge' is a degree more interior than the first one.

(3) The third stage is 'knowledge of God in regard to His attributes'. This is simply called 'knowledge' *maʿrifah*. Its locus is the 'inner heart' *fuʾād*, which is within the 'heart' *qalb*.

---

67. pp. 6–7.

68. *Rasāʾil fī al-ʿAqāʾid*, ed. Y. Z. Yörükān, Istanbul, 1035, pp. 15–16.

69. This is based on the Koranic verse (XXXIX, 22): 'Is a man whose bosom (*ṣadr*) God has expanded for the Surrender (*islām*) so that he be guided by a light from his Lord?' (meaning: Is such a man to be regarded as the same as a Kāfir?)

(4) The fourth stage is 'knowledge of God in regard to his Unicity (*waḥdāni-yyah*)'. It is called 'unification' *tawḥīd*, and the locus assigned to it is the 'innermost heart' *sirr*, which is said to be within the 'inner heart' *fu'ād*.

The Māturīdite commentator of the *Fiqh Akbar* I adduces here XXIV, 35 and asserts that these four stages of 'knowledge' are symbolically referred to in this verse. The verse, which is extremely beautiful in imagery, reads: 'God is the Light of the heavens and the earth. His light may be compared to a niche wherein is a lamp. The lamp is in a glass, and the glass looks as if it were a glittering star. It (i.e. the lamp) has been kindled (with the oil) from a blessed tree, an olive tree neither of the East nor of the West, whose oil almost glows forth of itself even if no fire touches it. Light upon light! God, indeed, guides unto His Light whom He will. Thus does God speak to men in allegories'.

In this allegorical passage, he says, the 'niche' *mishkāt* symbolizes the 'bosom' *ṣadr*, the locus of the first stage of 'knowledge'. Likewise, the 'glass' *zujājah* symbolizes the 'heart' *qalb*, the 'lamp' *miṣbāḥ* symbolizes the 'inner heart' *fu'ād*, and the 'tree' *shajarah* symbolizes the 'innermost heart' *sirr*.

The 'innermost heart' *sirr*, however, is not the ultimate end of the series. There is within the 'innermost heart' something still more interior. This something is called *khafiyy* which means literally 'hidden', that is, the 'hidden core of the innermost heart'. This is the locus of the Light of Divine guidance (*nūr al-hidāyah*). Man carries the *khafiyy* in himself, and yet it is absolutely beyond the control of man himself.

The process by which a man who is straying from the right path of belief is led to *īmān* and gradually becomes a perfect Muslim is described by reversing the order of the interiorization of the 'knowledge'. Six stage are distinguished here.

(1) The first stage refers to the very awakening of *īmān* in the human heart, which is, as we have just seen, an event entirely beyond the power of man. When God wills to guide an erring man to the right path, He throws His light into the 'hidden core' of the innermost heart. It is kindled and begins to shine forth. And this is the meaning of the expression 'a man guided by a light from his Lord' in the above-quoted Koranic verse.[70]

70. Koran, XXXIX, 22, cf. note (69)

(2) Then at the second stage, this light reaches the 'innermost heart'. When this happens, the man begins to do the work of 'unification' *tawḥīd*, that is, he realizes the absolute unicity of God and quits the worship of idols.

(3) The light does not stop at the second stage but continues to extend its brightness till it reaches the 'inner heart'. Then the man acquires the 'knowledge', that is, he comes to know God with all His attributes.

(4) From there the light still continues to shine forth until it reaches the 'heart'. This is the stage of *īmān* i.e. the knowledge of God with regard to His divine nature.

(5) From there the light reaches the 'bosom', and that is the stage at which *islām* is actualized.

(6) Finally, the light extends to the whole of the bodily members. When this stage is reached, the man avoids doing acts of disobedience and tries to comply with the commandments. Only when the man responds actively to this practical requirement, is he a God-fearing (*taqiyy*) Believer corresponding to the Koranic verse, 'Verily the noblest of you all in the sight of God is one who is the most God-fearing'.[71] If, on the contrary, he does not respond to it, he is deprived of the quality of *taqwá*. If he commits acts of disobedience, he is qualified with 'sinfulness' *fisq*; his destiny is in danger because of his *fisq*, but there is still some hope of salvation because of his *īmān*.

The four degrees of 'knowledge', i.e. *tawḥīd*, *maʿrifah*, *īmān* and *islām*, are called the 'four principles' *ʿuqūd arbaʿah*. They are not exactly one and the same thing, and yet they are not completely different from each other. The combination of the four constitutes 'religion' *dīn*. And this is what is meant by the Koranic verse, 'Verily the religion in the sight of God is Islam'.[72]

71. Koran, XLIX, 13.
72. Koran, XXX, 19.

CHAPTER VII

BELIEF AS ASSENT

I Knowledge and assent

Up till now we have been considering the first constituent of *īmān* as 'knowledge' *maʿrifah*. In the history of Islamic theology we remark another important current which is often consciously and positively opposed to the identification of the first element of *īmān* with 'knowledge'. The theologians of this second tendency prefer to define *īmān* by 'assent' *taṣdīq* instead of 'knowledge'. They point out invariably that the word *īmān* itself means etymologically 'assent', and that this must also be the basic theological meaning of the term.

It is really remarkable that even in the Ḥanafite school of theology which, as we have seen in the preceding pages, emphasizes so much the importance of 'knowledge', no less a theologian than Māturīdī himself takes the position that *īmān* should be understood in terms of 'assent', not 'knowledge'.

In his *Kitāb* al-*Tawḥīd* he begins by pointing out, as is commonly done, that *īmān* means in Arabic 'assent' *taṣdīq*.[1] Basing himself on this linguistic fact, he then goes on to develop his original argument against those who claim that what happens in the heart of a Believer is 'knowledge' only.

He draws attention first of all to the fact that the concept of *īmān* stands in opposition to the concept of *kufr*. This conceptual opposition of *īmān* and *kufr* is universally and unanimously acknowledged by all Muslims. Now 'knowledge' is a concept opposed to 'ignorance' *jahālah*. So if *īmān* is to be equated with 'knowledge', *kufr* would have to be equated with 'ignorance'. But in reality

1. fol. 386.

kufr does not mean 'ignorance'. *Kufr* means 'giving the lie' *takdhīb* or 'covering up (the truth)', *taghṭiyah*, and a Kāfir is a man who denies the truth of something, 'who gives the lie to somebody' *mukadhdhib* (lit. one who does *takdhīb*). A man who does not know a truth is never called for that reason a *mukadhdhib*; he is simply 'ignorant' *jāhil* of it.

This does not mean, however, that 'knowledge' has nothing at all to do with *īmān*. The two are intimately connected with each other. And the relation between them is a causal one. In other words, 'knowledge' is a cause of *īmān*, just as 'ignorance' is often a cause of *kufr*.

> *Īmān* with the heart is strictly speaking not 'knowledge'. Only 'knowledge' is a cause which induces 'assent', just as 'ignorance' induces in many cases the attitude of 'giving the lie'. …
>
> Not everybody who does not know something can rightly be described as a *mukadhdhib*, nor can everybody who knows it be justifiably described as a man who assents to it. Since, however, 'knowledge' tends to call forth 'assent' as 'ignorance' tends to call forth denial, *īmān* is often called 'knowledge' in regard to its 'cause'. This does not mean that 'knowledge' is really *īmān* itself. How could we otherwise explain the Koranic verse (XVI, 106)?: 'Whoso disbelieves in God after having believed in Him (lit. after his *īmān*)—except those who are forced thereto, their hearts being happily content with *īmān*—but whoso is happy with *kufr*, upon them will be wrath from God!' If what is in the heart were 'knowledge' only, *kufr* would not be able to remove and eliminate it. Moreover, the condition mentioned here (of their hearts being happily content with *īmān*) would be completely pointless. In fact, it happens very often that a man, in order to protect himself from suffering wrongful treatment, adopts something which is quite different from what he knows to be the truth. He does so only for self-protection. In such a case the 'happy contentment of the heart' is his condition (i.e. is the evidence that he still keeps his *īmān* intact.)[2]

In brief, according to Māturīdī, *īmān* may actually be caused by 'knowledge', but the latter is far from constituting the essence of *īmān*; *īmān* is rather an 'assent' which is of such a nature that the man who has it feels in himself a profound contentment (*ṭuma'nīnah*) arising from the unshakable conviction.

---

2. *Ibid.* pp. 390–391.

As a typical example of a more elaborate and theoretical argument against the equation of *īmān* and 'knowledge', we shall examine Taftāzānī's discussion of this problem, which he develops in his commentary on the Creed of Nasafī.

> Some of the Qadarites[3] assert that *īmān* is nothing but 'knowledge' *maʿrifah*. The authorities of our school[4] are agreed that this position is untenable.
> The reason why they think so is as follows. The people of Scripture[5] (at the time of Muḥammad) *knew* very well that Muḥammad was a Prophet 'just as they knew their own sons'.[6] And yet they were Kāfirs because they lacked *taṣdīq*.
> Another reason is that there were among the Kāfirs those who *knew* the truth perfectly and yet denied it because of stubbornness and arrogance, as the Koran says (XXVII, 14): 'They denied them (i.e. the signs) because of stubbornness and arrogance, although their souls had no doubt that they were true'.
> Thus it is clear that there is a fundamental difference between simply 'knowing' some propositions and being certain of their truth on the one hand and 'assenting' *taṣdīq* to them and 'believing' *iʿtiqād* them. So that only the latter deserves the name of *īmān*, not the former.[7]

It is not Taftāzānī's intention, however, simply to dismiss 'knowledge' as something alien to *īmān*. Just as Māturīdī recognizes 'knowledge' as a cause inducing to *īmān*, Taftāzānī recognizes it as the ground and basis of *īmān*. The latter contains something additional to mere 'knowledge'. And that something is a 'free choice' *ikhtiyār*. Suppose somebody has given you a piece of information. You *know* it. But it is not yet your *belief*. Only when you 'bind your heart' to that information, which you already know is true, does it become *īmān*. And that is the meaning of 'assent' *taṣdīq*.

> As some of the authoritative scholars have said, 'assent' means the binding the heart to a piece of information given by somebody else, which one already knows to be true. In this sense 'assent' is an act of acquisition (*kasbī*) which is realized by the free and voluntary choice of one who assents.

---

3. I.e. the Muʿtazilites.
4. Taftāzānī is speaking here as a representative of Ashʿarite Orthodoxy.
5. like the Jews and the Christians.
6. Reference to II, 146: 'Those unto whom We have given the Scripture recognize (the Koran) as they recognize their sons. And yet some of them conceal the truth 'knowingly.'
7. Taftāzānī, p. 446.

> And because it is an act of acquisition, it is likely to be rewarded (by God), and it is placed at the head of all religious duties. In this respect it is quite different from 'knowledge', for the latter often occurs without any act of acquisition on the part of man, as for example when one happens to see some material object and it produces immediately the 'knowledge' that it is a wall or a stone.
>
> 'Assent' is that you attribute truth by your free and voluntary choice to a piece of information in such a way that if exactly the same thing occurred in your heart without involving your free choice, it would not be 'assent' though it might very well be 'knowledge'.[8]

The problem of *taṣdīq* is made complicated by the fact that it is also one of the most basic terms in the science of logic. *Taṣdīq* in the purely logical sense is the occurrence of a certain psychological state, and in that sense it does not involve any voluntary act. It occurs when we first represent in our mind a (logical) relation between two things,[9] being in doubt whether to affirm or negate the relation, and then there comes to us a proof in favor of affirming the relationship. What occurs in such a case in our mind is the rational acknowledgment of the existence of the relation between the two terms. And this is the meaning of *taṣdīq* in the logical sense. As a pure logical process, it does not seem to involve any act of free and voluntary choice.

> And yet there is a certain respect in which the occurrence of the psychological state here in question is induced by an act of free and voluntary choice in that it involves a process of examining the possible causes, speculating, removing the obstacles and the like. It is in this respect that *īmān* assumes the nature of a duty imposed upon man. And it is because of this aspect that *īmān* is said to be a matter of acquisition and voluntary choice. Mere 'knowledge' is not sufficient to produce *taṣdīq* in this sense, because the former can very well occur without the latter.

And thus Taftāzānī reaches the conclusion that *taṣdīq* is a 'positive knowledge acquired by free choice' and that *īmān* is nothing other than that.[10]

---

8. *Ibid.* p. 446. [ref. number missing in the original text.]

9. meaning thereby two terms one of which will form the subject of a proposition and the other the predicate.

10. *Op. cit.* pp. 447–449.

Are we justified then in equating *īmān* and *taṣdīq* completely? Taftāzānī's argument seems to endorse this equation. Some theologians take objection to it. Ibn Ḥazm is one of them. Here again his objection is based on his original linguistic theory. As we saw in an earlier context, his linguistic theory consists, in brief, in asserting that when God used Arabic as the language of the Koranic revelation, He assigned to each one of the key-terms a very peculiar meaning which specialized it in a definite way. Starting from the originally given meaning of a word, He transferred and transposed the word semantically from its proper place, and made out of it a special kind of technical term. Thus we have in the Koran a set of divinely-instituted technical terms. And since the meanings of these technical terms have been determined by God Himself, no one has the right to interfere with them.

Thus in regard to the words of this kind, Ibn Ḥazm distinguishes between lexical meaning and technical meaning. Confusion between the two is, in his opinion, largely responsible for confused thinking in the field of theology. The word *īmān* affords a typical example of such a case.

> Lexically, the most basic meaning of *īmān* is *taṣdīq* both by the heart and by the tongue. In this sense, when a man assents to anything whatsoever, that is *īmān*. There is no specification at all as to what he assents.
>
> However, God has, through the intermediary of His Apostle, narrowed down the meaning of the word *īmān* to believing with the heart in a specifically limited number of things. In this particular sense it is no longer mere believing in anything whatsoever. Furthermore, He has included in the meaning of *īmān* the verbal acknowledgment of these narrowly specified things.[11] God has also included therein 'works' done by bodily members as an expression of exclusive obedience to God.[12]
>
> In the context of the Divine Law God has thus transposed (*naqala*) the name of *īmān* from its proper original place in Arabic to a different place, and prohibited in the field of theology and jurisprudence the application of this word to mere *taṣdīq*. If it were not for this Divine transposition of the word *īmān*,

11. These specified objects of *taṣdīq* are given in *Fiṣal* IV, p. 190. They are: God, His Apostle, all that is taught in the Koran, the final resurrection, the Garden, the Fire, worship, *zakāt*, and all other things without assenting to which no one, according to the unanimous Consensus of the Community, can be considered a Believer.

12. *Fiṣal* IV, p. 192.

> even all Kāfirs on the earth would have to be called Believers (men of *īmān*), and we would have to admit that there is *īmān* in them, because they too believe undoubtedly in many things in this world and assent to them.[13]

In truth, however, no one is entitled to be called a Believer unless he fulfils all the conditions laid down by God in the Koran. This is why, Ibn Ḥazm goes on to assert, the Christians and the Jews are not Believers in the true sense of the word, and their belief cannot be regarded as true *īmān*. The Jews, for example, acknowledge the Unicity of God and the prophethood of Moses, but that does not make them Believers.

> We admit readily that a Kāfir may have belief in God in the sense of *taṣdīq* and that to that extent he is a *muṣaddiq* (assenter) to God. But that does not make him a Believer nor is there *īmān* in such a man.[14]

Thus as the result of the semantic specification done by God Himself, *īmān* is no longer mere *taṣdīq*, and a man can very well be a *muṣaddiq* without being a Believer. But *taṣdīq* itself has not suffered any semantic specification by God and so it preserves its original meaning without any change.

> The semantic value (*ḥukm*) of *taṣdīq* remains as it has always been in the Arabic language. And in regard to *taṣdīq*, there can be no difference between a human being, a jinni, a Kāfir and a Believer. Anybody who has given assent to something is a *muṣaddiq*. He who has given assent to God and His Apostles without giving assent to all other things that constitute the essential conditions of *īmān*, is merely a *muṣaddiq* to God and His Apostle. He is neither a Believer nor a Muslim. Nay, he is a Kāfir and a Mushrik.[15]

II Ashʿarī's theory of *īmān*

As an example of the theory of *īmān* in which the concept of *taṣdīq* plays a central role, I would like to take up here Ashʿarī's thesis and analyze it carefully. In view of the tremendous historical importance of Ashʿarism in Muslim theology, his position deserves careful attention. Moreover, Ashʿarī's position

13. *Ibid.* p. 205.
14. *Ibid.* pp. 205–206.
15. *Ibid.* p. 212.

regarding the concept of *īmān* is much more difficult to ascertain than it appears at first sight.

Ibn Ḥazm, who regards Ashʿarī not as an orthodox leader but as an abominable representative of heterodoxy, puts him and Jahm together and ascribes to both of them the thesis that *īmān* is nothing but 'believing firmly with the heart' *ʿaqd bi-al-qalb*, and that it does not matter essentially whether a man manifests by the tongue *kufr* and a belief in the Trinity, or worships the Cross in the domain of Islam without *taqiyyah*.[16] The attribution of this thesis to Ashʿarī is certainly wrong. What then was the real teaching of Ashʿarī? To give a proper answer to this basic question is, as I have just said, far more difficult than it looks.

The difficulty just mentioned comes from the fact that divergent descriptions of the Ashʿarite position have been handed down to us. Ashʿarī himself, to begin with, gives two completely different definitions of *īmān* in his two main theological works, *Kitāb al-Ibānah* and *Kitāb al-Lumaʿ*. Besides it seems to have been even a common knowledge among his later followers that he gave divergent definitions to *īmān* on various occasions. *Al-Rawḍah al-Bahiyyah*, for instance, explicitly states that Ashʿarī explained the meaning of *īmān* by *taṣdīq*, but as to the meaning of this latter word itself, he gave different answers.[17]

In the *Ibānah* he, as a conscious representative of Orthodoxy, states formally:

> We assert that *islām* is a wider concept than *īmān*, not all *islām* being *īmān* (while all *īmān* is necessarily *islām*), and that *īmān* is 'saying' and 'doing', and is capable of increasing and decreasing.[18]

In this statement the most important part for our present concern is the sentence '*īmān* is saying and doing' *Alīmān qawl wa-ʿamal*. It is really remarkable

16. *Ibid.* II, pp. 111–112. In another place (IV, p. 188) he uses the phrase 'knowledge (*maʿrifah*) of God by the heart' instead of *ʿaqd bi-al-qalb* in his description of the Ashʿarite thesis. Here again he puts Ashʿarī and Jahm in the same class of heterodoxy, and says, '(According to Jahm, Ashʿarī and the Ashʿarites) *īmān* is nothing other than knowledge of God by the heart. It does not matter whether a man manifests by his tongue and by his way of worship Judaism, Christianity or any other form of *kufr*. As long as he knows by his heart God, he is a Muslim belonging to the people of the Garden.'

17. p. 24.

18. *Kitāb al-Ibānah*, Haydarabad, 2ed. 1948, p. 7.

that he does not even mention *taṣdīq*. In other words, of the three basic elements of *īmān* he only mentions the second, i.e. 'verbal confession' and the third, i.e. 'good works', and completely omits the first. Examination of another definition of *īmān* given in *Luma'* makes it clear that this omission does not imply that he does not consider *taṣdīq* essential. On the contrary, he considers *taṣdīq* so important and essential that it needs no explicit mention. We must keep in mind that Ash'arī's intention in this first definition of *īmān* is chiefly polemical. Here he is only interested in arguing against the Murji'ites and in emphasizing that the second and the third element should not be excluded from the conceptual structure of *īmān*.

In his *Luma'*[19] Ash'arī mentions neither 'saying' nor 'doing'. This time his definition is: '*Īmān* … is *taṣdīq* to God'. He emphasizes that this is linguistically the only legitimate interpretation of the word *īmān*. He reminds us that the Koran was revealed in Arabic, implying thereby that in interpreting the key Koranic terms we must respect the common linguistic usage of the Arabs. The Arabs say, for example, 'So-and-so believes (*yu'minu*, a verbal form corresponding to *īmān*) in the chastisement in the grave and intercession (by the Prophets)'. The word *yu'minu* in such a context. Ash'arī says, means *yuṣaddiqu*, i.e. 'he considers it true', a verbal form corresponding to *taṣdīq*.

What then was Ash'arī's real teaching about *īmān* in its definite and full form? Perhaps some positive hints may be obtained from what the later theologians of his school report on this problem.

Shahrastānī is definite in saying that for Ash'arī *taṣdīq* is the only essential thing while 'saying' and 'doing' are merely of secondary importance, though they are not to be excluded from the definition of *īmān*.

> Ash'arī holds: *īmān* is essentially *taṣdīq* by the heart, whereas 'saying' by the tongue and the 'doing' of the cardinal duties (*arkān*) are merely its 'branches'. So the true Believer is he who gives assent (*ṣaddaqa*) to the Unicity of God by his heart, i.e. he who acknowledges its truth, and accepts the Apostles as truthful (*taṣdīq*) in regard to what they have brought from God. The *īmān* of such a man is true belief.[20]

---

19. *Kitāb al-Luma' fī al-Radd 'alá Ahl al-Zaygh wa-al-Bida'*, ed. Richard J. McCarthy, Beirut, 1953, §180.

20. *Milal*, pp. 138–139.

This account combines the two different definitions given in *Ibānah* and *Lumaʿ* into one, giving each of the three elements its proper place.

Somewhat different from this is the account given by Baghdādī in his *Uṣūl al-Dīn* in that it introduces the concept of 'knowledge' *maʿrifah* as the very basis of *taṣdīq*. But apart from this point, Baghdādī's account coincides with Shahrastānī's. Here again we see *taṣdīq* emphasized; no mention at all is made of 'saying' and 'doing'.

> Abū al-Ḥasan al-Ashʿarī says: *īmān* is the *taṣdīq* to God and to his Apostles with regard to their reports, but this *taṣdīq* is not sound unless accompanied by a 'knowledge' of God. *Kufr*, in his view, is nothing other than 'giving the lie' *takdhīb* (i.e. to God and the Apostles).[21]

Baghdādī in his *Farq* is more explicit. In a chapter in which he enumerates fifteen essential dogmas that are common to all the People of the Sunnah, he says:

> They all agree that the fundamentals of *īmān* are 'knowledge' *maʿrifah* and 'assent' *taṣdīq* by the heart. The only point in which they differ is the question of whether 'verbal confession' *iqrār* and the 'acts of obedience' *ṭāʿāt* performed by external bodily organs are also to be called *īmān*, although they unanimously admit that all the prescribed acts of obedience are obligatory and that the performing of the ordained supererogatory acts are preferable.[22]

If by the expression 'they differ, etc.', he suggests that Ashʿarī does not regard 'saying' and 'doing' as of primary significance to the concept of *īmān*, this explanation of Baghdādī only corroborates the above-quoted statement of Shahrastānī.

Shahrastānī himself gives a more detailed account of the Ashʿarite position in his *Nihāyah al-Iqdām*.[23] He begins by saying, as indeed many others do, that the proper original meaning (*waḍʿ al-lughah*) is nothing but *taṣdīq*, and he adds that this meaning has been acknowledged and confirmed by the Divine Law.

The question to solve then is: What should we understand concretely by *taṣdīq*? According to Shahrastānī, Ashʿarī gave to this question a number of answers, the main ones being the following three:

(1) *Taṣdīq* is the 'knowledge' of the existence of the Creator, His Divinity,

21. *Uṣūl al-Dīn*, p. 248.
22. *Farq*, p. 343.
23. Ed. Alfred Guillaume, London, 1934, pp. 471–473.

> His eternity (*a parte ante*), and His attributes.
> (2) It is (primarily) a mental speech (*qawl fī al-nafs*) containing the 'knowledge'. Then (at the second stage) this mental speech is uttered with the tongue. And this verbal confession, too, is called *taṣdīq*.
> (3) The 'doing' of the basic religious duties is also a kind of *taṣdīq* in the sense that it is an outward indication (of the *taṣdīq*), just as the verbal confession is *taṣdīq* in that it is an outward indication of the mental assent.[24]

From this Shahrastānī draws the conclusion that, in Ashʿarī's view, the idea subsisting in the heart is the root, of which 'verbal confession' and 'work' are but outward indications.

Then Shahrastānī gives another definition of *īmān*, which is, as he says, attributed to Ashʿarī by some of his followers, and which equates *īmān* and *shahādah* or the 'formal confession of faith'.

> *Īmān* is essentially a 'knowledge' that God and His Apostle are truthful in whatever they have said. The minimum measure by which a man becomes (formally) a Believer, and which constitutes the general obligation upon both the common people and the learned, is that he testifies that there is no god but God, there being no partner in His kingdom nor an equal in all His Divine attributes nor anyone to share with Him His acts, and that Muḥammad is His Apostle whom He has sent with guidance and the religion of truth so that he might make it overcome all other religions.[25]

Does this mean that, according to Ashʿarī, the *shahādah* or the formal confession of faith by the tongue is the most fundamental part of *īmān*? Shahrastānī says No. Here again Shahrastānī tries to convince us that what is important is not merely the *shahādah* itself, but the *shahādah* as the direct expression of the inward acceptance and attestation. In other words, '*taṣdīq* with the heart is the most fundamental element'.[26] Simple verbal confession is valueless unless it is based on the particular state of the mind called *taṣdīq*.

> We all know that the Prophet explicitly invited men to say the *shahādah* with its two parts, namely, that there is no god but God and that Muḥammad is the Apostle of God. However, we know definitely also that he was never satisfied

24. *Ibid.* p. 472.
25. *Ibid.* p. 472.
26. *al-taṣdīq bi-al-qalb huwa al-rukn al-aʿẓam*, p. 473.

> with people saying the *shahādah* as mere words, while concealing in the heart what contradicts it. Both the Koran and the Prophet call such people 'hypocrites' and the Koran denies the existence of *īmān* in them, and accuses them of 'lying' and calls them 'liars'.
>
> From this it is known for certain that *taṣdīq* by the heart is the most important thing, while confession by the tongue is but an expression of it. The mental acceptance (*ʿaqd*) is the real source, and 'saying' only serves to express it outwardly. When it is impossible to attest by the tongue, the mental acceptance suffices.[27]

Thus the last two passages which we have quoted has made it clear that according to Shahrastānī, Ashʿarī recognized as the minimum requirement for the existence of real *īmān* in the heart just the amount of inner conviction which, when expressed verbally, would assume the form of *shahādah*. The comparison of the two passages also makes it clear that the 'knowledge' *maʿrifah* to which reference is made at the beginning of the first quotation is nothing but this inner conviction, that is, *taṣdīq*. The 'knowledge' here does not mean a perfect and fully detailed knowledge of God. It would be too much to demand of the people anything like a perfect knowledge of God.

> It is true that the Prophet was not satisfied with mere saying of the *shahādah* which was not based on inner conviction, but, on the other hand, he did not impose upon all men the duty of 'knowing' God as He really is, for that was evidently something far beyond the capacity of all men.
>
> The best way to convince us of this is for us to see that God knows all the objects of His knowledge in full detail, and knows that He is the Creator of all that is created individually, and knows all that he wills from the creatures and for the creatures, whereas man does not and cannot know these things. All that is required of him is to know that there is no god but God.
>
> This kind of 'knowledge' depends upon the most evident proofs which the Divine Revelation itself has given him. Otherwise, the imposition of the duty of 'knowledge' would simply be asking for something which is beyond the reach of the ability of the ordinary human.[28]

Here we see 'knowledge' and 'assent' completely identified with each other on a certain level of understanding which is within the reach of the common

---

27. *Op. cit.* p. 473, p. 474.
28. *Ibid.* pp. 473–474.

people. At the same time we see that, if Shahrastānī's account of the Ashʿarite position is true, it would be quite wrong to ascribe to Ashʿarī the thesis of the *kufr al-ʿāmmah*.

In any case, the *shahādah*, backed by *taṣdīq*, is for Ashʿarī the practical standard by which one could judge whether a man is a Believer or not. This implies, of course, that anybody who says the *shahādah* in a meaningful way should not be lightly called a Kāfir.

> Anybody who does that (i.e. the *shahādah*), without denying anything which the Prophet has brought or which God has revealed, *is* a Believer. And if such a man dies in this state, he is a Believer both in the sight of God and of man. Only when a man—God forbid!—does something which would contradict this kind of *īmān*, is he to be judged a Kāfir.
>
> In case a man belongs to a school of thought which compels him, because of some theoretical principle peculiar to it, to oppose any of the fundamentals of Islam, he must not be judged a Kāfir in the absolute sense. He must be regarded rather as a man of error and innovation. His final judgement in the Hereafter as to whether he should stay in the Fire eternally or merely temporarily is in God's hand.[29]

The last few paragraphs have introduced the concept of the *shahādah*. Now in whatever way we understand the word, it is certain that the *shahādah* is a kind of 'saying' *qawl*. And *qawl* is, as I remarked several times, the second constituent of the concept of *īmān*. The next chapter will be devoted to a discussion of the problems raised in the history of Muslim theology by this aspect of *īmān*.

29. *Ibid.* pp. 472–473.

CHAPTER VIII

BELIEF AND VERBAL CONFESSION

I Which is more important, *taṣdīq* or *iqrār*?

As we have seen in the preceding pages, by far the most important constituent of *īmān* is, in the view of Ashʿarī, definitely 'assent' *taṣdīq*, i.e. inner conviction. *Taṣdīq* is the 'pillar' *rukn* of *īmān*. The remaining two elements, 'verbal attestation or confession' *iqrār* and 'work' *ʿamal* are also important, but not to the degree of constituting side by side with *taṣdīq* what we might call the 'pillars' *arkān* of *īmān*. There is only one 'pillar' in *īmān*, and *iqrār* and *ʿamal* are after all of secondary importance. We are not absolutely sure that such was really the personal opinion of Ashʿarī himself, because in those of his works that have come down to us, Ashʿarī does not seem to be very much interested in discussing the problem of the essential conceptual constitution of *īmān*. But at least such is his view as we understand it from Shahrastānī's description.

The same interpretation of Ashʿarī's position on this problem is offered also by Taftāzānī in the above-mentioned commentary on Nasafī's *Creed*. Commenting on Nasafī's statement that *īmān* is the *taṣdīq* of what has come from God and the *iqrār* of it, a statement which, as we see, regards the two elements as equally important, Taftāzānī tries to interpret it in such a way that we should feel forced to admit the existence of a remarkable difference in importance between them. The following is the interpretation which he offers.

> However (there is a difference between the two) in that *taṣdīq* is the 'pillar' which does not allow of being neglected at any time, whereas *iqrār* allows of it depending upon circumstances, like when one is under compulsion. … True, there are some scholars who assert, just as Nasafī does, that *īmān* consists of

> *taṣdīq* and *iqrār* equally. But the majority of the most reliable authorities take the position that *īmān* is essentially nothing but *taṣdīq* by the heart and that *iqrār* is only a condition for a man being recognized formally as a Muslim as far as the life of the present world is concerned. Because in their view *taṣdīq* by the heart is a matter of mental state which necessarily requires an outward sign.
>
> In the light of this, he who does *taṣdīq* by the heart and yet does not express it by the tongue must be regarded as a Believer in the sight of God although he is not a Believer from the point of view of the qualifications peculiar to the present world. He who makes a confession of belief by the tongue but does not do *taṣdīq* by the heart, as in the case of a hypocrite, is exactly the opposite of this (i.e. he may pass for a Believer in this world, but is not one in the sight of God) and this is the position represented by Abū Manṣūr (Māturīdī).[1]

Against this one may argue by saying, 'Yes, *īmān* is certainly *taṣdīq*. But *taṣdīq* according to the common linguistic usage of Arabic can be nothing other than *taṣdīq* by the tongue. Besides, the Prophet and his Companions were quite satisfied with the two sentences of the *shahādah* as a definite sign of a Believer, and readily recognized this person's *īmān* without probing further into what was hidden in his heart'. Taftāzānī's reply to this objection is as follows:

> A man who only confesses by the tongue is fully entitled to be called a Believer from a purely linguistic point of view. There can be no dispute about that. Such a person is to be regarded and treated as a Believer as far as outward rules of social life are concerned. The real issue, however, turns round the question of whether such a man is a Believer before God.
>
> It is true that the Prophet and those who followed him used to judge anybody who pronounced the formula of the *shahādah* to be a Believer. But it is also true that they judged all hypocrites to be Kāfirs. This indicates that the mere action of the tongue is not at all sufficient to constitute *īmān*.
>
> Furthermore, the Consensus confirms the *īmān* of one who has *taṣdīq* in the heart and intends to confess it verbally, but who is impeded by an obstacle like natural dumbness and the like.
>
> Thus it is clear that the essence of *īmān* is not the mere matter of pronouncing the *shahādah* as the Karrāmites claim it to be.[2]

---

1. Taftāzānī, *op. cit.*, pp. 438–439.
2. *Ibid.* pp. 440–443.

The last sentence of the passage just quoted refers to the Karrāmites, the followers of Muḥammad b. Karrām,[3] as those who claim that *īmān* is nothing but a matter of pronouncing the *shahādah*-formula.

In fact, the Karrāmites *are* the real representatives of the thesis that *īmān* is nothing but 'saying' *qawl*. They stand out so conspicuously in the history of Muslim theology because they formulated this thought in such an extreme form. But in a more or less moderate form, the element of 'saying' was often emphasized by non-Karrāmites as well. There were even a few who went to the same degree of extremism as the Karrāmites.

According to Ibn Ḥazm,[4] for example, the Fuḍaylites or *Fuḍayliyyah*, a sub-sect of the *Ṣufriyyah*, who were themselves a sub-sect of the Khārijites, held:

> He who says 'There is no god but God and Muḥammad is the Apostle of God' by his tongue is a true Muslim and Believer in the sight of God, even if he does not believe that in his heart, nay, even if he believes in *kufr* or materialistic Atheism or Judaism or Christianity. Whatever he believes with his heart, it does not matter so long as he says by the tongue what happens to be true.

And Ashʿarī, who divides the Shīʿite *Rawāfiḍ* into three main groups, says that the first group, which comprises the majority of the *Rawāfiḍ*, take the following position:[5]

> *Īmān* is essentially the *iqrār* of God, His Apostle, and the Imām, together with all that has come from these three.
>
> But the 'knowledge' *maʿrifah* of all this is also obligatory. So he who acknowledges verbally and has, in addition, the obligatory kind of 'knowledge' is a Believer-Muslim, while he who merely acknowledges verbally and does not 'know' is a Muslim but not a Believer.

As a moderate form of the emphasis on 'saying', I think we may mention the attitude peculiar to the school of Abū Ḥanīfah. It is highly remarkable in this respect that the Ḥanafite Creeds usually put 'saying' in the first place in the definition of *īmān*. In order to understand the significance of this fact we must remember that the commonly accepted orthodox definition invariably puts

3. Cf. Chap. V, I, [XII]
4. *Fiṣal* IV, p. 190.
5. *Maqālāt*, p. 53.

taṣdīq in the first place, then *iqrār*, then finally *ʿamal*, this order being the index of the relative importance of the three elements.

Viewed in this light, it is significant that the Ḥanafite Creeds usually give 'saying' the first place. *Waṣiyyah Abī Ḥanīfah*, for example, defines *īmān* as follows: '*Īmān* consists in (1) *iqrār* by the tongue and (2) *taṣdīq* (var. 'and *maʿrifah*') by the heart'.[6] It is not that the Ḥanafite Creeds of this type put an exclusive emphasis on verbal confession as the Karrāmites do. The definition just quoted mentions *taṣdīq* and *maʿrifah* as the second constituent element of *īmān*. Besides, immediately following the definition the Creed makes its own position quite clear by remarking: '*Iqrār* alone does not constitute *īmān*, for, if it did, all the hypocrites would be Believers. Neither does *maʿrifah* alone constitute *īmān*, for if it did, all the People of Scriptures would be Believers'. What really matters is the relative importance of *taṣdīq* and *iqrār*. By giving *iqrār* the first place in the order, the Creed suggests that it is the most important element in *īmān*.

The fact that the Ḥanafite theologians attached an extremely great importance to *iqrār* is shown still more clearly by the *Fiqh Akbar* II. It is really remarkable that the commentator goes to the length of stating explicitly that *iqrār* is a 'pillar' of *īmān*.

Instead of adopting the usual form of the definition of *īmān* ('*īmān* consists in *taṣdīq*, *iqrār*, and *ʿamal*'), this Creed defines it in a very original way. From the outset it emphasizes the importance of 'saying' itself as the pivotal point of the monotheistic belief (*tawḥīd*), and then enumerates the cardinal tenets which a true Believer is supposed to 'say' that he believes in.

> The root of the monotheistic belief and the very basis on which stands the true faith consist in a man's saying 'I believe in God, His angels, His books, His Apostles, the resurrection after death, the decree by God of both good and evil, the final account, the balance, the Garden and the Fire, and that all these things are true.[7]

Concerning the expression 'consist in a man's saying …', the Ḥanafite commentator makes the following very interesting remark:

---

6. *Waṣiyyah Abī Ḥanīfah*, Haydarabad, 1321 A.H., p. 75. Cf. Wensinck, *op. cit.* p. 125. This Creed, by the way, regards 'work' as essentially extraneous to *īmān* (cf. Wensinck, pp. 125–126, Article 5). We shall come back to this point in the next chapter.

7. *al-Fiqh al-Akbar* attributed to Abū Ḥanīfah, to which reference has been made earlier as the *Fiqh Akbar* II, pp. 31–33.

> Note that the author does not say here 'the root of the monotheistic belief etc. consists in a man's *believing in God*. He says, instead, '... consist in a man's *saying*'. The underlying intention is to show that *iqrār* is a 'pillar' of *īmān*, for the essence of *īmān* consists in the *iqrār* and the *taṣdīq* of the six things mentioned.[8]

Similarly in the *ʿAqīdah* attributed to Māturīdī,[9] the first place is given to *iqrār* by the tongue, *taṣdīq* by the heart being put in the second place, although both are considered equally essential to *īmān*.

> *Īmān* consists in *iqrār* by the tongue and *taṣdīq* by the heart. If a man does not confess by the tongue despite his ability to do so (i.e. when there is no natural hindrance like dumbness, etc.), he is not a Believer. Likewise, if he confesses without any inner conviction and dies in that state, he is not a Believer. For the neglect of expressing himself explicitly, without there being any reasonable excuse for the neglect, is a sign which shows that there is in fact no *taṣdīq*.[10]

It is clear that, with the Ḥanafites, the first place given to *iqrār* is simply a matter of psychological emphasis. In other words, of the two elements of *īmān*, *iqrār* receives psychologically a slightly greater emphasis than *taṣdīq*. Otherwise both are equally essential. Although *iqrār* is of primary importance, it is not important to such an extent that it would dispense with inner conviction. When the importance of *iqrār* is pushed to such an extreme degree, we obtain the typically Karrāmite thesis.

II The Karrāmite theory of *īmān*

The Karrāmites are notorious for their thesis that *īmān* is 'saying' by the tongue, nothing else. In this respect they form a striking contrast within the same camp of Murji'ism with the Jahmites who hold that *īmān* is inner conviction, nothing else.

---

8. *Ibid.* p. 32.
9. *Rasāʾil fī al-ʿAqāʾid* referred to earlier, Chap. VI, note 68.
10. *ibid.* §20. The last sentence refers of course to the case in which man does not confess by the tongue.

Ibn Ḥazm, who regards the Karrāmites and Jahmites as the two extremes of Murji'ism, brings out the basic contrast in the following way:

> The Karrāmites assert: *īmān* is nothing but 'saying' by the tongue. (As long as a man declares verbally that he believes) he is a Believer in the sight of God even if his inner conviction be *kufr*. He is a 'friend' of God, and (in the Hereafter) he will be among the people of the Garden.
> The Jahmites assert: *īmān* is nothing but a matter of mental conviction (*ʿaqd bi-al-qalb*). Even if a man openly declares *kufr* without *taqiyyah*, even if he worships idols or attaches himself to Judaism or Christianity in the midst of the domain of Islam, even if he adores the Cross and expresses his belief in the Trinity in the midst of the domain of Islam, and dies in that state, (as long as he has the right kind of conviction in his heart) he *is* in the sight of God a Believer with perfect *īmān*, and a 'friend' of God, a member of the people of the Garden.[11]

This description of the Karrāmite thesis by Ibn Ḥazm represents the typical form in which it has been pictured by the popular mind. In this sense, it gives us an idea of the most common popular reaction against the Karrāmite heresy. However, as a description of the historical fact about the latter, it is not correct, particularly in one point.

From the fact that Ibn Karrām taught that whoever did *iqrār* was a true Believer, many people jumped to the conclusion that in his view a man who *said* 'I believe' by the tongue, without having *taṣdīq* in his heart, was *a Believer in the sight of God* and *would be in the Hereafter in the Garden forever*. But this is simply a distorted picture of the Karrāmite position, because it ignores, whether wilfully or unconsciously, the most important point in the Karrāmites' conception of *īmān*. And by the most important point I mean their clear distinction between the point of view of the present world and that of the Hereafter. Here is what Shahrastānī writes about it.

> The Karrāmites assert: *īmān* is *iqrār* by the tongue, nothing else; it does not include *taṣdīq* by the heart nor any external works.
> But they make a distinction between the problem of calling a man a Believer in so far as the formal matters of the present world and the obligations of religious life are concerned on the one hand, and, on the other, (the same

11. *Fiṣal* IV, p. 204.

> problem) in so far as it concerns the conditions of life in the Hereafter and the final reward and punishment. Thus a hypocrite is, in their view, a Believer in the true sense of the word as long as he lives in the present world, but he is doomed to an eternal punishment (in the Fire) in the Hereafter.[12]

Ibn Taymiyyah's understanding of the Karrāmite position is far more exact and precise in this respect than Ibn Ḥazm's. He takes fully into consideration this distinction between the two points of view and emphasizes the pivotal importance of it in evaluating the seemingly horrifying Karrāmite theory of *īmān*. Because of this basic distinction they make, he considers the Karrāmite thesis not so bad as it is commonly thought to be. It is certainly an 'innovation', *bidʿah* and a wrong view, but the Jahmite thesis is far worse.

> The Karrāmites assert that a hypocrite (Munāfiq) *is* a Believer, but they add that he will be in the Fire forever because he merely believes formally or externally, not internally. Only a man who believes externally as well as internally will enter the Garden.[13]

It is important to see, he says, that according to the Karrāmites, a hypocrite is doomed to Hell. This means that in this world a hypocrite is to be classified as a Believer officially, but in the Hereafter his destiny will be totally different from that of a true Believer. In fact, a man who has in his heart *taṣdīq* but never confesses it by the tongue does not deserve the name of Believer. But *taṣdīq* without confession is exactly the standard of *īmān* for the Jahmites. In this sense, the Karrāmite thesis is far better than the Jahmite one. From the fact that the Karrāmites call a hypocrite a Believer, some draw the conclusion that according to the Karrāmite thesis a hypocrite will go to Heaven. But to say such a thing is simply to tell a lie against the Karrāmites. They themselves never make such a statement.[14]

> He who 'assents' by his heart but does not openly confess his assent has absolutely no relation at all to any aspect of *īmān*, neither in this world nor in the Hereafter. Nor is such a man among those to whom God has addressed His words: 'O you who believe!'
>
> Thus we know that if the Karrāmite theory of *īmān* is fundamentally a mis-

12. *Milal*, p. 168.
13. *Kitāb al-Īmān*, p. 118.
14. *Ibid.* p. 118.

> taken view and an 'innovation' which nobody before them has ever asserted, the Jahmite theory is still more mistaken. At least the Karrāmites are more in conformity than the Jahmites with the usage of Arabic, the teaching of the Koran and Reason.
>
> There is no doubt that the Jahmites are more corrupted than the Karrāmites in many respects from the points of view of the Divine Law, the Arabic language, and Reason.[15]

But of course, Ibn Taymiyyah hastens to add, all this is merely a matter of relative superiority. The plain truth is that both theories of *īmān* are wrong. What then is the right view on this particular problem? To this question Ibn Taymiyyah gives the following answer:

> People have produced many evidences to prove that the Karrāmite thesis is wrong—though, to be sure, evidences of this kind are more numerous in the case of the Jahmite thesis—one of them, for example, is God's words: 'And of men there are some who say: We believe in God and the Last Day, when in reality they believe not' (II, 8). They point out that here clearly God denies the existence of *īmān* in the hypocrites. In my opinion this is right. For in truth a hypocrite cannot be a Believer. He who calls him a Believer is surely in the wrong. Likewise[16] those in whose heart is 'knowledge' and *taṣdīq*, but who (outwardly) deny the Apostle and oppose him obstinately like the Jews and others, have been called Kāfirs by God Himself. God has never called them Believers. And they have no formal relation at all to any aspect of *īmān*, whereas a hypocrite comes at least under the formal conditions of *īmān* in this world.
>
> The truth of the matter is that (both the Karrāmites and the Jahmites are mistaken, for) God has denied the name of *īmān* to those who confess with the tongue and (assent) with the heart as long as they do not 'act' accordingly.
>
> God says: 'The Bedouins say: We believe. Say (unto them): You do not believe; say rather: We have surrendered. ... The (true) believers are those only who believe in God and His Apostle and then never doubt, but strive with their possessions and lives in the way of God. They are the sincere (believers)'.[17]

---

15. *Ibid.* p. 118.
16. Reference to the Jahmite thesis.
17. Koran, XLIX, 14–15.

> Thus God has denied the name of *īmān* to anybody who is not of these people. There are many other places both in the Koran and the Ḥadīth, in which *īmān* is denied to those who do not 'act' in a proper way, just as there are many places in which the hypocrites are denied the attribute of *īmān*.[18]

The upshot of Ibn Taymiyyah's argument is that 'work' *ʿamal* is as essential an element as *taṣdīq* and *iqrār*, and that consequently only when a man combines in himself all the three is he entitled to be called a Believer in the full sense of the word. The Karrāmite thesis is in this respect evidently a mistake just as the Jahmite thesis is a mistake.

There is one more point of primary importance in the Karrāmite theory of *īmān* which is mentioned by some heresiographers as particularly characteristic of the Karrāmites. It is in fact a strange view, but it is something quite understandable if we examine carefully the logical process by which the Karrāmites reached it, concluding it from the basic thesis that *īmān* is essentially a matter of verbal acknowledgment.

The starting-point of the whole argument is not anything that might shock the common-sense. The problem concerns the validity of the *first* confession of faith. Suppose a man becomes a Muslim by openly confessing his belief in God and the Apostle. Will this first confession of his be valid for the rest of his life? Or should he repeat the same confession from time to time?

> The Karrāmites assert that (what is decisive) is only the single confession (*iqrār fard*) made at the very beginning. After that repetitive confession does not produce *īmān* except in the case of an apostate who does the same *iqrār* for the first time after his apostasy.[19]

So far so good. Everything is quite reasonable. But here breaks in a reflection which leads the Karrāmites to a very interesting but strange conception of the matter. The assertion that only the first act of confession is valid and that it actually invalidates all subsequent acts of the same kind brings into their minds the Koranic verse (VII, 172) which reads:

> And (remember) when thy Lord produced from the children of Adam, from

18. *Op. cit.* pp. 119–120.
19. Baghdādī, *Farq*, p. 211. Following Dr. Abraham Halkin (*Moslem Schisms and Sects*, Tel-Aviv, 1935, p. 27), I read *baʿda riddati-hi* instead of *bi-qudrati-hi*.

> their loins, their progeny, and made them testify of themselves, 'Am I not your Lord?' They answered, 'Yes, indeed (*balá*)!' (This happened) so that you should never say on the Day of Resurrection, 'Verily of this we have been unaware'.

Does this verse not imply that all the children of Adam 'from his loins' have verbally acknowledged, at the beginning of human history, God as their Lord? And is this not the very first of all acts of verbal confession? If so, this first verbal attestation would invalidate and make unnecessary all acts of attestation by individuals, because the whole of mankind has already at the beginning of history made, so to speak, a group confession of faith. But this would simply destroy the Karrāmite thesis of *īmān* itself, for everyone, according to this interpretation, is a Believer, whether or not he himself has confessed his faith individually. Were the Karrāmites aware of this logical consequence? In any case, Baghdādī describes their position in the following way:

> The Karrāmites assert: *īmān* is a matter of single confession, and by this they refer to the 'saying' of mankind 'Yes, indeed!' in the first generation in reply to the question of God, 'Am I not your Lord?'
> They assert that this first confession continues to be effective forever till the Day of Resurrection in everyone who confesses even if he be silent or dumb. Its validity does not cease to exist except in the case of apostasy.
> When someone apostatizes, then makes his confession again, his first confession after apostasy alone is effective, and all the acts of confession that occur subsequently do not produce *īmān*.[20]

The famous Shīʿite (Imāmite) philologist, al-Sharīf al-Murtaḍá (d. 1044), known also for his Muʿtazilite position in theology, offers an interesting interpretation of this part of the Karrāmite theory of *īmān*. He thinks that all this is based on a grave misunderstanding of the above-quoted Koranic verse.

The Karrāmites, he says, maintain that the meaning of the verse is that God (in the beginning) brought forth from the loins of Adam the whole of his descendants (i.e. the whole of mankind) in the state of seeds,[21] and while they were

---

20. *Uṣūl*, p. 250.

21. In other words, all of them have been produced not actually but merely *in potentia*; they are at this stage still in a pre-natal state, so to speak, to be brought forth into actuality one after another in the course of history.

yet in that state, God made them confess their knowledge of Him and testify for themselves.

Now this interpretation would seem to imply that those of the children of Adam who are actually brought forth from the state of seeds to actual existence forget completely about the attestation which they themselves have made in the presence of God in the earlier stage.[22] Murtaḍá says that this interpretation is contrary to both the plain meaning of the Koranic verse itself and Reason. To prove it he draws attention to the following points.

The Koran, in the first place, says 'when thy Lord produced *from the children of Adam, from their loins …*', and not 'from Adam, from his loins'. Furthermore, God says '*their* progeny'. And He adds that He arranged the matter this way in order that they might not say on the Last Day, 'Verily, we were totally unaware of this!' (v. 172) or 'Our fathers had been polytheists in the past and we were merely their seeds after them. Dost Thou (now) destroy us on account of what the wrong-doers (i.e. our fathers) used to do?' (v. 173) This makes it clear, Murtaḍá says, that the problem only concerns those who had polytheists as their fathers. In other words, only some of the descendants of the children of Adam are in question here.

In the second place, the Karrāmite interpretation of the verse contradicts Reason, too. For the 'seeds' that are said to have been produced 'from the loins of Adam' and addressed by God and made to confess, must have been, already at that stage, perfectly endowed with mature Reason and all the necessary conditions for the imposition of religious duties. Otherwise, it would have been absurd on the part of God to address them and try to make them confess. But if, on the other hand, they were perfectly endowed with mature Reason so much so that they fulfilled all the conditions for the imposition of religious duties, it must necessarily be the case that these people remember all that happened in the previous (pre-natal) state, even after they are actually born into this world, grow up, and acquire mature Reason. For generally, a man equipped with Reason does not forget this kind of event after the lapse of a long period of time, just as the intervention of sleep, drunkenness, or temporary insanity do not sweep away anything from the memory of an intelligent man.[23]

---

22. This would imply further that because everybody has completely forgotten about his own pre-natal attestation, he is, as it were, in the state of apostasy, and that this is why his first *iqrār* after birth is valid as an act of *īmān*.

23. Al-Sharīf al-Murtaḍá, *Amālī*, I. Cairo, 1954, pp. 28–29.

What then is the right interpretation of the Koranic verse? It is quite simple, Murtaḍá replies. In reality it allows of two different interpretations. And whichever of the two we may choose, the verse does not afford any basis at all for this strange Karrāmite thesis.

The first interpretation is this. God is simply speaking here of some of mankind. He created them, brought them up to the age of maturity, made their Reason perfect, then sent an Apostle who informed them of that which had to be known about God and of those acts of obedience that were obligatory. Then they acknowledged all this and made a formal confession of faith.

According to the second interpretation, the verse means that God created some men and equipped them with everything in such a way that their very constitution might prove His knowledge and testify to His power and the necessity for them to worship Him, then He showed them a great many 'signs' both in themselves and in the outer world in such a way that these signs in themselves were so to speak making attestation and confession on their behalf even if they did not actually confess by the tongue. Thus understood, the verse is not in any way a description of a historical event, but a simple description of the wonderful creative work of God, nor does it mean an actual act of the *shahādah*.[24]

The part of the Karrāmite theory of *īmān* which has been examined in the last paragraphs is an attempt to trace the 'first' confession of faith (which alone is the significant act of *iqrār* in the life of a man) back to the first historical confession made by the forefathers of mankind. This part of the theory is left out of consideration in the common understanding of the Karrāmite thesis. Nor even the fact that for the Karrāmites what is valid is only the first *iqrār* in life is usually taken account of. Their thesis is ordinarily presented, discussed, and criticized in the extremely simplified form: *īmān* is *iqrār* by the tongue, nothing else, with the necessary consequence that the Hypocrites would all be real Believers. That this is an oversimplification we have already observed.

24. *ibid.* pp. 29–30. For this use of the word *shahādah*, Murtaḍá refers us to IX, 17.

CHAPTER IX

BELIEF AND WORK

I The Muʿtazilites and the Murjiʾites

One of the most controversial questions raised by Murjiʾism was that of the significance of *ʿamal* (pl. *aʿmāl*), i.e. 'work' or 'action'. Is *ʿamal* to be included in the essential constitution of the concept of *īmān*? Or is it to be recognized only as a necessary sequel to *īmān*? Or is it to be dismissed altogether as simply irrelevant to the constitution of *īmān*? These are questions that were hotly argued among the post-Murjiʾite theologians. And the name of Jahm b. Ṣafwān almost symbolizes the heretical view that *ʿamal* is entirely unnecessary. Jahm in this respect is representative of one extreme of Murjiʾism, forming a clear contrast with Ibn Karrām who represents its another extreme. The thesis defended by Ibn Karrām is, as we saw in the preceding chapter, that *īmān* is nothing but 'saying' by the tongue. The Jahmite thesis is that *īmān* is nothing but inner conviction, and that no other thing, whether 'saying' or 'doing', counts as a constituent element of *īmān*. As Ibn Ḥazm says in the above-quoted passage, 'even if a man declares *kufr* openly, even if he worships idols and attaches himself formally to Judaism or Christianity, even if he adores the Cross and expresses his belief in the Trinity and dies in that state, he is a Believer in the sight of God if only he has in his heart a firm inner conviction'.

If it were not for the activity of Jahm and his followers, the problem of 'doing' would probably not have caused so much discussion in Islam, nor perhaps would it have occupied such a definite and important position in the system of scholastic theology. The Jahmites, however, were not the only persons who devoted attention to the problem of 'doing'. In truth, the problem had been prepared by the Khārijites from the very beginning. For the Khārijite theory of the 'grave sinner' *murtakib al-kabā'ir* was, after all, a theory of 'doing', and their practice of 'condemnation' *takfīr* was based on man's actions. This attitude was continued by the Muʿtazilites who developed it more or less theoretically and incorporated it into their conception of *īmān*. It is remarkable that most of the leading thinkers of Muʿtazilism, like Abū al-Hudhayl,[1] Hishām al-Fuwaṭī,[2] ʿAbbād b. Sulaymān,[3] Naẓẓām,[4] Jubbā'ī,[5] and Abū Bakr al-Aṣamm,[6] defined *īmān* in terms of the acts of obedience, i.e. religious duties. In this respect we might say that the Muʿtazilite concept of *īmān* was of a legalistic nature, although, as we have already seen, it had some other important aspects as well. The only basic difference between the Khārijites-Muʿtazilites and the Jahmites was that the latter took a negative attitude toward the significance of 'doing' while the former positively emphasized the decisive importance of 'doing' in *īmān*.

The general Muʿtazilite conception of *īmān* is given by Taftāzānī[7] in a concise form: 'The acts of obedience constitute a 'pillar' of the real essence of *īmān* in such a way that whoever neglects them is not a Believer'. And the Muʿtazilite Zamakhsharī, commenting on Sūrah X, v. 9,[8] says: 'The verse shows definitely that the kind of *īmān* by which man deserves Divine guidance, help, and light on the Day of Resurrection is *īmān* specified by a condition, that is, *īmān* accompanied by good deed, with the implication that a man whose *īmān* is not accompanied by good deed will not be accorded Divine help nor Divine light'.

It is easy to imagine how this strong emphasis on 'doing' led to the rise among the Muʿtazilites of a group of radicals known as the *Waʿīdiyyah* or the 'threateners'. The central point of their thesis is the view that one act of disobedience will put a Muslim who does it into the Fire with the Kāfirs and make

1. Ashʿarī, *Maqālāt*, pp. 266–267.
2. *Ibid.* p. 268.
3. *Ibid.* p. 268.
4. *Ibid.* pp. 268–269.
5. *Ibid.* p. 269.
6. *Ibid.* p. 270.
7. *Op. cit.* p. 444.
8. 'Those people, their final abode will be the Fire because of what they have been acquiring (i.e. doing)'. Zamakhsharī, *al-Kashshāf*

him stay there forever, and that neglect of even one act of obedience is enough to negate a man's *īmān*.[9] This *Waʿīdiyyah* thesis is combatted and rejected by Shahrastānī in the following way:

> Such a thesis invalidates the majority of the Koranic verses, the Ḥadīths and the Sunnah, closes the door of Divine mercy, and leads to utter despair and hopelessness. … Besides, the Koran distinguishes between the word *īmān* and the word *ʿamal*.[10]
>
> Know that *īmān* and *ʿamal* have their own essences which are quite distinct from each other. God often addresses (in the Koran) the grave sinners (Fāsiqs) by calling them Believers: 'O you who believe, do not do such-and-such a thing!' From this is known for certain that if *īmān* were the same thing as *ʿamal* or if *ʿamal* were a fundamental 'pillar' in the essential constitution of *īmān*, God would never have made such a clear distinction between the two.
>
> Moreover, it would follow from the *Waʿīdiyyah* thesis that there would be in the whole world no Believer except an infallible Prophet, because nobody except the Prophets is free from errors. Besides, the conclusion would also follow from it that the name 'Believer' is not applicable to anyone until he has gathered in himself all the virtuous qualities, in both 'doing' and 'saying', without a single exception. And this could only imply that the application of the name 'Believer' depends upon (not only the past and present works of a man but also upon) all the works he is to do in the future.[11]

What is the true relation of *ʿamal* to *īmān*? We can easily guess the Ashʿarite answer to this question from what we have seen in the preceding chapter of Ashʿarī's conception of *īmān* as primarily *taṣdīq*, and secondarily *qawl* and *ʿamal*. Here is Shahrastānī's presentation of the problem:

> It is certain, on the one hand, that *ʿamal* does not enter into *īmān* as a 'pillar', constituting it in such a way that the absence of it turns a man immediately into a Kāfir, deprives him of the name of 'Believer' in this world, and dooms him to the eternal chastisement of the Fire in the Hereafter. But, on the other hand, *ʿamal* is not extraneous to *īmān* in such a way that he who neglects

---

9. Shahrastānī, *Nihāyah*, p. 474.

10. *Alladhīna āmanū wa-ʿamilū al-ṣāliḥāt* 'those who believed and do good works' is one of the most frequently used phrases in the Koran.

11. *Op. cit.* pp. 474–475.

> *ʿamal* may be said to deserve no punishment and chastisement in the next world.[12]

Shahrastānī considers absurd the *Waʿīdiyyah* thesis which affirms that 'doing' is so important that the commission of even a single grave sin will send a man to an eternal Hell although his punishment may be alleviated (*takhfīf*) because of other good works he may have done.

> If all the acts of obedience are invalidated (by a single act of disobedience), how can they conceivably bring about the alleviation of punishment? And how can there be alleviation when the man is to stay in Hell forever? Besides, how is the eternal punishment in Hell justifiable for an act which is temporally delimited? When a Kāfir has been a Kāfir for one hundred years, for instance, sending him to Hell forever will be sheer injustice.
> Why not measure out to him a punishment of one hundred years? Suppose a man steals a hundred dinars, is it just to take back from him two hundred dinars?[13]

Now Shahrastānī sees the Murjiʾite theory of *ʿamal* as the exact antithesis of the Waʿīdite position. In a certain sense, he says, the Muʿtazilites of the Waʿīdite type fully deserve the appellation of 'Murjiʾites', i.e. the 'Postponers', because they 'put *īmān*[14] behind *ʿamal*', just as the Murjiʾites 'put *ʿamal* behind *īmān*'. Before we go on to examine the Murjiʾite thesis, we must say a few more words about the Muʿtazilites' position. The Waʿīdites are after all the extremists among the Muʿtazilites in regard to this particular problem, and they do not represent the whole of Muʿtazilism.

Zamakhsharī, for example, defines *īmān* in a way that is remarkably close to the orthodox position.

> The true *īmān* consists in a man being convinced of the truth, then expressing his inner conviction by the tongue, and then confirming it by his deed.
> A man who lacks the inner conviction is a Hypocrite, however much he may attest verbally and do good works. He who lacks the verbal confession is a Kāfir, while he who lacks 'doing' is a Fāsiq.[15]

12. *Ibid.* p. 475.
13. *Ibid.* p. 475.
14. More exactly, this should be *taṣdīq*, not *īmān*.
15. *Kashshāf*, on II, vv. 2–4.

The famous Shīʿite-Muʿtazilite, al-Sharīf al-Murtaḍá, to whom reference has been made earlier, points out that although the Muʿtazilites lay great emphasis on the importance of 'doing', yet they do not believe that 'doing' has an absolute power over man's destiny. One cannot be a Believer without 'doing', but 'doing' alone does not make one enter Paradise. To prove this scripturally, he interprets in a characteristic way a Ḥadīth in which the value of 'doing' appears minimized.

> The Ḥadīth which is traced back to Abū Hurayrah: "(The Prophet) once said, 'Whatever a man does[16] will not make him enter the Garden, nor will it rescue him from the Fire'. Thereupon somebody asked the Prophet, 'Even you yourself, O Apostle of God?' He replied, 'Not even me!' (and added to this) 'Unless God covers me up with mercy and grace'. He repeated this last sentence three times." (Murtaḍá's explanatory remark:) The pivotal point of this Ḥadīth is to make clear that all those who are legally responsible (are not independent, but) are in need of God, that they need God's grace, help and aid. It purports to show also that if God were to cut off all help and grace from man, leaving him to himself alone, man would never be able to enter the Garden and escape the Fire by his own *ʿamal*. So the (first part of the) Ḥadīth must be understood in the sense that man will never enter the Garden by his work which he does without God's help, grace, and guidance.[17]

This explanatory remark of Murtaḍá is obviously designed to serve a double purpose. On the one hand it purports to prevent those who are inclined to belittle *ʿamal* from utilizing this Ḥadīth for the justification of the thesis that *ʿamal* is essentially something extraneous to *īmān*. On the other hand, it aims at safeguarding the Muʿtazilites from the accusation, which they actually incurred upon themselves on many other points, that in their view man is made an autonomous being capable of acting freely and independently of all Divine intervention.

Diametrically opposed to the Muʿtazilite position on the value of 'doing' is the Murjiʾite thesis to which Muqātil b. Sulaymān[18] gives, according to Ibn Ḥazm,[19] the following terse formulation: As long as there is *īmān*, no evil act,

16. *ʿamalu-hu* lit. 'his work'.
17. *Amālī* I, p. 344.
18. a leading Murjiʾite of Baṣrah (d. 757)
19. *Fiṣal* IV, p. 205.

whether grave or light, can do any harm at all, just as with *shirk* no good act is of any use at all.

As I have remarked, it is wrong to ascribe such a thesis, particularly in such an extreme form, to all the Murjiʾites indiscriminately. On the contrary, many of the leading Murjiʾite thinkers recognized the importance of 'doing'. But the Murjiʾites' almost exclusive emphasis of 'knowledge' and their inclination to relegate 'doing' to a secondary position, led their opponents to interpret the name *Murjiʾah*, originally an essentially political title, in the sense of 'those who look at *ʿamal* in a disparaging way'. And this Murjiʾite tendency was given a most daring expression by the Jahmites and the Karrāmites, and a number of surprising consequences were drawn from it by both the Jahmites and the Karrāmites themselves and their opponents. We have already fully examined the Karrāmite position in the foregoing chapter. We have seen that, for the Karrāmites, the only decisive element in the constitution of *īmān* is 'saying'. The Jahmites assert that the decisive element is 'knowledge', and that nothing other than 'knowledge' is to be included in the concept of *īmān*.[20] Thus whichever position we choose, we arrive at exactly the same result in regard to one point, i.e. the complete irrelevance of 'doing' to *īmān*. This theoretical conclusion affords the anti-Murjiʾites an unlimited scope for imagining all kinds of evil acts in the most concrete forms and arousing widespread public indignation by telling the people, 'Look, these people assert shamelessly that none of their evil acts affects the perfection of their *īmān*!' As an example of this sort of argument I give here Malaṭī's criticism of the Murjiʾite position.

> Some of the Murjiʾites claim that they are the most perfect Believers and that no harm whatsoever is done to their *īmān* even if any of them should have sexual relations with his own mother or sister, even if he should commit all sorts of horrible crimes, mortal sins and atrocities, even if he should drink wine, murder, eat the forbidden things, take usury, neglect ritual worship and *zakāt*, nay all the religious duties together, even if he indulges in backbiting, slandering, calumniating and gossiping.[21]

Of a less emotive and more theoretical nature is the criticism of the same thesis by Ibn Ḥazm. The positive side of his argument rests on a simple con-

20. Cf. Chap. V, I, [I]
21. Malaṭī, *Tanbīh*, p. 145.

viction that 'doing' is as much an essential constituent of *īmān* as 'saying' and 'assent'. 'All works of piety (*aʿmāl al-birr*) are *islām*, and *islām* is identical with *īmān*. So all works of piety are *īmān*'. As a proof-text for this assertion he quotes Sūrah IV, v. 65: 'Nay, by thy Lord, they are not true Believers until they make thee (Muḥammad) arbiter of whatever dispute happens between them'. He points out that 'making somebody an arbiter' is quite different from 'assenting by the heart', and yet this Koranic verse affirms that it is something without which there can be no *īmān*. Thus it is clear, he says, that *īmān* is a name that covers all acts in all branches of the Sacred Law.[22]

The critical side of his argument is more original and interesting. He begins by asserting on the basis of linguistic observation, that the argument of those who exclude 'doing' from *īmān* boils down to one fundamental point.

> The Koran was revealed 'in plain Arabic language' (XXVI, 195, etc.), and both God and His Apostle addressed us in the language of the Arabs. Now in this language, *īmān* means only 'assent' *taṣdīq*, nothing else. Any 'bodily work' is not called *taṣdīq* in Arabic, so it is not *īmān*. (In a more specifically Islamic context,) *īmān* means 'unification' *tawḥīd* (i.e. pure monotheism). But no one would call any 'work' *tawḥīd* in Arabic. So 'work' cannot be *īmān*.
> (Such is their main line of argument,) but the (linguistic) fact is not as they imagine it to be. In Arabic, to begin with, *taṣdīq* by the heart which is not accompanied by *taṣdīq* by the tongue has never been called *īmān*. Suppose there is a man who acknowledges something as true (*taṣdīq*) but expresses by the tongue the view that he thinks it to be a lie. Would a true Arab call such a man a *muṣaddiq* (lit. man who does *taṣdīq*) or a Believer? Never! Likewise, *taṣdīq* by the tongue which is not accompanied by *taṣdīq* by the heart is never called *īmān* in Arabic. Thus according to the linguistic usage of the Arabs, only the acknowledgement of the truth of something by both heart and tongue is called *taṣdīq* and *īmān*.[23]

Against this view, Ibn Ḥazm expects an objection from his opponents who might say: If 'work' constituted *īmān*, he who has lost even a part of it would have lost *īmān* itself and consequently would no longer be a Believer. Ibn Ḥazm replies to this objection with his favorite theory of Divine 'naming' *tasmiyah*,

22. *Fiṣal* IV, p. 195; cf. also IV, p. 221.
23. *Ibid.* IV, pp. 189–190.

which has been explained earlier. The theory consists in emphasizing that nobody is allowed to interfere with the naming of those things to which God Himself has given special names in the Koran. Removing a name from the place to which God has assigned it constitutes what the Koran condemns as a heinous act of *kufr* under the name of *iftirā' al-kadhib*, i.e. forging a lie (against God).

> We should not call anybody a Believer unless God has called him a Believer. Nor should we remove the 'name' of *īmān* from anybody after he has deserved the name, unless God Himself removes it from him.
> Now God has called a number of 'works' *īmān*. And yet among these *īmān*-constituting works we find some which are of such a nature that even if a man neglects to do them, God does not take away the 'name' of *īmān* from him. In such a case, we should not remove the name from him. We should simply say, instead, that the man has lost some of his *īmān*, not the whole of it.[24]

Far more comprehensive, thoroughgoing and systematic than this is the argument brought forth by Ibn Taymiyyah against the Murji'ite thesis here in question. His criticism of Murji'ism forms part of his larger theory of *īmān*, constructed with a special emphasis on the importance of 'doing'. In this respect, his theory has already been partially examined in an earlier context from a different angle. In what follows, we shall examine it as an attempt at systematic refutation of Murji'ism.

II Ibn Taymiyyah's theory of *īmān*

Almost everybody starts his discussion of the meaning of *īmān* with a philological or semantic observation. And the general rule is, as we have seen abundantly, that the word 'assent' *taṣdīq* is brought forward as the only exact synonym of *īmān* in Arabic. Ibn Taymiyyah combats this equation. It is interesting to remark that in doing so, he, too, bases his argument in the first place on a semantic examination of the behavior of the two words, *īmān* and *taṣdīq*, in the Arabic language.

24. *Ibid.* IV, p. 191.

> The Murji'ites, having lost touch with the true knowledge of the words of God and His Apostle, have begun to talk about *īmān*, *islām*, etc., in an entirely arbitrary way. Regarding *īmān*, for example, they argue in this way: *īmān* is linguistically nothing other than *taṣdīq*, and the Apostle has addressed the people in the Arabic language without changing it; so what is meant by *īmān* must be *taṣdīq*.
>
> Now, according to what they assert, *taṣdīq* occurs either by the heart and the tongue or by the heart alone. In either case, 'work' is not included in *īmān*.
>
> And the basic proof-text on which rests their equation of *īmān* and *taṣdīq* is: 'thou believest (*mu'min*)[25] not our (words) even when we speak the truth' (XII, 17), where the word *mu'min* is apparently synonymous with *muṣaddiq*.[26]

Against this Ibn Taymiyyah brings forth the following argument based, as I have said, on a semantic observation.

First of all, *īmān* is not a synonym of *taṣdīq*. It is to be noticed that the latter word is essentially indifferent to whether a report given be about the visible world or about the Unseen. Whenever a man gives a report about anything, visible or invisible, we say, 'He has told the truth (*ṣadaqa*)', or, as the case may be, 'He has told a lie (*kadhaba*)'. In other words, we either 'regard his words as true' (*taṣdīq*) or 'regard them as false' (*takdhīb*).

The word *īmān*, on the contrary, is never used except with regard to a report about the Unseen. When, for example, somebody tells us, 'The sun has arisen' or 'The sun has set', we may regard his words as true (*taṣdīq*), but we never 'believe in' (*īmān*) his words, because the matter concerns a visible phenomenon.

All this comes ultimately from the fact that the word *īmān* is a derivation from *amn*, having the meaning of 'feeling safe and secure', 'the mind being peacefully at rest'. Thus the word *īmān* is usable only with regard to a report, the reporter of which is to be trusted and relied upon. A report about the Unseen is just the case. In the same way, when two persons share between them the same knowledge about something, we describe the situation by saying, 'They

25. a participial form corresponding to *īmān*.

26. a participial form corresponding to *taṣdīq* which means literally 'regarding something as true'. The whole passage that gives the Murji'ite interpretation of *īmān* is from Ibn Taymiyyah, *op. cit.* p. 243.

saḍḍaqa each other', and not 'They *āmana* each other', because it is not a matter concerning the Unseen, in which each one of them would have to trust and rely upon the other without himself seeing it. All the Koranic examples of the usage of the word attest to this.

Thus the word *īmān* includes the meaning of 'putting confidence' *i'timān* and 'reliance' *amānah* in addition to the element of *taṣdīq*. And the above-quoted Koranic verse must be understood in this sense, namely 'you (father) do not acknowledge our report as true, you do not put confidence in it, nor is your heart at rest with it'. This because in the eye of their father, they were not those in whom he could place confidence.

Ibn Taymiyyah goes on to point out that the essential difference between *īmān* and *taṣdīq* can also be perceived clearly when we consider them from the reverse side. The contrary of *taṣdīq* is *takdhīb*, i.e. 'giving the lie to something', while *takdhīb* is not the contrary of *īmān*.

In ordinary Arabic usage, he says, *ṣaddaqnā-hu* 'we regard him as truthful, we acknowledge what he says to be true' and *kadhdhabnā-hu* 'we regard him as a liar' are the alternatives that may be said of anyone who has made a report. This is not the case with the pair *āmannā la-hu* and *kadhdhabnā-hu*, for the real antithesis of *īmān* is *kufr*, and *kufr* does not necessarily involve *takdhīb*.[27]

> It may very well happen that someone says: 'I know perfectly well that what you say is true, yet in spite of that I will not follow you. I will rather fight against you, hate you, oppose you; I will never agree with you!' His *kufr* would be far worse than simple *takdhīb*. Thus *kufr*, which is the antithesis of *īmān*, is not exactly identical with *takdhīb*, and so it is clear that *īmān* is not a simple negation of *takdhīb*.
>
> It is true that *kufr* can sometimes be *takdhīb*, but it can also be opposition, antagonism and refusal without *takdhīb*. So *īmān* must necessarily be *taṣdīq* plus agreement, concord, and submission. In other words, mere *taṣdīq* is not enough to form *īmān*.
>
> Thus *islām* (i.e. in the sense of 'surrender' and submission') constitutes part of the meaning of *īmān*, just as refusal to submit, despite *taṣdīq*, forms part of the meaning of *kufr*. And the conclusion to be drawn from this is: every Believer is a Muslim who submits and obeys the (Divine) command. And the

27. *Op. cit.* pp. 246–247.

last part of this statement corresponds to *'amal*.[28]

Even if we concede to the Murji'ites that *īmān* is simply synonymous with *taṣdīq*, even then, Ibn Taymiyyah says, the Murji'ite thesis would be unacceptable, for this thesis rests upon a false understanding of the word *taṣdīq*. The Murji'ites assert that *taṣdīq* (which is the same as *īmān*) does not occur except by the heart or the tongue. Authentic Ḥadīths show that this is wrong; 'works' are often called *taṣdīq*. In such a case, *taṣdīq* means that man 'makes true' *yuṣaddiqu* his words by his work.[29]

Then Ibn Taymiyyah quotes the famous statement of Ḥasan al-Baṣrī: '*Īmān* does not consist in showing off or mere wishing, but it is something grave, established deeply in the heart, which is "made true" by what one really does'. And he interprets this as follows:

> As for a man who says by the tongue something beautiful but does wrong things, God turns his words back to him. As for a man who says something beautiful and does good, his deed raises him up (to God). This is what is meant by God's words: 'Unto Him ascend good words, and good works God raises them up'. (XXXV, 10)
>
> What Ḥasan al-Baṣrī really means by saying that '*īmān* does not consist in mere wishing (*tamannī*)' is that *īmān* is not simply 'saying'. And by 'showing off (*taḥallī*)', he means making a beautiful show outwardly without there being anything corresponding to it in the heart. So the whole statement may be paraphrased as: *īmān* is not a matter of saying something outwardly, nor is it external embellishment, but it is something grave, established deeply in the heart and confirmed by the deed'. The last part of this statement is based on the observation that whatever is in the heart must needs be expressed externally by 'doing' and the absence of a natural necessary sequel proves the absence of that to which it is the sequel.[30]
>
> Thus, in admitting that the most basic element of *īmān* is *taṣdīq*, we must also admit that it is a very particular kind of *taṣdīq* in the sense that ritual worship (*ṣalāt*) is a particular kind of prayer, the pilgrimage (to Mecca) is a particular kind of intention, and the fasting (of Ramaḍān) is a particular kind of abstinence. And this particular kind of *taṣdīq* has a number of natural and neces-

28. *Ibid.* p. 247.
29. *Ibid.* p. 248.
30. *Ibid.* pp. 248–249.

> sary sequels which form an integral part of the meaning of the word *taṣdīq* when it is used 'absolutely',[31] for the absence of the necessary sequel of a thing indicates the absence of the thing itself. Thus the dispute as to whether 'doing' is included in *īmān* or is only a 'necessary sequel to *īmān*', is reduced to a verbal question.[32]

The discussion of the problem of 'doing' as an essential constituent of *īmān* brings Ibn Taymiyyah to his favorite theory of *īmān* and *islām*, which we have analyzed earlier in a preliminary way. Indeed the distinction itself between these two rests upon, and is made possible by, the introduction of the concept of 'doing' into the picture. His theory of *īmān* as distinguished from *islām* turns round this concept so much so that one is almost tempted to say that it is a theorizing about the value of 'doing'.

The gist of his thesis is that a solid steadfast *taṣdīq* is enough to make a man a Muslim (i.e. man of *islām*), but that it does not turn him into a Believer (i.e. man of *īmān*) unless it is accompanied by good works.

Islām in his view is something that can be very formal and superficial. A man who is converted to Islam because of fear of the sword is a Muslim in this sense. This illustrates the formal and external kind of *islām*, but not the lowest. For in the most superficial type of *islām* even the Hypocrites are included, not to speak of those in whose hearts *īmān* and 'hypocrisy' *nifāq* coexist. Nay, in certain cases, even *kufr* can exist in the heart side by side with *īmān* without the *kufr* being strong enough to drive the man out of the religious community of Islam.[33]

This does not mean of course that such a Muslim, though he *is* to be considered a Muslim, is as good as a perfect one. Perfection in this matter should always be sought after. A steadfast *taṣdīq* is a first step toward such perfection.

> And yet we must remember that *īmān* is not constituted by mere *taṣdīq*, but that it must be accompanied by the 'works of the heart' *ʿamal qalbiyyah* which, in their turn, necessarily demand external bodily acts. Thus love of God and His Apostle is part of *īmān*. The same is true of the love of what

31. The fundamental distinction made by Ibn Taymiyyah between the 'absolute' and the 'conditioned' use of a key-term has been explained above in detail in Chap IV.

32. *Op. cit.* p. 251.

33. *Ibid.* p. 258, p. 264.

> God has commanded man to do, and the disliking of what He has prohibited. And these are among the most characteristic traits of *īmān*. To this refer a great many Ḥadīths of the Prophet; for example: 'He who feels delighted by his good deed, and is grieved by his evil deed, is a Believer'. Such a man loves a good deed and is delighted by it. Such a man hates an evil deed, and feels sad and sorry if he has done anything wrong, even if he has done it driven by an irresistible desire. This kind of love and hate, I say, is among the specific characteristics of *īmān*.

It is interesting to note that Ibn Taymiyyah introduces here the concept of the 'work of heart' *ʿamal qalbī* as a kind of connecting link between the purely interior and static *taṣdīq* and the purely exterior and active *ʿamal* of the body. Against those who assert that *īmān* has nothing to do with *ʿamal* (understood in the sense of bodily act), Ibn Taymiyyah points out that, on the contrary, *ʿamal* begins even at a deeper level than external bodily members, that the heart (*qalb*) itself has its own deed. Love of God and the Apostle, for instance, is a psychological 'act', and the various kinds of psychological acts are *aʿmāl* in the real sense of the word, just as external bodily acts are *aʿmāl*. Once we admit this, there can be no reason why we should make a sharp essential distinction between two kinds of *aʿmāl*, internal and external, and exclude the latter from our definition of *īmān*.

In fact, this thesis of psychological acts is but a theoretical elaboration of the very old conception of *īmān*, which is reflected in the Ḥadīth, and in which there is no clear-cut distinction made between *ʿamal* as an external act and *īmān* or *taṣdīq* as something internal. In *Ṣaḥīḥ al-Bukhārī*, just to give one or two examples out of a number, we read:

> (The Prophet) was asked, 'Which act is the best (*ayy al-ʿamāl afḍal*)?' He replied, '*Īmān* in God and His Apostle'. 'What next?' the man asked. He replied, 'Fighting (the Kāfirs) in the way of God'. 'What next?' the man went on asking. He replied, 'The pilgrimage (to Mecca) duly performed'.[34]

Here we are given three items in a descending order of importance: (1) *īmān* in God and the Apostle, (2) *jihād*, (3) pilgrimage. According to the usual classification of the later theologians, (2) and (3) would evidently belong to the

34. *Kitāb al-Īmān*, Ḥadīth 25.

category of *ʿamal* in the sense of bodily deed, while (1) would be *taṣdīq*. In this Ḥadīth, however, all three are given as an answer to the question of *which of the acts* is the best. In other words, *īmān* is treated as an *ʿamal*.

Likewise in the following famous Ḥadīth which depicts the agreement on the night of *ʿAqabah* and which probably reflects the oldest form of the Muslim conception of *īmān*, no distinction whatsoever is made between inner and outer acts.

> The Apostle of God, surrounded by a group of his companions, said, 'pledge allegiance to me! The conditions (I propose to you) are that (1) you should not associate anything with God; (2) you should not steal; (3) you should not commit adultery, (4) you should not kill your own children, (5) you should not tell a lie, forging it without any ground, (6) you should not disobey (when you are commanded to do) a good thing. He among you who fulfils all these conditions will surely get his reward from God'.

In this Ḥadīth, of the six basic conditions for a man being recognized as a member of the newly arisen religious community around Muḥammad, only (1) concerns *taṣdīq*, all the remaining conditions being commandments regarding right conduct.

As for the idea that *taṣdīq* or *maʿrifah* is an 'act of the heart', the introductory words to Ḥadīth 19 of the same book are quite explicit.

> Chapter concerning the fact that 'knowledge' *maʿrifah* is an act of the heart (*ʿamal al-qalb*) because of God's words: 'But He will hold you responsible for what your hearts have acquired'. (II, 225)

Let us now go back to Ibn Taymiyyah and see how he cleverly utilizes this concept of psychological act as a connecting link between *taṣdīq* and external acts, so that *īmān* might include both within its semantic structure.

We may recall at this point the long passage from his *Kitāb al-Īmān* which we quoted at the end of chapter IV. There he points out that an adulterer, when he commits adultery, does so only because he loves this act in his heart. He would not commit adultery if there were in his heart a real fear (*khashyah*) of God strong enough to repress his concupiscence, or a love of God powerful enough to overcome it. And this, he says, must be the meaning of what God says about Joseph: 'In this way did We ward off from him evil and atrocity.

Verily he was one of Our sincere and faithful servants'. (XII, 24)[35]

Thus, he who is really sincere and faithful to God will never commit adultery. A man commits adultery because he lacks this quality. And this is the kind of *īmān* which man may lose, although he may never lose *taṣdīq* itself. This is why it is said of such a man that 'he is a Muslim (i.e. man of *islām*) but not a Believer (i.e. man of *īmān*).

So a Muslim who really deserves Divine reward must necessarily be a man of *taṣdīq*, for otherwise he would simply be a Hypocrite. However, not every man of *taṣdīq* is one in whose heart there are firmly established the necessary states of *īmān* (*al-aḥwāl al-īmāniyyah al-wājibah*) like a perfect love of God and His Apostle, a profound fear of God, a perfect sincerity in his deed toward God, and an absolute reliance upon Him.

Ibn Taymiyyah goes on to say that whoever does not have in his heart all the necessary states of *īmān*, although he may have *taṣdīq*, is the kind of man in whom the Apostle did not see the existence of *īmān*. The *taṣdīq* is merely a part of *īmān*. There must be some other things in addition to *taṣdīq*, like love of God and fear of God. The *taṣdīq* which is devoid of these things is not *īmān* at all.[36]

Ibn Taymiyyah gives in support of his view some terse remarks made by Waqīʿ b. al-Jarrāḥ on this problem. One of them reads: 'The people of the Sunnah say that *īmān* consists in "saying" and "doing", while the Murjiʾites say that *īmān* is "saying",[37] and the Jahmites say that it is "knowledge", (but such a view is *kufr*)'.[38] Another remark is a little more original and interesting. It reads: 'The Murjiʾites are those who assert that "verbal confession" *iqrār* makes "doing" unnecessary. But (in my view) whoever makes such an assertion is doomed to perdition, while he who asserts that "intention" *niyyah* makes "doing" unnecessary is a downright Kāfir. This latter is the position taken by Jahm'. To this Ibn

35. *min 'ibādi-nā al-mukhlaṣīna*. The verb *akhlaṣa*, from which the participle *mukhlaṣ* (pl. *mukhlaṣīna*) is derived, means 'to make something (or someone) pure and sincere'. Here the word is used in the passive form, meaning 'those who (have been made) pure and sincere'.

36. *Op. cit.* pp. 259–260.

37. Here Waqīʿ evidently identifies the Murjiʾites with the Karrāmites. It is to be noticed also that the Jahmites are treated as a non-Murjiʾite sect.

38. This addition is given in a variant.

Taymiyyah adds that such was also the view of Aḥmad b. Ḥanbal.[39]

As we have just seen, the concept of the 'works of the heart' or, we might say, 'psychological works' as distinguished from 'bodily works', plays a decisive role in the thought of Ibn Taymiyyah. Once one admits that the heart (*qalb*) has its own works or actions, like love of God and fear of God, and that they go into the very structure of *īmān*, then one is necessarily forced to admit that the works of the body too are included therein, because the latter are no other thing than the outer expressions and necessary sequels of the former. We must admit, he says, the supreme importance of the heart; it is the 'root' *aṣl*. And yet the heart has not the sole function of knowing. It has its own peculiar 'doing'. Nay, it has even its own 'saying'.

> No doubt, the very basis of *īmān* is the *īmān* which is in the heart. But we must remember that this latter consists of two things: (1) *taṣdīq* by the heart, and (2) the *iqrār* (acknowledgement) of it and the *ma'rifah* (knowledge) of it. The (2) is called the 'saying of the heart'.[40] (In addition to these two there is also the 'work of the heart'.) Junayd b. Muḥammad has said: '*tawḥīd* (i.e. the pure monotheistic Belief in God) is a "saying of the heart" *qawl al-qalb*, while *tawakkul* (i.e. a complete reliance on God) is a "doing of the heart" *'amal al-qalb*'.
>
> Thus there can be no doubt that there is 'saying' as well as 'doing' of the heart. ... The 'doing of the heart' includes things like love of God and His Apostle, fear of God, the love of what God and His Apostle love, and the hate of what God and His Apostle hate, devoting all one's actions to God and God alone, a complete reliance of the heart upon God, and other psychological acts which God and His Apostle have imposed upon us as religious duties and made parts of *īmān*.
>
> The heart, in this way, is the very root (of *īmān*). But (it does not exhaust the whole of *īmān*, because) whenever 'knowledge' and 'will' are in the heart, they necessarily seek an outlet in the body. The body cannot stay aloof from what the heart wills.
>
> So when the heart is really good (*ṣāliḥ*) in the sense that real *īmān* exists in it, including both 'knowledge' and the 'doing of the heart', then it cannot

39. *Op. cit.* p. 260.
40. in contrast to the more common notion of 'saying by the tongue'.

> but result in a good body, functioning with external (i.e. verbal) 'saying' and (external) 'doing' in accordance with the true *īmān* (in the heart). … The external (*ẓāhir*) always follows the internal (*bāṭin*). When the internal is good the external is necessarily good, and when the former is corrupt the latter is also corrupt. And to this refers what one of the Companions of the Prophet said concerning a man whose way of participation in ritual worship was quite vain: 'If the heart of this man were humble, his body would be humble'. …
>
> And thus is disclosed to our eyes the mistake of the thesis of Jahm b. Ṣafwān and his followers, who assert that *īmān* is a mere matter of *taṣdīq* by the heart and the 'knowledge' in the heart, and exclude all 'works of the heart' (and consequently all 'works of the body' too) from *īmān*. They are of the opinion that a man is a Believer with a perfect *īmān* if he has *taṣdīq* (and 'knowledge') in the heart. It does not matter, in their view, if this man should revile God and His Apostle, show enmity to the friends of God, make friends with the enemies of God, kill the Prophets, demolish the mosques, treat the copies of the Book with contempt, entertain Kāfirs with utmost courtesy, and look down upon the Believers with utmost disdain.
>
> They assert that all these things are merely acts of disobedience which do not affect the *īmān* in the heart. Such a man may do all these things while being in his 'interior' a good Believer in the sight of God.[41]

It is interesting to remark that Ibn Taymiyyah notices an affinity between what he calls the 'works of the heart' and the so-called 'states' *aḥwāl* of the Sufis. What is generally known in Sufism under the various names of 'states', 'stages' *maqāmāt*, 'alighting places' *manāzil* of the travellers toward God, etc., refers to nothing other than the 'works of the heart'. Some of these Sufi psychological 'states', he says, are those 'works of the heart' which God and the Apostle have made obligatory. They form part of the 'obligatory *īmān*'. Some other 'states' are those that God and the Apostle have liked but have not made obligatory. These belong to the 'preferable *īmān*'. The psychological acts of the first category are incumbent upon every Believer, while those of the second category are only for those 'admitted to closest proximity (*muqarrabūn*) to God. But, of course, every Believer is not supposed to reach such a high status. He who confines himself to the psychological acts of the first category *is* a real

41. *Op. cit.* pp. 155–157.

Believer, one of the Fellows of the Right (*aṣḥāb al-yamīn*).[42] By far the greatest mistake committed by the Murjiʾites is, Ibn Taymiyyah says, that they do not consider the psychological acts of the first category, which are common to the Sufis and the non-Sufis, as an essential part of *īmān*.[43]

This last-mentioned accusation, however, is obviously an oversimplification. We have seen earlier in chapter V how much importance was attached by most of the leading Murjiʾites to the 'works of the heart' like love of God, fear of God, humble submissiveness, etc. In making the above statement, Ibn Taymiyyah is thinking most obviously of the Jahmite position. And he himself is conscious of it. This is shown by the fact that a few pages down in the same book, he sets about to criticize the Murjiʾite theory of *īmān* in a more comprehensive way.

He begins by dividing the Murjiʾites into three main groups in regard to the problem of the structure of *īmān*: (1) those who assert that *īmān* is nothing other than what is in the heart, (2) those who assert that it is merely 'saying' by the tongue, (3) those who assert that it consists in *taṣdīq* by the heart and 'saying' by the tongue.

The first group is further sub-divided into two groups. The first are those who include the 'works of the heart' in *īmān*. The majority of the Murjiʾite sects are of this type. And the second are those who exclude the 'works of the heart' from that which they understand by 'what is in the heart'. This position is taken by Jahm and those who follow him like Ṣāliḥī.

After dividing the Murjiʾites into three main groups in this way, Ibn Taymiyyah goes on to subject their theory of *īmān* to a thoroughgoing critical examination. He finds therein three basic mistakes.

(1) The first big mistake which he points out is that the Murjiʾites regard the *īmān* of all men as identical. Here is what he writes about this point:

> One of their chief mistakes is their thought that the *īmān* which God has imposed upon his servants is equal and identical in very person, that the kind of *īmān* which is incumbent upon one man is equally incumbent upon every other man. This is wrong. For the kind of *īmān* which God required of the followers of the Prophets of the preceding ages is different from what he

42. Reference to the Koran, LVI, 27.
43. *Op. cit.* pp. 158–159.

requires of the followers of Muḥammad, just as God has imposed upon the Community of Muḥammad what He has not imposed upon others. Furthermore, the *īmān* which was obligatory before the revelation of the whole of the Koran was completed must have been different from the *īmān* which has become obligatory after the completion of the revelation of the Koran.

Besides, the *īmān* which is obligatory to those who know all the concrete details of what the Apostle has reported is necessarily different from the *īmān* which is obligatory to those who have only a broad general knowledge about it. This is because of the following fact. *Īmān* cannot exist without man's regarding as true (*taṣdīq*) all that of which the Apostle has informed him. But a man, for example, who has accepted the Apostle as truthful (in the first moment, without waiting for any further information) and died immediately after conversion is not required to have more than that much of *īmān*, while he to whom the Koran and the Ḥadīths have reached with all the information and commandments that are contained in them in concrete details is required to have a concrete detailed *taṣdīq* of every individual piece of information and commandment. To such a man is obligatory what is not at all obligatory to a man who dies with incomplete knowledge, and is thus required to have only a broad, general sort of *īmān*.

Even if we suppose that everybody were allowed to live (long enough to acquire a detailed knowledge of the Koran and the Ḥadīths), it is wrong to think that every one of the common people is required to know all the commandments, prohibitions, and the information given by the Apostle. All that is required is that everybody should know what is incumbent upon him and what is prohibited, (each according to his individual conditions).

He who, for instance, does not possess any wealth is not required to know the details of the commandment about *zakāt*. He who has no ability at all to go on pilgrimage is not required to know the details about the ritual acts connected with the pilgrimage. He who is not married is not asked to know the detailed regulations about marriage life. Thus the kind of *īmān* required, both *taṣdīq* and 'doing', differs from one person to another.[44]

These considerations lead Ibn Taymiyyah to an extremely interesting crit-

44. *Ibid.* pp. 163–164.

icism of Platonic Idealism. The main point of his argument is that *īmān* as something identical in all men, something fixed once for all and not allowing of any individual variation, is but a Universal. He takes the position that Universals exist only in the human mind, that they have no existence at all in the outer world. In the outer, i.e. physical, world of reality, there are only Particulars, each one of which has its own peculiar individual traits. *Īmān* is no exception to this general rule.

> The Murjiʾites imagine that the kind of *īmān* which is obligatory to all men is a single species, and some of them have come to think that since it is a unique species, it does not allow of various degrees. One of them once said to me, '*Īmān*, in so far as it is *īmān*, does not allow of increase and decrease'. I replied to him in the following way:
> What you are speaking of is *īmān* as a universal concept. It is the same as 'man' as man, 'animal' as animal, 'existence' as existence, 'blackness' as blackness, etc. Things of this sort allow neither increase nor decrease. We admit that these thing do possess an absolute existence free from all (individualizing) conditions and attributes. However, they possess no reality in the outer world. They are merely things which man posits in his mind, just as he posits (in his mind) an existent which is neither eternal nor temporal, neither subsisting in itself nor in another. He can even posit a man who is neither existent nor non-existent, and say that the 'essence' *māhiyyah* in itself is something which is qualified neither by existence nor by non-existence. We must keep in mind, however, that an 'essence' in itself is merely something posited by the mind and that it has no reality in the outer world.
> The same is true of positing an *īmān* which is not an attribute of any Believer, being free from all limitations. This is like positing a man who is neither existent nor non-existent.
> No, in reality there is no *īmān* without it being the *īmān* of some individual Believer, just as there can be no 'human-ness' apart from any individual man whom it qualifies. Every individual man has a 'human-ness' which is peculiar to him. In the same manner, every Believer has an *īmān* which is peculiar to him. Thus the 'human-ness' of Zayd is *similar* to the 'human-ness' of ʿAmr, but the two are not one and the same thing. If the two are said to share the unique species of humanity, the meaning of this is that they look alike as two existents in the outer world, and that they participate in a Universal which exists only in the mind.[45]

In the particular context of the present section, this kind of discussion, although interesting, may seem a digression. And we must admit that it has a more proper place in the following section in which we shall deal with the problem of the increase and decrease of *īmān*. There we shall also discuss the problem, touched upon in the passage just quoted, of whether there can be a divergence of degrees among men in regard to *īmān*. However, the above discussion is not without direct relevance to the topic of the present section. The point is that, in Ibn Taymiyyah's view, the individual differences in *īmān* come mainly from the inclusion of 'works' in *īmān*. *Taṣdīq*, in itself and as an abstract entity, may be one and the same, but it is materialized through the 'works of the heart' and the 'works of the body' in a myriad of individual forms.

The second of the big mistakes committed by the Murjiʾites is the Jahmite thesis that the psychological aspect of *īmān* is exhausted by *taṣdīq*. The thesis simply ignores the existence and the function of the 'works of the heart'.[46] This point has been already discussed fully in the foregoing pages.

The third mistake consists in their asserting that the *īmān* which is in the heart is perfect by itself and does not need any 'work' at all for its perfection. Of course, in practice, good 'works' are done by every Believer, but they are, so to speak, the 'fruit' *thamarah* of *īmān*, not the necessary requirement of *īmān* itself.

Against this view Ibn Taymiyyah emphasizes, as we have seen above, that a perfect *īmān* in the heart necessarily requires outward acts in accordance with it.[47] The nature of the relation between *īmān* and 'work' is explained as follows:

> The relation between them may be assimilated to that of the heart with the body. Neither of the two can exist without the other. As there is no being with a living body that does not possess a heart, so there is no being possessed of a heart without a body. And yet they are two different things; they are distinguishable from each other both in function and conception.
> One may also compare the relation to the outside and the inside of a grain. (The

45. *Ibid.* pp. 346–347.
46. *Ibid.* p. 170.
47. *Ibid.* pp. 170–171.

> two are different and yet) they are one. Nobody regards a grain as two grains because its outside and inside have different properties.
> Likewise, the 'works' of *islām* are but the outside of *īmān*. They are the 'works' of the body, while *īmān* is the inside of *islām* and it is the 'works' of the heart.
> This is what is meant by the Prophet's words: '*Islām* is an external matter, while *īmān* is in the heart'.[48] ... *Islām* here means nothing but the 'works' of *īmān*, and *īmān* nothing but the inner conviction of *islām*. There can be no *īmān* without 'work', and no 'work' without an inner conviction (*ʿaqd*).
> The same idea is expressed by another Ḥadīth: 'The (value of a) work is to be measured by the intention (or motive, *niyyah*)'.
> It means simply that there can be no 'work' (in the religious sense) without it being backed by an inner conviction or intention. By this the Apostle of God affirmed and recognized both the 'works' of the body and the 'works' of the heart, i.e. 'intentions'.
> The relation of 'work' to *īmān* is like that of the lips to the tongue. No speech is possible without them, because the lips gather together different sounds and the tongue emits them in the form of speech. If either of them is damaged, speech itself is lost. In exactly the same way if 'work' is dropped, *īmān* disappears.[49]

As we have remarked a few paragraphs back, the question of whether *īmān* increases or decreases is inextricably bound up with the question of whether or not 'works' are included in the concept of *īmān*. The next section will be devoted to an examination of this problem.

III The increase and decrease of *īmān*

'Is *īmān* capable of increasing?' 'Does *īmān* decrease also?' 'Is there a difference of degrees (*tafāḍul*) among men regarding their *īmān*?' These are questions which Muslim theology has inherited from the Murjiʾites. As we saw

48. Cf. Chap. IV, note 9. It is worthy of note that in the particular context of this passage, the famous Ḥadīth is given a very peculiar coloring.
49. *Op. cit.* p. 283.

in chapter V, most of the Murji'ites were characteristically interested in the problem of whether *īmān* increases and decreases. And the raising of this question itself was the direct result of their discussion on the significance of 'doing' in *īmān*. The answer to this question varied naturally according to whether one included or excluded 'doing' from the essential constitution of *īmān*. It was quite natural for those who excluded it to choose the negative answer, while those who admitted that 'doing' is an integral part of *īmān* chose the positive answer.

In this sense, the problem of the increase and decrease of *īmān* is but a corollary of that of *ʿamal*. The question of the existence or non-existence of different degrees in *īmān* is a further corollary of the question of increase and decrease. For if we admit that *īmān* can increase and decrease, i.e. that it can vary, we admit almost automatically that there are degrees in it, while if *īmān* is incapable of increase and decrease, *īmān* must necessarily be exactly the same in all men.

The very basis of the thesis of increase and decrease is, therefore, the thought that *taṣdīq* itself is invariable and remains always the same, while 'work', which is another constituent of *īmān*, is constantly changing, i.e. growing or diminishing. In other words, *īmān* in this conception is composed of an unchanging constant core which is surrounded, so to speak, by a large area of changing elements. This is the most commonly accepted picture of this matter.

Concerning the idea that *taṣdīq* itself never changes, Ibn Ḥazm remarks:

> It is absolutely impossible that increase or decrease should occur in *taṣdīq* of any kind, that is, *taṣdīq* of anything (whether religious or otherwise). The *taṣdīq* of the Unicity of God and the Prophethood of Muḥammad is no exception to this general rule. There can also be no increase and decrease in this *taṣdīq*. ... This comes from the fact that the meaning of *taṣdīq* is nothing other than that a man has an unshaken conviction of the existence of whatever he considers truth. Obviously there can be no 'more or less' in this kind of property. For, unless he is absolutely sure of his being in the right, he is a doubter, not a *muṣaddiq* (i.e. man of *taṣdīq*). And if he is not a *muṣaddiq*, he is not a Believer.[50]

Against this one may raise an objection and say, 'How can you be so sure

50. *Fiṣal* IV, p. 193.

that *taṣdīq* does not allow of any variation?' *Taṣdīq* is, after all, an attribute. And attributes in general allow of various degrees.

> It is a matter of ordinary experience (the opponent goes on to argue) that some green is 'more green' than other green; some courage is greater than some other courage. Particularly worthy of notice is the fact that courage and *taṣdīq* are both 'modes' of the mind and belong to the same category of mental attributes. (How can you differentiate them from one another in respect to the possibility of their having 'more or less'?).
>
> (To this objection Ibn Ḥazm replies: The 'qualities' *kayfiyyāt* can be divided into two kinds in this respect, i.e. those that allow of 'more or less' and those that do not.) If some of the qualities allow of 'more or less', they do so simply because they allow, by nature, of some other quality coming into them and mixing with them. This occurs only in those cases where there are a number of intermediate stages between a quality and its opposite in which they mingle with each other in varying dosages, or where the two opposite qualities can mingle with each other directly.
>
> But as for those qualities that do not allow of any mixture at all, there can be no varying degrees. God has created them in that way. … The quality of 'truthfulness' *ṣidq*, for instance, turns into a 'lie' *kadhib* immediately if it is mixed with anything else. Likewise, if *taṣdīq* is mixed with anything else, it changes immediately into 'doubt' *shakk*, and the *taṣdīq* itself is invalidated.[51]

Thus *taṣdīq* is a constant element which never allows of even the slightest variation. And yet in the Koran we find many references to the 'increase' of *īmān*.[52] So there must be in *īmān* some other thing that does change. And that changing element is 'work'. As I have remarked above, this is the typical answer given by those who regard 'work' as an essential constituent of *īmān*. Ibn Ḥazm is one of them. Thus he concludes: *Īmān* is not only *taṣdīq*, but it includes side by side with *taṣdīq* many other things (i.e. 'works'). And the "more or less" comes into *īmān* through the greater or smaller amount of these things'.[53] The concept of 'increase' *ziyādah* is applicable only to 'quantity' and

51. *Ibid.* IV, pp. 220–221.

52. For example, 'Whenever a Sūrah is revealed, some of them say: "Which one of you has this increased in *īmān*?" As for those who (really) believe, it has increased them in *īmān*.' (IX, 124)

53. *Op. cit.* IV, p. 221.

'number'. Within the conceptual range covered by *īmān*, only the element of 'work' admits of 'quantity' and 'number'.[54]

An excellent illustration of this fact is afforded, Ibn Ḥazm says, by a famous Ḥadīth in which the Prophet describes the woman as 'deficient in both Reason (*'aql*) and Religion (*dīn*)'. On being asked what he meant be 'deficiency in Religion', he answered, 'Do you not see? Women have a certain number of days and nights[55] in which they neither perform fasting nor participate in ritual worship. This is their deficiency in Religion'. According to Ibn Ḥazm, this can only refer to deficiency in 'works', which are here conceived of in terms of the number of days. It does not mean that, in the woman, *taṣdīq* itself is deficient. If *taṣdīq* is deficient even in a small portion, the whole *taṣdīq* will be lost, for '*taṣdīq* has no parts'.[56]

Now the deficiency and the perfection of *īmān*, thus understood, are evidently relative concepts. And the number of the degrees is illimitable. The *īmān* of a man who does, for example, *A-B-C-D* of all the possible 'works' of piety, is more perfect than the *īmān* of one who does only *A-B-C*, the difference between the two being only one act (D). But the *īmān* of the first man is more deficient than that of a man who does *A-B-C-D-E*. All this of course rests on the basic supposition that all these three men share one and the same *taṣdīq*. Ibn Ḥazm explains this relativity of the perfection of *īmān* by an imaginary dialogue between himself and an opponent who would not include 'work' in *īmān*.

> (The opponent:) Tell me, what do you think of a man who says, 'There is no god but God and Muḥammad is the Apostle of God', and dissociates himself from all religions except Islam, and regards as true everything the Prophet has brought, believes in it with his heart, and then dies immediately after this. Do you think he is a Believer or not?
> (Ibn Ḥazm:) My answer is: Yes, he is without any doubt a Believer in the sight of both God and man.
> (The opponent:) Tell me then, is he deficient in his *īmān* or perfect? If you reply that he is perfect in his *īmān*, that is precisely what we assert. But in case you say that his *īmān* is deficient, I will ask you, 'What is the thing which is missing from his *īmān*? And what is still there in his *īmān*?'

54. *Ibid.* p. 194.
55. Reference to menstruation.
56. *Ibid.* p. 197.

> (Ibn Ḥazm:) He is a Believer deficient in *īmān* in comparison with another man whose *īmān* is more than his by the acts which the former has not done. More generally, every man is deficient in *īmān* in comparison with another who is superior to him in regard to 'works'. And the series continues until it finally reaches the Apostle of God with whom no one can compete in the perfection of *īmān*, in the sense that he is superior to any other man in regard to 'works'.
>
> Thus the question, 'In what is his *īmān* deficient?' must be answered by saying, 'It is deficient in those acts which (he has not done and) others have done, and the quantity of which is known best to God'.[57]

The argument presented by Ibn Ḥazm represents a typical form in which the problem of the increase and decrease of *īmān* is dealt with in the orthodox circles though with noticeable difference of details in each case. Taftāzānī, to give one more example, also takes the position that 'this problem is a branch of the more basic one of whether the acts of obedience (*ṭāʿāt*) form part of *īmān*'. Commenting on Nasafī's text: 'As for "works" they increase in themselves, but *īmān* neither increases nor decreases', he writes:

> The very essence of *īmān* neither increases nor decreases ... because it (i.e. the essence of *īmān*) is the *taṣdīq* of the heart which has reached the utmost limit of decisiveness and submission. It is inconceivable that there should be increase or decrease in this kind of thing. So much so that when a man has once reached the *taṣdīq* in the real sense of the word, it makes no difference any longer whether he does all the works of obedience or commits disobedience, for in either case, his *taṣdīq* remains firm in the same state without any change at all.[58]

The 'increase' *ziyādah* of *īmān*, which is mentioned in a number of verses in the Koran, must be understood in accordance with this basic observation. Here Taftāzānī says that he is, on the whole, following Abū Ḥanīfah who interprets these verses in this way:

> (In the first period of Islam, when the Koran was being revealed little by little,) the people believed only in very broad principles. Then one religious duty after another was revealed, and the people progressed, believing those duties

57. *Ibid.* IV, pp. 210–211.
58. Taftāzānī, *op. cit.* pp. 444–445, 446.

one by one (as they were revealed). As a result, *īmān* went on increasing as the objects which had to be believed increased in number. Such a situation, however, is inconceivable except in the lifetime of the Prophet.

But this last statement (Taftāzānī says) is problematic. For the process of obtaining a concrete knowledge of individual religious duties can very well occur in other than the Prophet's lifetime. *Īmān* is obligatory in a broad and general way regarding things that are known only in a broad and general way. It is also obligatory in a detailed way regarding matters that are known in a detailed way. And no one can doubt that in the concrete detailed *īmān*, there is 'increase' *ziyādah*, and that it is, further, more perfect (than the broad and general *īmān*).[59]

Ghazālī's proposed solution to the same problem[60] is somewhat different from the two preceding in its approach, although in the main, and as a whole, all three belong to the same line of thought. Ghazālī's starting-point is the Aristotelian theory of *ishtirāk*, i.e. equivocality. In his view, the divergence of opinions on this problem arises from the ignorance of the fact that the word *īmān* is equivocal. So the confusion will be removed as soon as we distinguish clearly between the different meanings in which this word is actually used. There is no point in quarrelling over a problem caused by the equivocality of a word without first making an effort to disentangle the various meanings that are lumped together under the form of one and the same word.

Ghazālī isolates three major meanings of *īmān* in theological thinking. They are: (1) *taṣdīq* which is firmly established, being based on an apodictic proof; (2) *taṣdīq* which, based originally on uncritical reliance on authority, has reached the stage of a firm and determined conviction; (3) *taṣdīq* accompanied by 'work' which is required by the *taṣdīq* itself.

The first kind of *īmān* occurs when a man, for example, knows the existence of God by a logical proof. The second is that of the common people in Islam. The third is mainly based on Ḥadīths in which bodily actions are also included in the meaning of *īmān*.

Now *īmān* in the first sense is a kind of absolute certainty (*yaqīn*), and here increase and decrease are inconceivable. For an absolute conviction, once it

59. *Ibid.* p. 445.
60. *Iqtiṣād*, pp. 225–228.

has attained to perfection, does not allow of any increase, and before it attains to perfection it is not yet absolute conviction. *Īmān* in this sense is a single homogeneous unit which neither increases nor decreases, unless we mean by 'increase' a greater degree of clarity, i.e. an increase in the subjective feeling of reliance and the peace of mind.

Īmān in the second sense allows of 'more or less'. No one can deny this because it is a matter of daily experience. We see constantly how certain people, whether Jews, Christians or Muslims, stand firm in their religious conviction, never being moved by any kind of threat or persuasion, while certain others are weaker in their conviction, show greater flexibility, or are inclined to fluctuation. Conviction in this second sense is like a knot. Just as a knot can be made stronger or weaker, so there are stronger convictions and weaker convictions.

As for *īmān* in the third sense, it goes without saying that 'work' admits of individual differences. The question is rather: Does assiduous practice (*muwāẓabah*) of a 'work' affect *taṣdīq* itself and bring into it individual differences? Ghazālī's answer to this question is in the affirmative.

> I think as follows. Assiduous practice of the acts of obedience affects *taṣdīq* gravely in that it strengthens the subjective feeling of absolute confidence in the conviction based on authority, and helps it take deeper root in the soul.
> The best and the only way to know this is for us to reflect and observe our own states of mind, and compare the state of consciousness at the moment when we are assiduously engaged in doing a certain act of obedience, and the consciousness when we are slack. We observe a clear difference by introspection. And thus we come to know that assiduous practice of an act increases the sense of familiarity with the things we believe in and strengthens the feeling of reliance and the peace of the mind. The result is that a man who is convinced of something and who has been engaged for a long period of time in doing things in accordance with his conviction proves far more resistant than those who have not done so, to any attempt from outside to alter the conviction or to make it look dubious.[61]

Far more elaborate and detailed is Ibn Taymiyyah's examination of the meaning of 'increase' or varying degrees of *īmān*. We know by now that the

61. *Ibid.* p. 228.

pivotal point of this theory is the inclusion of 'work' in the concept of *īmān*. The thesis that *īmān* allows of many degrees and individual differences is but a natural consequence of this understanding of *īmān*. The question before him now is: What do we actually mean when we say that *īmān* is capable of having 'more or less'? Ibn Taymiyyah isolates a number of different respects in which *īmān* may be said to increase and decrease.

(1) The first to mention is the contrast of *ijmāl* with *tafṣīl*, that is, the difference between a broad and general knowledge and a more detailed concrete knowledge concerning the Divine Commandments.

> It is true that *īmān* in God and His Apostle is incumbent upon all men, and that it is also incumbent upon every community to obey what their own Apostle has commanded them to do in a broad and general way. But we know on the other hand that (historically) there was a wide difference between the obligations at the very beginning of Islam and the obligations after the completion of the Koranic revelation. And there are also individual differences between men regarding the details of what they have to believe in.
>
> Thus he who knows the whole of the Koran and the Sunnah and all the implications of them is obliged to have a detailed *īmān* which is not incumbent upon others. So if somebody has just come to believe in God and the Apostle inwardly as well as outwardly, then dies without having the chance of knowing the items of the religious Law, he dies as a Believer fulfilling all that is incumbent upon him of *īmān*. That which is incumbent upon such a man and that which he does, are not the same as the *īmān* of one who knows all the items of the Law, believes in them, and acts in accordance with them. On the contrary, the *īmān* of the latter is more perfect (than that of the former,) both in regard to obligations and deeds.
>
> The Divine words: 'This day have I perfected for you your religion' (V, 3), means only that God has finished establishing all the rules of what man has to do and what he is forbidden to do. The verse does not mean that every individual member of the community is obliged to do all that is incumbent upon the rest of the community.[62]

62. *Kitāb al-Īmān*, pp. 193–194.

(2) Individual differences arise from the practice and non-practice of what God has commanded man to do. This is again a question of *ijmāl* and *tafṣīl*, but with particular reference to what man actually does.

> (Suppose there are three men. The first) is a man who believes without reservation in what the Apostle has brought and never denies anything of it, who, however, neglects all effort to obtain a knowledge of what the Apostle has commanded him to do and what he has forbidden him to do. He does not make any effort also to know about the Apostle, neither does he try to seek the knowledge which is obligatory to him, so he does not know what is obligatory and, consequently, does not do it, but simply follows his vain desires. The second is a man who tries to obtain the knowledge of what the Apostle has commanded him to do, and does put it into practice. The third is a man who seeks for the knowledge, obtains it, believes in it, but does not put it into practice.
>
> Evidently all these three share (the minimum of) what is obligatory. And yet he who seeks for a knowledge of the details (about the commandments and prohibitions) and acts accordingly (i.e. the second man) has a more perfect kind of *īmān* than the one who knows all that is obligatory, obeys and acknowledges it, but never puts it into practice (i.e. the third man).
>
> And the man who, though he acknowledges all that the Apostle has brought, (does not act accordingly,) though conscious of his sin and afraid of Divine chastisement for the neglect of the work,[63] has a more perfect *īmān* than the one who never tries to obtain the knowledge of what the Apostle has commanded him to do, never acts accordingly, has no fear of the coming chastisement, and is completely careless of the details of what the Apostle has brought, although he admits his Prophethood inwardly and outwardly (i.e. the first man).
>
> Thus the process by which the human heart goes on acquiring a knowledge of what the Apostle has brought and what he has commanded, and goes on accepting (every item) as a duty is in reality an 'increase' in *īmān* as compared with the case in which a man does not materialize his knowledge although he accepts and acknowledges all these things as a duty in a broad and general sense. (Nay, even within the domain of 'knowledge' itself there can be an

63. I think this refers to the third man under a particular condition: a man who does not act properly but is clearly conscious of his sinfulness.

> 'increase' of *īmān*). For instance, he who knows all the names of God and their meanings and believes in them has a more perfect *īmān* than a man who believes in the Divine names in a vague sense without knowing (the exact meanings) of all or some of them. Thus as a man goes on increasing his knowledge of the names of God, His attributes, and His signs, his *īmān* too goes on increasing accordingly.[64]

(3) Ibn Taymiyyah is against the view, which we have studied above, that *taṣdīq* does not change, and that if *īmān* varies from one person to another, it is because it includes 'work' which *is* variable. He takes the position that *taṣdīq* itself allows of various degrees.

> Both 'knowledge' and *taṣdīq* admit of individual differences. The *taṣdīq* of one person may be stronger or weaker than that of others; it can be firmer and farther removed from doubt and hesitation in one person than in another.
> Everybody can perceive this individuation by introspection. Take the case of the sense perception of one and the same object by many men, the seeing of the new moon by a group of people, for example. Although all of them participate in the event, the vision differs in perfection from man to man. The same is true of the hearing of one and the same sound (by many), the perception of one and the same smell, the tasting of one and the same kind of food. And so 'knowledge' and *taṣdīq* vary from man to man. Nay, 'knowledge' and *taṣdīq* in many ways show more of individual differences than sense perception.
> As for the meanings of God's names and His speech, people differ one from another in their 'knowledge' far more than in the knowledge of other matters.

(4) There is another respect in which *taṣdīq* varies individually. The kind of *taṣdīq* which requires a 'work of the heart' is more perfect than the kind which does not.

> The *taṣdīq* which necessarily causes a 'work of the heart' is more perfect than the *taṣdīq* which does not cause any, and a 'knowledge' that results in an action is more perfect than another that is not put into practice.

64. *Op. cit.* pp. 194–195.

> Suppose there are two persons who know that God is the Truth, that His Apostle is true, that the Garden really exists, and that the Fire really exists. Suppose, further, that this same knowledge necessarily causes in one of them love of God, fear of God, the desire to go to the Garden, and the desire to escape from the Fire, while in the other, it does not cause anything of the sort. Evidently, the former is more perfect than the latter, for we can judge the strength of the cause by the strength of the result.[65]

(5) Once we admit that the 'works of the heart' are included in *īmān*, we must admit that *īmān* varies from individual to individual, for people differ greatly from each other in matters such as love of God and His Apostle, fear of God, etc.

(6) The external, i.e. bodily 'works' follow the internal, and they, too, are part of *īmān*. And in external 'works' there is a great deal of individual difference.

(7) Another factor which causes 'more or less' in *īmān* is the greater or lesser attentiveness of men to the Divine commandments.

> When a man remembers in his heart what God has commanded him to do and keeps it constantly present in his mind, never being forgetful of it, his *taṣdīq* or 'knowledge' is more perfect than that of a man who regards it as true (*taṣdīq*) and yet forgets about it. Forgetfulness or carelessness is the opposite of the perfection of 'knowledge', *taṣdīq*, and consciousness. And keeping something constantly in mind brings 'knowledge' and certainty to perfection.
> This must be what was meant by ʿUmar b. Ḥabīb, one of the Companions of the Prophet, when he said, 'Whenever we remember God, praise Him, and glorify Him, there occurs an increase of *īmān*, and whenever we are heedless, forgetful and neglectful, there occurs a decrease of it'.
> The same is true of the words which Muʿādh b. Jabal used to say to his companions, 'Sit with us for a while so that we might believe'![66] God says, 'Do

65. *Ibid.* pp. 195–196.

66. I.e. let us sit together and talk about religious matters so that we might increase in *īmān* for the moment.

not obey him whose heart We have rendered forgetful of Us, who follows his own vain desires' (XVIII, 29), and 'Make (them) remember, for remembrance profits the Believers' (LI, 55) etc. …

(It is a matter of common experience that) when a man reads the Koran again and again, even (such a short Sūrah as) the 'Sūrah of the Opening', new meanings occur to him during this process, which have never occurred to his mind before. And this new awareness often causes the man to feel as though the Sūrah were being revealed for the first time at that very moment. He believes in these (new) meanings, and both his 'knowledge' and 'work' increase. Those who read the Koran carelessly do not experience this, but anyone who reads it with any attentiveness does have experiences of this kind. And as the man goes on practising what he has been commanded to do, his consciousness that he has been commanded to do it grows keener and keener, and his *taṣdīq* becomes more and more firmly established. When such a stage is reached, he has in his mind a *taṣdīq* for what he has not been clearly aware of, even if he has never denied it before.[67]

(8) Increase in *īmān* occurs also when a man comes to realize that something against which he has hitherto been fighting, is in reality God's commandment, and completely changes his attitude toward it.

It often happens that a man denies and gives the lie to a certain thing without knowing that the Apostle has informed men of it and commanded them to do it, while if he but knew this, he would never deny it, for his heart firmly believes that the Apostle does not tell anything except truth and does not command anything except what is really obligatory.

If such a man happens to hear a Koranic verse or a Ḥadīth, or reflects upon the matter by himself, or the meaning is explained to him by somebody else, or he understands the real meaning of it in any other way, and if as a result he regards as true what he has been considering false, and comes to know (the truth of) what he has been denying, this marks the birth of a new *taṣdīq* and a new *īmān* by which his (former) *īmān* has increased. This, of course, does not mean that he has hitherto been a Kāfir. He has simply been ignorant (*jāhil*).[68]

67. *Op. cit.* pp. 196–198.
68. *Ibid.* p. 198.

One might be tempted to say that this case resembles very much the first one in which individual differences of *īmān* have been attributed to the difference between a broad general knowledge (*mujmal*) and a concrete knowledge of details (*mufaṣṣal*). But the two cases are not the same because:

> Many people, even the most pious and learned ones, happen to have in their minds a lot of details which are opposed to the Apostle's teaching, without having the slightest idea that they are against the Apostle's teaching. In such a case, if they come to realize this, they would certainly withdraw from their wrong views.
>
> To this category belong all those who—although they believe in the Apostle, know his teaching and believe it, and do not deviate from it—put forward a theological thesis which proves to be a mistake or do some 'work' which is an error. In general, every 'innovator' who acts with the good intention of following the Apostle faithfully, belongs to this category.
>
> (This being the case, it is natural that there should be degrees in *īmān*,) for a man who knows the Apostle's teaching and acts in accordance with it is evidently more perfect than others who commit a mistake in this respect; and a man who comes to know the truth after a mistake and begins to act in accordance with the former is more perfect than those who are still in error.[69]

After this detailed analysis of the eight ways in which individual differences occur inevitably in *īmān*, we are now in a better position to understand why Ibn Taymiyyah criticizes Platonic idealism so severely. What he wants to emphasize in particular is that *īmān* is a strictly personal and individual affair. The *īmān* of Zayd is not identical with the *īmān* of ʿAmr. The *īmān* of each individual person is something peculiar (*mukhtaṣṣ*, *muʿayyan*) to him, and to him alone. *Īmān* in this sense allows of 'increase and decrease'.

> Those who deny the existence of degrees in this and similar matters are people who mentally picture an 'absolute *īmān*', or an 'absolute man', or an 'absolute existence' devoid of all particular attributes. And then they imagine that this is the unique *īmān* which exists in all men. Of course, *īmān*, thus understood, admits of no varying degrees, nor does it allow of any plurality, because it is nothing but a particular representation subsisting in a mind which

69. *Ibid.* p. 198.

> pictures it that way.
> This misleads many people into thinking that a number of things that participate in one and the same thing[70] must also be one and the same in the domain of Individuals and Particulars.
> As a result, some of the most learned men have come to imagine that 'existence' itself must be of the same nature. They represent all the existent things as participating in the idea of 'existence'. This idea they picture in their minds, and then (project it into the outer world) thinking that it exists in the world of reality exactly as it is pictured in their minds. Then they go a step further, and think that it (i.e. the 'existence' itself) is God, and thus they turn their Lord into the (Idea of) 'existence' which is not found in the outer world, but exists only in the mind that pictures it.
> In like manner, many Philosophers represent abstract numbers and abstract entities in their minds, and call them 'Platonic Ideas' *al-muthul al-aflāṭūniyyah*. They picture in this way 'time' which has reference neither to movement nor to a moving thing, and 'dimension' without any reference to bodies and their attributes, and then posit these abstract things as existing in the world of reality. All these people are victims of confusion between mental and real entities. ... Exactly the same thing can be said of those who assert that *īmān* is a single entity which is identical in all children of Adam. Their mistake consists in their thinking that *īmān* is one, and that it is identical.

In this respect, the error into which Jahm and his followers fell regarding the problem of *īmān* was of the same nature as the error into which they fell in regard to the Lord in whom all Believers believe, His speech, and His attributes. God is indeed far above all that the wrong-doers say about Him![71]

Before I close this chapter, I would like briefly to mention two other positions which admit the possibility of an 'increase' of *īmān* in a very different way from the theories that we have been examining.

One is that of the Atomists, mentioned by Taftāzānī. For the Atomists *īmān* is just an accident which continues to subsist by the continual renewing of a countless number of *īmān*-s, each one of which is similar to the preceding one. In their view, each *īmān*, like any other atom, does not continue to exist after

70. I.e. one mental picture, which is a Universal.
71. *Op. cit.* pp. 347–348.

it has been created except for a single unit of time, and then disappears to be replaced by a new *īmān* similar to it. And yet those of the Atomists who admit the increase of *īmān*, assert that, as this process of continual renewing goes on, a kind of firm perseverance in *īmān* is naturally produced. And this, they say, is an 'increase' hour by hour, and thus, as a whole, the *īmān* of a man goes on increasing as time increases.

Against this view, Taftāzānī points out that the occurrence of something similar to what has just been annihilated, however much it is repeated, does not constitute 'increase' at all.

The second position is that of the Māturīdites. We have remarked above how the Māturīdite concept of *īmān* is influenced by psychological theories peculiar to Sufism. We have also observed that they like very much the metaphor of 'light', and that they develop their peculiar conception of *īmān* in terms of this basic metaphor.

The problem which we have been discussing in this section is also approached from this particular angle. They do not admit the 'increase and decrease' of *īmān*. However, this does not mean that they refuse to admit in any sense the existence of 'more or less' in *īmān*. On the contrary, they do readily admit that there are individual differences in *īmān*, but only in terms of 'light' and 'brightness'. Some hearts are more illuminated by the light of God than others.

The famous Ḥadīth is explained in this way, in which the Prophet says: 'If we weigh on a scale the *īmān* of Abū Bakr with the *īmān* of the whole of mankind, the scale of the former will certainly outweigh the latter'. The scale of the *īmān* of Abū Bakr weighs more in the sense that it exceeds in 'light' and 'brightness' all the *īmān*-s of men put together. The Ḥadīth, they add, must not be understood in terms of 'increase and decrease'.[72]

72. *Fiqh Akbar* I, p. 8.

CHAPTER X

'I AM A BELIEVER, IF GOD WILLS'

The problem we are going to deal with in the present chapter is known technically as the problem of *istithnāʾ* in *īmān*. The word *istithnāʾ* means literally 'making an exception of something'. As a technical term in Muslim theology, however, it is used in a very narrowly limited sense. It means, namely, turning the definite statement of faith, 'I am a Believer (*anā muʾmin*)' into a conditional form by adding the short clause, 'if God wills (*in shāʾa Allāh*).

The problem, in other words, is whether one should straightforwardly express one's firm conviction by declaring, 'I am a Believer' or 'I am really (*ḥaqqan*) a Believer', or mitigate the force of the expression by saying, 'I am a Believer, if God wills', indicating thereby that everything, including one's own personal belief, is ultimately dependent on God's will. The latter attitude has been suggested by the Koranic verse which reads: Do not say of anything, 'Lo, I shall do it tomorrow,' except (you add) 'if God wills' (XVIII, 23–24).

This problem, which might look trivial to some, raises an extremely serious issue, because it touches upon the very core of the subjective aspect of one's own *īmān*. It concerns the personal existential decision about one's faith. Historically it did raise a vital issue in Islam because of the sharp disagreement on this problem between the Ashʿarites and the Māturīdites. As a matter of fact, it is counted among the main points of difference in theology between the two rival schools of Orthodoxy. The Ashʿarites affirmed the necessity of the conditional phrase while the Māturīdites denied it.

I shall begin by presenting the Māturīdite position. It is usually traced back to Abū Ḥanīfah's teaching, as is the case with the majority of the Māturīdite positions.

In the *Waṣiyyah* attributed to Abū Ḥanīfah, we find the following definite statement:

> The Believer is really a Believer and the Kāfir is really a Kāfir, for there can be no doubt about *īmān* or regarding *kufr*. And this is based on the Divine words: 'These are really Believers' (VIII, 74) and 'These are really Kāfirs' (IV, 151).[1]

The Ḥanafite-Māturīdite argument based on this statement may conveniently presented as follows. The first point which is invariably emphasized is that *istithnā'*, i.e. the addition of a conditional clause, indicates 'doubt' *shakk*. The indication of 'doubt', however, goes against the statement of the *Waṣiyyah*. Indeed, it goes against the general Consensus which holds that there can be no 'doubt' in *īmān*. This is shown by the fact that he who says, 'I believe in God, if God wills' or 'I witness that Muḥammad is the Apostle of God, if God wills', is considered a Kāfir by the Consensus.[2]

The second point is that, even in ordinary social life, the conditional clause invalidates all contracts and transactions. If we add, for example, the conditional clause to the statement 'I hereby sell such-and-such a thing' and say, 'I hereby sell such-and-such a thing, if God wills', the business transaction is immediately invalidated. Likewise expressions such as 'I hereby manumit my slave, if God wills', 'I hereby divorce my wife, if God wills', etc. In exactly the same way, the conditional clause invalidates *īmān*.[3]

The third point is that the adding of this clause indicates *ta'līq*, i.e. suspending (the matter upon a condition) or leaving the matter undecided. But 'suspension' is possible only in reference to an event which is expected to happen later. The Koranic verse quoted above is an example in point. No 'suspension' is imaginable in regard to what has already been realized, that is, past events and the present situation. The expression, 'I am a Believer' is a description of the subjective situation in which the speaker stands at present. So the conditional clause is here inadmissible.[4]

The fourth point, which is mentioned by the Ḥanafite commentator of the

1. *Waṣiyyah Abī Ḥanīfah* with a commentary by the Ḥanafite Mollā Ḥusayn b. Iskandar, Ḥaydarabad, 2 ed., 1365 A.H., p. 77. Cf. also Wensinck, *Muslim Creed*, p. 125, and Wensinck' remarks on this article of faith, pp. 138–139.

2. *al-Rawḍah al-Bahiyyah*, p. 6.

3. *Ibid.* p. 6; cf. also the commentary on the *Waṣiyyah*, p. 77.

4. *Ibid.* p. 6.

Waṣiyyah, concerns the case in which the use of the conditional clause is permissible. He says that not only is the use of the clause permissible but it is even recommended when the statement does not concern the very 'root' of *īmān*, but some particular circumstances accompanying the event of *īmān*. In expressions like, 'I shall be a Believer tomorrow, if God wills,' 'I shall die a Believer, if God wills,' 'My *īmān* will be accepted, if God wills,' etc., the conditional clause is to be considered preferable because the problem here is not about the 'root' of *īmān* but about the continuance, perseverance, and acceptance of *īmān*. Ḥusayn b. Iskandar summarizes the Ḥanafite-Māturīdite position in the following way:

(1) When a Believer declares, 'I am really (or actually) a Believer' (*anā mu'min ḥaqqan*), he is incontestably doing the right thing.

(2) When he says, 'I am a Believer, if God wills,' there are two possibilities:

(a) If his intention is to 'suspend' the matter on (Divine) Will regarding the actual situation, he is wrong.

(b) But if his intention is to refer to a future situation, he is right.[5]

Among the most important theoreticians in Islam, Ibn Ḥazm is one of those who take basically the same position as Māturīdism on this particular question. But his thought, as on many other points, shows a touch of originality.

> Each Believer is conscious of the existence in himself of this attribute (i.e. the attribute of being a man of *īmān*). And as long as he is sure that he believes in God, Muḥammad, and all that the latter has brought, and if he is ready to confess all this by the tongue, it is incumbent upon him to declare it openly. This is based on the Divine commandment:
> 'As for the favor of thy Lord, talk openly about it!' (XCIII, 11) We have to remember that there is no favor greater, and more gracious, and more deserving gratitude, than that of *islām* (*īmān*).
> Thus it is incumbent upon every Believer to declare, 'I am surely a Believer-Muslim in the sight of God at this present moment'. Properly speaking, there is no difference between the statement 'I am a Believer-Muslim' and the statement 'I am black', or 'I am white'. The same applies to all the attributes of which there is no doubt. The statement has nothing at all to do with self-

5. *Sharḥ Kitāb al-Waṣiyyah*, p. 77.

> praise or self-complacency.[6]

It is related of a famous Companion of the Prophet, (ʿAbd Allāh) Ibn Maṣʿūd, that he disliked the expression, 'I am a Believer', and used to add the conditional clause. Ibn Ḥazm justifies this attitude of Ibn Maṣʿūd by applying to it his original theory of *īmān*, which we have studied earlier.

> In my opinion, Ibn Maṣʿūd's attitude is right, for both *islām* and *īmān* are names that have been removed (by God) from their proper places in the Arabic language so that they might cover all the acts of piety and obedience. He disliked the blunt expression, 'I am a Muslim-Believer' only because it might be taken to mean that he exhausted in practice all the acts of obedience without leaving even a single item. This attitude of his is certainly right, for whoever claims for himself such a thing is no doubt a liar.[7]

Against the Māturīdites, who take the position that no *istithnāʾ* is necessary in the normal type of declaration of one's *īmān*, the Ashʿarites insist on the necessity of adding the conditional clause. Wensinck, in his *Muslim Creed*,[8] gives four arguments that were put forward by Ghazālī (*Iḥyāʾ ʿUlūm al-Dīn*, I, 114–117) in defense of the Ashʿarite position. The first is that such an absolute declaration is akin to self-elevation and self-sufficiency. The second is that the use of the conditional form is recommended by both the Koran and the Ḥadīth, as an expression of wish or desire, and not of 'doubt' in the sense in which the opponents understand it. The third is that it does express 'doubt', but it is a doubt about the perfection of one's *īmān*. And 'doubt' in this sense is surely justified. The fourth is that the conditional clause is necessary in reference to the 'last act' of man.

It is interesting to note, in connection with the second and the third point, that the Māturīdites call the Ashʿarites *Shakkākiyyah*, i.e. the Doubter-sect,[9] because of their insistence on the necessity of the conditional clause. In their view, the

6. *Fiṣal*, IV, pp. 227–228.

7. *Ibid.* p. 228.

8. p. 139.

9. Professor Tritton (*Theology*, p. 106) quotes from *al-Ghunyah* the following interesting remark about this nickname. The Murji'ah called the followers of custom and the community (i.e. the Orthodox) 'doubters' (*Shakkākiyyah*) because they qualified their claim to be Muslims by the addition 'if God will.'

Ashʿarites do so because they have doubts about their own *īmān*. Significantly enough, the above-mentioned *Creed*, attributed to Māturīdī himself, opens the section which deals with this problem by saying: 'The problem of *istithnā'* in *īmān* is a point of dispute between us and the *Shakkākiyyah*'.[10]

Ghazālī defends Ashʿarism against this charge by pointing out that the clause 'if God wills' is not indicative of 'doubt' in the sense that the Ashʿarites have only a very weak and shaky kind of *īmān*, but that it expresses rather an ardent wish to be more perfect in *īmān*. If, he says, it is 'doubt', it is a reasonable doubt about the perfection of one's *īmān*. It would be presumptuous of a man to suppose that his *īmān* is perfect in every respect in the sight of God.

In defense of Ashʿarism, Abū ʿUdhbah draws attention to the fact that the Ashʿarites have illustrious predecessors in the use of the conditional clause, like the Caliph ʿUmar, ʿAbd Allāh b. Masʿūd, and ʿĀ'ishah among the Companions, and among the Followers, Ḥasan al-Baṣrī, Ibn Sīrīn, Sufyān al-Thawrī, Ibn ʿUyaynah, Awzāʿī, Mālik b. Anas, Shāfiʿī, Aḥmad b. Ḥanbal, and many others. All these people, he says, used to declare their *īmān* in the conditional form. And yet nobody would claim that they were 'doubters'. On the contrary, the conditional clause was in them a natural overflowing of the strength of their *īmān*. It was a manifestation of the sense of 'being a humble servant' *ʿubūdiyyah*, and an expression of the basic thought that everything is dependent on God's Will.

The fourth point mentioned by Ghazālī is also worthy of special attention. It is related to a very particular theological problem, known technically as *muwāfāt*. It is, in brief, a theory of *īmān* which lays an exclusive emphasis on the 'final act' *khātimah* of man in determining the nature of his *īmān*. It stresses, in other words, that what is decisive in this matter is the last act a man does at the moment of death or the state in which he dies. If a man dies a perfect Believer, he *is* a Believer no matter what he has been doing all through his life. If, on the contrary, he dies in the state of *kufr*, he *is* a Kāfir however pious a Muslim he has been throughout his life.

The importance of the conditional clause is obvious for those who take this position on the problem of *īmān*. For how can we know now in which state we

---

10. *ʿAqīdah*, §25, p. 17.

shall die? All that we can do at present is to wish for a good end. Even if a man is a good Believer at present, and even if it is quite natural for him to wish that he should persevere in his *īmān* without wavering till the very last moment of his life, he can never be absolutely sure of such perseverance. His state at the last moment of his life is still a mystery (*ghayb*), something unpredictable. The conditional clause, 'if God wills' refers precisely to the *khātimah*.[11]

This theory of *istithnā'* is, as we have remarked, based on a very peculiar conception of *īmān*, namely, that one's *īmān* or *kufr* is determined solely by the state in which one finds oneself at the moment of death and that nothing preceding the last moment is of any significance in this respect. The conception of *īmān* presented in this form is evidently an 'innovation', for such is not by any means the Koranic conception of *īmān*.

Ibn Taymiyyah, who traces this conception back to Jahm,[12] criticizes it as follows:

> The majority of the later theologians who support Jahm's position assert the necessity of *istithnā'* in *īmān*. Their argument is that *īmān* as a technical term in the Divine Law means that with which a man finally comes (*muwāfāt*) to his Lord, although the word has a wider meaning linguistically.
> In this way they bring into the problem of *istithnā'* a peculiar understanding of the word *īmān* which they claim to be its meaning in the Divine Law. And thus they deviated (arbitrarily) from the common usage of Arabic. ...
> The conception that the word *īmān* means only the state in which a man dies has no support in the Divine Law. It is just a new conception which none of the great authorities of the past has ever upheld. From the fact that some of the leading authorities of the past used to practise *istithnā'* they have drawn the (wrong) conclusion that such must have been the basic understanding of *īmān* among the Ancients. This mistake is due to their lack of knowledge about the real opinion of the Ancients. They simply take the surface of the Ancients' words and interpret them in accordance with what they have learnt from the Jahmites and other similar men of 'innovation'. Thus the outward form is still the thesis of the Ancients, but the underlying idea is that of the

11. *al-Rawḍah al-Bahiyyah*, p. 8.

12. The famous Mu'tazilite, Fuwaṭī is said to have been the first to teach the doctrine of *muwāfāt*. (See Tritton, p. 115, note 1)

Jahmites, whose theory of *īmān* is the worst imaginable thing.[13]

Ibn Taymiyyah's ascription of this theory of *istithnā'* to the Jahmites is problematic. He himself seems to commit a contradiction when he counts in another place[14] 'the Murji'ites and Jahmites' among the representative thinkers who definitely forbid *istithnā'* in *īmān*. Here is what he says about the Jahmite position on the problem of *istithnā'*:

> Those who forbid the use of the conditional clause are represented by the Murji'ites, the Jahmites and the like, who regard *īmān* as a single entity of which man is conscious in himself, like *taṣdīq* to the Lord and other things that are in his heart. The typical form of their argumentation is as follows:
> I know that I am a Believer just as I know that I have pronounced the *shahādah*-formula, that I have recited the first Sūrah of the Koran, that I love the Apostle of God, and that I hate the Jews and the Christians. There is no difference at all between my saying, 'I am a Believer' and my saying, for example, 'I have recited the first Sūrah of the Koran, or 'I hate the Jews and the Christians' and the like, all of which belong to those things of which I am actually conscious, and which I know definitely to be true.
> And just as it is absurd to say, 'I have recited the first Sūrah, if God wills', it is absurd to say, 'I am a Believer, if God wills.'
> This clause is used only when the speaker is doubtful of the matter. In that case, he says, 'I have done it, if God wills'.
> And thus they conclude: Whoever adds the conditional clause in the declaration of *īmān* does so because he is doubtful of his own *īmān*. This is why they call the people who practise *istithnā'* 'the Doubters' (*Shakkākah*).[15]

It goes without saying that Ibn Taymiyyah does not subscribe to the view of those who are resolutely against the practice of *istithnā'*, because such a rejec-

13. *Īmān*, pp. 120–121.

14. I.e. in the last chapter of the book, in which he deals specifically with the problem of *istithnā'*. Here he ascribes the *muwāfāt*-theory to the later followers of Ibn Kullāb (Abū Muḥammad b. Saʿīd d. shortly after 854) who was one of the leading theologians among the Traditionists before Ashʿarī. See also page 100 of the same book where Ibn Taymiyyah describes Ashʿarī as a representative theologian who follows and supports Jahm in his theory of *īmān* (referring thereby to Jahm's exclusion of 'work' from *īmān*), but who differs from Jahm in the problem of *istithnā'* and supports the view taken by the people of the Sunnah.

15. *Op. cit.* p. 366.

tion rests on the Jahmite theory of *īmān* which excludes 'work' and make *īmān* an homogeneous entity shared by all who 'believe' at all.

However, he also rejects the view which allows the practice of *istithnā'* basing this allowance on the 'last act' theory. He attributes this view of *istithnā'*, in the last chapter of his book, to the Kullābites, the followers of Ibn Kullāb. There he gives the following summary of the Kullābite theory of the 'last act'.

> *Īmān* refers exclusively to the state in which man dies. Every man is either a Believer or a Kāfir in the sight of God solely in respect to *muwāfāt* and to what is in God's foreknowledge regarding his last state. Nothing that precedes the last state is of any account.
>
> If the *īmān* of a man is followed later by *kufr*, and if he dies a Kāfir, that *īmān* is not *īmān* at all. Such an *īmān* may be compared to a ritual worship done by a man who invalidates it before it is accomplished, or to the fasting of a man who breaks it before sunset. (Even while still a Believer) such a man is a Kāfir in the sight of God because of the Divine knowledge of the state in which he will die. And the same is true of *kufr*. ...
>
> Since God knows that such-and-such a man will die a Kāfir (even if he be at present a pious Believer), He has been from the very beginning intending to chastise him. So that kind of *īmān* which he has at the present moment is vain and of no avail, nay, its existence is equivalent to non-existence. And the man is not a Believer at all. Likewise, since God knows that such-and-such a man is going to die a Believer (even if he be now a Kāfir), God has been from the beginning intending to reward him. So in regard to the kind of *kufr* which he has at present, its existence is the same as non-existence. Such a man has never been a Kāfir.
>
> Based on such a conception, these people practise *istithnā'* in *īmān*. (Strangely) some of the authorities of this school (go even a step further and) practice *istithnā'* regarding *kufr*, too. Māturīdī is a representative thereof. This they do because they think that theoretically there can be no difference between *īmān* and *kufr* in this respect.[16]

---

16. *Ibid.* pp. 367–368.

The Kullābites and people of similar opinion justified the practice of *istithnā'* in *īmān* by pointing out the fact that the practice was widespread among the Ancients, i.e. the great authorities of the past. Ibn Taymiyyah admits that. So there is nothing wrong with the practice itself. Only the theory of *īmān* on which these people base it is, according to Ibn Taymiyyah, completely wrong.

It is true, he says, that the Ancients used to practise *istithnā'*, but they did so on an entirely different ground. Not even one of them is related to have used the conditional clause having in mind the final state in which he would leave his life on earth. But these people thought that the idea of *muwāfāt* was precisely the motive for which the Ancients used to practise *istithnā'*. In reality, what they took for the conception of the authorities of the past was nothing but a basic conception of *īmān* peculiar to Jahm.[17]

What then was the real thought of the Ancients underlying their practice of *istithnā'* in *īmān*? To this Ibn Taymiyyah gives the following answer:

> It is known through authoritative traditions that many of the Ancients used to practise *istithnā'*, such as Ibn Maṣʿūd and his followers, Thawrī, Ibn ʿUyaynah, the majority of the scholars of Kūfah and some scholars of Baṣrah, Aḥmad b. Ḥanbal, and others of the authorities of the Sunnah. But none of them has ever said, 'I practise *istithnā'* because of *muwāfāt*, because *īmān* in my view is nothing other than the name for that in which a servant goes to meet his Lord.' On the contrary, the authorities of the past are quite explicit in declaring that *istithnā'* is deemed necessary and appropriate because *īmān* includes 'doing' of the acts of obedience. They dared not attest formally that they were doing all the acts of obedience without exception, just as they dared not attest to the perfection of their piety. Because nobody could be sure of that, and because, if they had attested to such a thing, it would have been an act of presumption on their part.
>
> As to the idea of *muwāfāt*, no one of the Ancients, as far as I know, has sought therein justification for *istithnā'*. But in recent times, *muwāfāt* has been often made the theoretical ground for *istithnā'*, both by Traditionists of the schools of Aḥmad b. Ḥanbal, Mālik, Shāfiʿī, and others, and by theoreticians like Ashʿarī and most of his followers.[18]

---

17. *Ibid.* p. 372. Note that here again Ibn Taymiyyah ascribes the wrong theory to Jahm.

18. *Ibid.* p. 374.

The explanation of the matter by Ibn Taymiyyah is based on his favorite semantic theory of the distinction between *iṭlāq* and *taqyīd*, that is, between the 'absolute' and the 'conditioned' use of a word. The word *īmān*, when used 'absolutely', includes naturally all that God has commanded man to do as well as all that He has forbidden him to do. If a man says 'I am a Believer' in this sense without *istithnā'*, it would mean that he considers himself a perfect and impeccable Believer. And this would be nothing but 'self-elevation' *tazkiyah al-nafs*. If he is entitled to make such an attestation, why does he not attest that he will surely go to the Garden?[19]

Aḥmad b. Ḥanbal made it clear that he practised *istithnā'*, not because he had doubt about his belief, but because 'doing' was included in *īmān*. He used to add 'if God wills' because he was not absolutely sure whether he fulfilled all the necessary conditions of 'doing'. But sometimes he dropped the conditional clause intentionally. And that was when he used the word *īmān* in a 'conditioned' way, that is, when he referred to his inner conviction itself, without regard to the element of 'doing'. Thereby he' showed that he had no doubt at all about what he knew of his inner state.[20]

The matter will best be understood if we consider the use of the conditional clause in daily circumstances. When, for example, I have made up my mind to do something to-morrow, I say, 'I will do it to-morrow, if God wills'. The conditional clause here refers to the realization of the act, not to my will and determination. I have no doubt whatsoever of my will to do the thing, because I actually feel and know the existence of the will in myself. But, however firm my determination may be, I am not yet able to assure myself absolutely that the intended thing will materialize tomorrow without fail. The clause 'if God wills' refers to uncertainty of this type. Exactly the same reasoning applies to the sentence, 'I am a Believer, if God wills'.[21]

19. *Ibid.* p. 383.
20. *Ibid.* p. 386.
21. *Ibid.* pp. 390–391.

CHAPTER XI

CREATION OF *ĪMĀN*

I The origin of the question

The rise and the prosperity of Muʿtazilism in the early days of the Abbasids raised a number of serious problems in all quarters of speculative theology. The concept of *īmān* could not remain unaffected by the Muʿtazilite way of thinking.

Of all the major tenets upheld vigorously by the Muʿtazilites, two deserve particular attention with regard to the influence they exercised on the concept of *īmān*. The first to mention is the typically Muʿtazilite tenet of Divine 'justice' *ʿadl*. On the face of it, the thesis seems quite harmless, for it is simply an emphatic assertion of the perfect justice of God, i.e. His being absolutely free from all injustice. The concept raises a serious problem, however, because, on its reverse side, it implies human responsibility and consequently, human freedom. Thus understood, the thesis must necessarily impair the absolute sovereignty and omnipotence of God to a significant degree.

Originally, the thesis of Divine justice was put forward with the intention of shifting from God to man the burden of the responsibility for the evil acts of man. But it soon led to the heretical view that whatever man does, he does it with his own power and on his own responsibility, that, in short, man is the 'creator' of his own deeds. This view stands in sharp contrast to that professed by Jahm, who asserts that no act or deed belongs to anyone other than God, that acts are attributed to man only metaphorically, and that in reality man does not *do* anything; he is simply the locus in which God causes the event to occur.[1]

1. See Baghdādī, *Farq*, p. 199.

In such a situation it is easy to see how the question arises as to whether *īmān* and *kufr* are created in man by God or whether they are entirely a matter of human responsibility. As we might expect, the Muʿtazilites give almost exclusive attention to the birth of *kufr* in the human heart. ʿAbbād b. Sulaymān, for example, is said to have asserted: 'It is a mistake to say of God that He has created the Kāfirs, for their *kufr* would not have been created by God'. It is unimaginable, they assert, that the absolutely righteous God should make a man a Kāfir by creating *kufr* in his heart. It is unimaginable that the absolute Lord of justice should willingly create a Kāfir and then punish His creature with Hell Fire for having been a Kāfir. It is unimaginable that He should have wished or willed the creation of the abominable sin of *kufr*. These and other related problems will be dealt with in detail in the third section of the present chapter.

Here I would like to remark only that the question of the Divine creation of *kufr* is closely related to that of the creation of *īmān*, which is but its reverse side, although the latter problem does not produce so acute a theoretical problem as the former. For the creation of a good thing does not in any way compromise the image of Divine justice, although it does compromise human freedom. The Muʿtazilites want to assert that whatever man does, whether good or evil, *is* man's doing, that it is something man decides upon by himself and executes on his own responsibility. *Īmān* should not be made an exception to this basic truth.

As a concrete example of the sharp opposition that existed in this respect between the Muʿtazilites and the non-Muʿtazilites, we shall take the Koranic verse II, 257 as interpreted by the two parties. It is taken from *Amālī*[2] by al-Sharīf al-Murtaḍá. The verse in question reads: 'God is the friendly Protector of those who believe. He brings them out of darkness into light.'

> (The anti-Muʿtazilites say: Does not the literal meaning of this verse force us to understand that God is the Creator of *īmān* in them? For the 'light' *nūr* here obviously stands for *īmān* and the acts of obedience, and the 'darkness' *ẓulumāt* stands for *kufr* and the acts of disobedience …
> And since (the grammatical subject of 'bring out' is God), He must be the producer of that by which they come out of darkness. And the verse thus understood is diametrically opposed to the Muʿtazilite thesis.

2. II, pp. 14–15.

> (To this Murtaḍá replies on behalf of the Muʿtazilites:) The best possible way of interpreting the 'light' and 'darkness' in this verse is to take the former as a symbol of the Garden, i.e. the reward, and the latter as a symbol of the Fire, i.e. the chastisement. If this is so, it is quite natural that God should be made the subject of 'bringing them out from darkness to light, for there is no doubt that He is the One who lets the Believers enter the Garden and leads them away from the way of Hell.
>
> (However, even if we concede to the opponents and admit that the 'light' is a symbol of *īmān* and the 'darkness' that of *kufr*, the verse would not necessarily mean what they want it to mean, i.e. the creation of *īmān* by God, because in that case the verb *ikhrāj*, i.e. 'bringing out', would be better understood in a different way.) Suppose in an ordinary situation I suggested to someone to go into a certain country and tried to awaken in him the desire to do so, telling him all the good things he would find there. I can correctly describe what I did by saying, 'I have made a man enter a certain country.' Likewise, if I tried to make a man avoid doing a certain thing, I can correctly describe my effort by saying, 'I have brought him out (*akhrajtu*) from such-and-such a thing.' In such a case, the expressions 'making a man enter' and 'bringing a man out' simply mean 'inducing' or 'encouragement'.
>
> (Thus the Koranic verse in question would mean that God induces men, or awakens a desire in them, to believe, not that He 'creates' *īmān* in their hearts.)

We have remarked at the outset that two of the major tenets of Muʿtazilism were involved in the question of the creation of *īmān* by God. We have just examined the first, i.e. God's justice and human responsibility. The second is the notorious problem of the 'creation of the Koran', a problem which raised a great scandal in the Muslim community in the early Abbasid age.

Theoretically this problem was in origin part of the theory of Divine attributes. The Muʿtazilites denied the existence of eternal attributes in God, because, in their view, to admit it would amount to admitting the existence of a number of eternal entities besides God. Since Speech (*kalām*) was one of the major Divine attributes, and since the Koran was after all God's Speech, the Muʿtazilites judged it proper to deny the eternal existence of the Koran. And thus they came to assert that the Koran, like all other things, was a created thing. This is in brief the Muʿtazilite thesis of the 'creation of the Koran' *khalq al-qur'ān*. And the question of 'whether the Koran was created or uncreated' was seriously discussed among the theologians—*Hal al-qur'ān makhlūq aw ghayr-makhlūq*?

Obviously the question of the 'creation of *īmān*' was modelled after that of the 'creation of the Koran'. And just as the question of 'whether the Koran was created or uncreated' was hotly debated, so the question about *īmān* was raised and discussed exactly in the same outward form, namely: Is *īmān* created or uncreated? And on this question Ashʿarī and the Māturīdites stood opposed to each other.

II Ashʿarī's position

A short treatise of Ashʿarī on this question[3] has come down to us. There he takes the definite position that *īmān* is uncreated (*ghayr-makhlūq*). There is a noticeable confusion in Ashʿarī's thinking in this treatise. But let us first follow his argument step by step as he develops it.

Among those who take the position that *īmān* is created, he counts Ḥārith al-Muḥāsibī, Jaʿfar b. Ḥarb, ʿAbd Allāh b. Kullāb, ʿAbd al-ʿAzīz al-Makkī and 'other theologians of a speculative nature'. Those who take the opposite position are mostly Traditionists, and the most representative thinker of this camp is Aḥmad b. Ḥanbal, whom Ashʿarī says he follows.

The argument of the former group is rather simple. They have observed carefully, he says, the existent things and found them all 'created' except God and His attributes. Now *īmān* is obviously a human act and a human property, and it cannot be an attribute of God. So it is among the 'created' things.

Representing the opposite position, Ashʿarī sets out to argue against the view which attributes createdness to *īmān*. The first point to consider is the exact meaning of the word 'created'. The adjective 'created' means 'what has come into being after having been non-existent.' He proposes: Let us try to apply this adjective in this particular sense to *īmān* and see whether the two can be harmonized with each other or whether they contradict each other. We find, he says,

3. *Risālah fī al-Īmān* published by Spitta in his *Zur Geschichte Abu'l-Ḥasan al-Ashʿarī's*, Leipzig, 1876, pp. 138–140. It is said to be one of the works which Ashʿarī composed in his Baghdad days.

that the latter is the case. The reason for this is as follows: If we are to say that *īmān* is 'created', that would imply that *īmān* had been non-existent before it was created. The implication is that before *īmān* was created, there was a state in which there was neither *īmān* nor *tawḥīd* (i.e. acknowledging God as One). In reality, however, there was, according to Ashʿarī, never a state in which there was no *īmān* and *tawḥīd*, neither before nor after the creation of the world.

It is quite evident that in this argument Ashʿarī is not thinking of *īmān* as a personal existential event which concerns each individual man, but rather as a cosmic event, a metaphysical entity which, once created, would continue to exist throughout the ages. This particular approach clearly indicates that the problem is being raised and discussed in this context after the model of 'the creation of the Koran'. Besides, Ashʿarī himself refers in the same treatise, to this parallelism between the two problems, as we shall see presently. In other words, *īmān* in this context is quite different from the *īmān* considered in terms of its constituent elements, *taṣdīq*, *qawl* and *ʿamal*. This fact indicates also that there is no real opposition between Ashʿarī and the Māturīdites, whose theory we are going to study in the next section. For the Māturīdites, when they discuss the createdness and uncreatedness of *īmān*, take the word *īmān* in the sense of a personal event.

Now to go back to Ashʿarī's argument, he expects his opponents to raise a serious objection to his thesis by saying, 'Your thesis has the obvious implication that there was once a time when *īmān* existed without there being a Believer. But how could *īmān* exist when there was no human being yet?'

The answer Ashʿarī gives to this question is based on an argument which seems surprisingly naive. Or rather we should say perhaps that it is nothing but a piece of sophistry. He begins by emphasizing that the most fundamental meaning of *īmān* is *taṣdīq* and *tawḥīd*. Then he points out that according to the testimony of the Koran, God has been from eternity declaring Himself to be One, (which is nothing other than *tawḥīd*), and He has been from eternity declaring Himself to be truthful (which is nothing other than *taṣdīq*). Before the creation of mankind, God had always been saying, 'I am God. There is no god except Myself!' and He had always been stressing His Truthfulness. In other words, although there was as yet no man to practise *tawḥīd* and *taṣdīq*, there existed *tawḥīd* and *taṣdīq* themselves, i.e. *īmān*.

After this point, Ashʿarī steps further into verbal confusion. He says that *īmān*, understood in an absolute sense and used without reference to any creature, *is* one of the Divine attributes. He quotes the Koranic verse: 'He is Allah other than whom there is no God, the Supreme Lord, the Holy One, Peace, the *mu'min*, the Guardian …' (LIX, 23). And he remarks that in this verse God calls Himself a *mu'min* and counts this latter among the Names which He applies to Himself.

It is quite evident that Ashʿarī in this argument is paying attention only to the outer form of the word *mu'min*. This word, as we have clearly seen, means in ordinary contexts 'One who believes' or a Believer, i.e. a man of *īmān*. In this verse, however, the word means quite a different thing, although derived from the same root. It means 'one who makes somebody feel safe', 'one who sets the mind of somebody else at rest', 'one who ensures and safeguards'.

The next point Ashʿarī makes is more interesting because it shows clearly that the problem is modelled after that of the creation of the Koran. Against those who say that *īmān* cannot possibly be a Divine attribute because it is an essentially human attribute, he argues as follows:

> Far be it from me to assert that God resembles the creatures and that He is qualified by an attribute which is peculiar to the contingent beings! The misunderstanding has occurred to those who are opposed to my thesis only through a wrong reasoning.
>
> They have been led to this mistaken view in the following way: they have examined all the created beings, the conditions and properties of which they have observed, and they have found them all to be 'created'. Furthermore they have ascertained that *īmān* is one of the attributes peculiar to the creatures. And from this they have concluded that *īmān* is 'created'. This is certainly a mistaken conclusion. They should have remarked that 'knowledge' and 'speech' too are among the human attributes, and yet these two are also among the Divine attributes, and as such they are 'uncreated' and not contingent. Whoever asserts that the 'speech' of God and His 'knowledge' are 'created' and contingent is a downright Kāfir.
>
> Exception may be taken to this on the ground that the thesis of *īmān* being 'uncreated' and non-temporal is the same as the assertion that *īmān* is 'eternal' *qadīm*, while in reality there can be nothing 'eternal' besides God, for in the beginning there was nothing other than God before He created the things.
>
> To this I would reply that this way of thinking is characteristic of those who assert that the 'speech' of God, His 'knowledge', and His attributes in general are contingent and 'created'. So the view can be refuted by exactly the same

argument by which is refuted the thesis that Divine attributes, like 'knowledge' and the Koran, are contingent and 'created'.

As a theory of *īmān*, this argument of Ashʿarī is extremely confusing because he himself is confused on a point of pivotal importance. He finds in the Koran the word *muʾmin* used in reference to God. He ignores the fact that in the particular context *muʾmin* means quite a different thing from a 'Believer', i.e. a man of *īmān*, and jumps to the conclusion that *īmān* is one of the eternal attributes of God on the same level as 'knowledge' and 'speech'. By doing so he confuses the issue completely.

This seems to have put some of his followers in an embarrassing situation. In order to ameliorate the argument and to give it a more reasonable look, Ibn ʿAsākir, for example, in his defense of Ashʿarī,[4] ascribes to his Master the thesis that *īmān* is of two kinds: the first is *īmān* of God which is 'eternal' according to the Koranic verse (LIX, 23), and the second is human *īmān* which is 'created' because it occurs on the initiative of man, for which man is either rewarded (when the *īmān* is sincere) or punished (when it is doubtful).

Then Ibn ʿAsākir assigns to Ashʿarī a 'middle position'[5] between the Muʿtazilites, the Jahmites, and the Najjārites, on the one hand, who assert that *īmān* is 'created' unconditionally, and the crude Anthropomorphists, on the other, who assert that *īmān* is 'eternal' unconditionally. In reality, however, this schematization itself cannot escape giving the impression that it rests on a semantic confusion. For, after all, the *īmān* of God and the *īmān* of man belong to entirely different orders of being and cannot, therefore, possibly constitute the two poles of opposition.

III The Māturīdite position

Unlike the Ashʿarite thesis, the position taken by the Māturīdites is consistent in that it is concerned with the nature of *īmān* as a human phenomenon. The central problem is: when a man 'believes in' God, is his *īmān* created in him

4. *Tabyīn Kadhib*, A. F. Mehren (*Exposé de la réforme de l'islamisme, commencée au troisième siècle de l'hégire par Abou'l-Hasan Ali el-Ashari*, St. Pétersburg 1876, II, pp. 113–114.

5. As he does in respect to all the major tenets of Muslim theology.

by God or is it rather something which he does by his power and on his own responsibility? The afore-mentioned *Creed* attributed to Māturīdī himself formulates the whole problem as follows:

> Since *īmān* consists in 'verbal confession' and 'assent', *īmān* is a created thing. Some people maintain that it is not created because it occurs only by God's 'assistance' *tawfīq* which is not created. To this we reply: That is true, and yet the act of man is not thereby turned into an act of God; it still remains a created thing, like fasting and ritual worship.[6]

We may do well to remember that this statement represents the opinion of the Samarqand school. The Māturīdites of Bukhārā took up a different attitude toward the same problem. Let us now turn to the details of the matter.

In his description of the Māturīdite situation, Bayāḍī, to whom reference has often been made before, goes back to the basic dictum traditionally attributed to Abū Ḥanīfah in the *Waṣiyyah*: 'We acknowledge that man, his works, his verbal confession, and his knowledge, are all created.'[7] And he points out that if 'verbal confession' and 'knowledge' are created, then we must say that *īmān* is created, because the latter is nothing but 'verbal confession' and 'knowledge'.[8]

The Māturīdite school of Samarqand is very straightforward in taking the position that *īmān* is 'created'. The school of Bukhārā, not content with this attitude, brings into the discussion a subtle complexity. They distinguish between two aspects in the structure of *īmān*. The one aspect is 'guidance' *hidāyah*, meaning Divine guidance as an active initiative on the part of God. The second aspect is 'being (rightly) guided' *ihtidā'*, which is the part played by man. These two aspects are based on the Koran.[9] And the people of Bukhārā assert that *īmān* in its first aspect is 'uncreated' while in its second aspect it is 'created'.[10]

According to Abū ʿUdhbah,[11] some of the authorities of Bukhārā school, like

---

6. *ʿAqīdah*, §22, p. 16.

7. *Waṣiyyah*, p. 84; cf. Wensinck, *Muslim Creed*, p. 128

8. Note that here Bayāḍī, faithful to the teaching of Abū Ḥanīfah, defines *īmān* as *iqrār maʿrifah* and excludes 'good works' from it. Cf. Chap. V, [IX], (3).

9. On the Koranic concepts of *hidāyah* and *ihtidā'* and the essential relation between them see my *God and Man in the Koran*, pp. 139–147.

10. *Bayāḍī*, p. 252

11. *al-Rawḍah al-Bahiyyah*, p. 71.

Ibn al-Faḍl and Ismāʿīl b. al-Ḥusayn al-Zāhid, went so far as to denounce those who professed the creation of *īmān* as Kāfirs on the ground that the thesis of the creation of *īmān* would lead to the open heresy of the creation of God's speech (i.e. the Koran). They are said to have been followed by the leading thinkers of Farghānah.

The interesting point about this is that these people of Bukhārā put the problem of the creation of *īmān* into direct connection with that of the creation of the Koran, i.e. God's speech. We remember that Ashʿarī intimately associated these two problems but the people of Bukhārā utilized this connection in quite a different way from Ashʿarī.

As a concrete example of the way they argued, Abū ʿUdhbah gives a thesis of Ḥashwī type which Nūḥ b. Abī Maryam upheld, attributing it to Abū Ḥanīfah himself. This thesis consists in stressing as a first step that *īmān* is nothing other than 'saying' the *shahādah*-formula, i.e. 'there is no god but God, and Muḥammad is the Apostle of God.' Now these words by which man attests to his own *īmān* are 'uncreated' because they are God's own speech. And this means that whenever a man pronounces this formula, there occurs in him something which is not 'created', and that is *īmān*. The process involved is the same as when a man recites the Koran. He thereby recites the speech of God, that is, he becomes really and not metaphorically, the reciter of God's speech. In exactly the same way, he who pronounces the *shahādah*-formula actualizes in himself something 'uncreated', which is *īmān*.[12]

Abū ʿUdhbah gives also the argument advanced by the people of Samarqand against this particular thesis. He who pronounces certain words which happen to coincide with words in the Koran, is not reciting from the Koran at all unless he has the clear intention of doing so. In the same way, the mere pronouncing of the *shahādah*-formula does not mean that something 'uncreated' subsists in the heart of the man. Furthermore, even when the *shahādah*-formula is backed by a firm conviction in the heart, what is in the heart is not the thing which is in the essence of God. Whatever occurs in the human heart is 'created' and contingent, because it is nothing but a knowledge of the meaning of the words. The Divine words, being essentially an 'inner speech' *kalām nafsī* subsisting in God, are 'uncreated', but the counterpart which is in the human heart is not Di-

12. *Ibid.* p. 72.

vine speech itself, but it is the meaning of the speech, which is 'created'.[13]

Against the distinction made by the people of Bukhārā between the 'created' and 'uncreated' aspects of *īmān*, Bayāḍī supports the Samarqand school. It is conceded that Divine 'guidance' *hidāyah*, being pre-eminently an act of God, is 'uncreated'. It is further conceded that 'guidance' is a necessary condition (*sharṭ*) without which *īmān* cannot be actualized. And yet it is not an essential constituent (*rukn*, 'pillar') of *īmān*. In this respect, 'guidance' is just like all acts of obedience in relation to *īmān*.[14] The thesis that 'guidance' is the 'uncreated' part of *īmān* owes its birth to a confusion between a necessary condition and an essential constituent.

Bayāḍī points out that *īmān* is something which God has commanded. God's command occurs only with regard to those things that are in His power. And whatever belongs to this category is 'created'. Divine 'guidance' and 'assistance' do not belong to this category. Therefore *īmān* cannot possibly be the name of these two things.[15]

In the particular theological context produced by the Muʿtazilite theory of Divine justice, this thesis of the creation of *īmān* raises a further very important problem. Suppose we have agreed that *īmān* is 'created'. Does it imply that man has no active part to play in the birth of *īmān* in his heart? In other words, is he *forced* to believe by the Divine creation of *īmān* in him, there being no freedom and, consequently, no responsibility on his part? Does the thesis lead to the *Jabriyyah* position?

The Jabrites, whose representative is Jahm b. Ṣafwān, assert that man does not 'do' anything in the real sense of the word, that he has no freedom of will nor power to do anything positively, and that all his actions are beyond his control just as the movements of feverish shiver and pulse. *Īmān* and *kufr* are thus quite 'involuntary'.[16]

---

13. *Ibid.* pp. 72–74.

14. Note again the Ḥanafite feature of excluding 'work' from the essential structure of *īmān*. It is an indispensable condition for its actualization, but not an essential constituent of it. Divine 'guidance' is put in the same position in regard to the occurrence of *īmān*.

15. Bayāḍī, *op. cit.* pp. 252–253.

16. *Ibid.* p. 253.

Against this Bayāḍī argues, basing himself on a passage in the *Fiqh Akbar* II which he attributes to Abū Ḥanīfah,[17] that man has a positive part to play in the birth of *īmān* in himself, although the latter is essentially 'created' by God. In the following quotation, Bayāḍī's explanatory remarks are given between parentheses.

> (Abū Ḥanīfah says in his *Fiqh Akbar* II:) God has not compelled any one of His creatures to *kufr* (by creating it in him and forcing him toward it) nor to *īmān*. He has not created anyone as a Believer (by creating in him *īmān* without leaving him any room for free choice and acquisition) nor as a Kāfir (by creating in him *kufr* without giving him any power to choose between it and its opposite).[18] God has created men as individuals (i.e. individual representatives [of one and the same species] provided with a certain number of essential characteristics as well as other distinguishing marks that are necessarily derived from the latter. *Īmān* and *kufr*, however, are not found among these specific characteristics of man which distinguish him from all other species of existent things. Thus it is clear that God has not created man in the state of either a Believer or a Kāfir without leaving him freedom of choice).
> So *īmān* and *kufr* are the 'work' of man (i.e. his 'acquisition', something which he acquires by using his power in a certain definite direction, and are not among those things that are determined fixedly beyond any interference on his part. This may be understood from the fact that there is a natural difference between the 'compulsory' kind of things which occur in man, like feverish shiver and the beating of the pulse on the one hand, and that which occurs in man in accordance with his intention and motive, on the other. *Īmān* and *kufr* are of the latter kind).[19]

This kind of discussion of the part played by God and man in the birth of

---

17. Article 6, cf. Wensinck, *Muslim Creed*, p. 191.

18. This last remark is very typical of the Māturīdite position on the problem of human power. It stands characteristically in sharp opposition to the Ash'arite position. In Ash'arism the human power for *kufr* is suitable only for *kufr*, it is not suitable for *īmān* at all. In Māturīdism, on the contrary, one and the same power is suitable both for *kufr* and *īmān*. And this gives man a certain degree of freedom, freedom of choosing between the two opposite directions.

19. *Op. cit.* p. 254.

īmān in man raises another serious question in the context of Islamic theology. And that is the question of the relation between God's will or volition and the creation of *īmān*. The problem may not appear serious as far as *īmān* itself is concerned. But it takes on an extremely serious aspect if we consider the opposite of *īmān*, that is, *kufr*. One may easily concede that *īmān* is a creation of God in an individual, making that individual a Believer. But is this true also of *kufr*? If God is the Creator of *īmān*, is He also the Creator of *kufr*? If God creates *kufr*, it would naturally imply that He wills it and wishes it. Certainly a Muʿtazilite would never concede such a thesis. What then is the relation between Divine will and the birth of *kufr* in man? We shall be occupied with this problem in the following section.

IV Creation of *kufr*

As I have remarked in the last paragraph, this question is, properly speaking, nothing but the reverse side of the problem of the creation of *īmān*. However the reverse side proves a more serious question because it involves Divine will and volition in the creation of the worst kind of sin. Is it at all imaginable that the infinitely righteous God should will the creation of such an evil as *kufr*? The Muslim theologians are here faced with a most grave and challenging problem.

As an interesting and convenient introduction to this problem I shall begin by quoting Ibn Ḥazm in his refutation of the thesis that *īmān* is 'uncreated'. The proof-text on which he bases his argument is the Sūrah of Yūnus (X), 100, which reads: 'It is not for any soul to believe except by the permission (*idhn*) of God'.

> This text is quite explicit in declaring that no one is able to believe except by the permission of God … So we know for certain that everybody who becomes a Believer does so by the permission of God and because God desires (*shāʾa*) that he should believe. This makes it clear also that whoever does not believe does not believe because God does not permit him to have *īmān* and because He does not desire him to have *īmān*.
>
> The 'permission' *idhn* of which the Koran speaks here, i.e. God's 'desire' *mashīʾah*, is nothing else than God's creation of *īmān* in whoever becomes a Believer. It is, in other words, God's saying 'Be!' to *īmān* so that it may occur. Conversely, absence of 'permission', i.e. absence of 'desire', would mean that

> God would refrain from creating *īmān* in a man, thus leaving him in unbelief. There is no other way of interpreting the text, for it is quite clear that 'permission' here does not mean 'command' *amr*.[20]

It is worthy of note that Ibn Ḥazm introduces in this passage the key-word 'desire' *mashī'ah* which plays an exceedingly important role in the Ḥanafite solution of the difficulty, as we shall see presently. But first let us examine what the Muʿtazilites have to say, for they are after all responsible for raising this problem in such a crucial form.

The nature and the locus of the difficulty within the *Qadariyyah* context are quite obvious. If God were the Creator of *kufr*, the responsibility for the existence of this greatest evil (and for that matter, the existence of all evils) in the world would lie with God, not with man. And God would have no right to punish the Kāfirs for being Kāfirs. The Muʿtazilites solve the question simply by negating the Divine creation of *kufr*.

Ashʿarī says that all the Muʿtazilites are agreed on the point that God creates neither *kufr* nor acts of disobedience (*maʿāṣī*). The only exception to this is Ṣāliḥ Qubbah, who asserts that God has created them in the sense that he has created a certain number of things that are designated by the words *kufr* and *maʿaṣī*, creating together with these things certain properties and qualifications that are peculiar to them.[21] Still Ṣāliḥ Qubbah may not have meant thereby that God creates these things that are designated by *kufr* in a man so that he might become a Kāfir. Even in a case like this, it is more in line with the main Muʿtazilite tendency to assert that God creates a man *and* the Kāfir-making properties, and that it is up to the man to choose the latter and become thereby a Kāfir. We shall see this point more clearly in what al-Sharīf al-Murtaḍá says about it in *Amālī*.[22]

Here the discussion turns around the Koranic verse (V, 60) which reads: 'Shall I tell you of something worse than that as a result of Divine chastisement? (I mean the case of) those whom God has cursed, and whom He with wrath has turned some into apes and some into swine, and who have become idol-worshippers'.

---

20. *Fiṣal* IV, pp. 138–139.
21. *Maqālāt*, p. 227.
22. II, pp. 180–181.

The anti-Muʿtazilites use this verse as one of the important proof-texts in favor of their theory that it is God who creates *kufr*, and makes a man a Kāfir.

> (They argue:) How could you deny that this verse shows conclusively that it is God who turns a man into a Kāfir, for He informs us here that He has made some men idol-worshippers, just as he has made (some of them) apes and swine? God cannot possibly turn a man into a Kāfir without creating his *kufr*.
> (To this Murtaḍá replies:) How is it possible to interpret the verse in the sense that God informs us that he has made them Kāfirs and created their *kufr*? The Divine words here purport to be a reproach against them, a severe remonstrance with them about their *kufr*, and an expression of an extreme disdain for them. God is simply reproaching them, and there is no place for the conception that He is the Creator of their *kufr*. God's reproach has nothing at all to do with His creating the object of the reproach.
> Besides, the Kāfirs would be perfectly innocent and excusable if God were the Creator of that for which He reproaches them. And the words would be sheer contradiction and nonsense. …
> The most that can be understood from the verse is the information that He has created and produced those who worship idols and that He has made some of them apes and swine.
> There is of course no doubt that God has created the Kāfir for there is no Creator other than God. And yet it does not follow necessarily from this that He has created his *kufr* and turned him thereby into a Kāfir.

The meaning of the last two sentences is that God is the Creator of *the man* who is potentially a Kāfir, i.e. who will become a Kāfir, but this is quite a different thing from saying that God has created *kufr* in him. God creates a man, but whether he really becomes a Kāfir or not is *his* affair, not God's.

> That by which a Kāfir becomes a Kāfir is not necessarily God's work. Nay, rather we have a definite proof that He is far too exalted to produce and create such a thing. The two (i.e. the creation of a man who is to become a Kāfir on the one hand, and the creation of that by which he becomes a Kāfir) are entirely different matters.

In the same book,[23] Murtaḍá deals with the problem of the Divine creation of

23. *Ibid.* II, pp. 25–28.

kufr from a slightly different angle. This time the proof-text is the Koranic verse (III, 8): 'Our Lord, do not cause our hearts to stray after thou hast guided us (to the right path).'

The verse would seem to give the anti-Muʿtazilites a good ground on which to assert that both *īmān* and *kufr* are God's creation. 'The very fact, they say, 'that the Muslims ask God not to cause their hearts to go astray shows very clearly that it is possible for God to cause their hearts to go astray from the *īmān* to which He has guided them.'

To this Murtaḍá replies on behalf of Muʿtazilism in the following way: the verse does not say that God directly creates *kufr* in their hearts; it says only that it is possible for God to produce such situations which might cause *kufr* in them. In other words, even in situations of that kind, man is always free not to choose the wrong way. If he chooses *kufr* under the pressure of a situation, it is essentially a matter of his own responsibility. On the basis of this understanding, Murtaḍá proposes a number of possible interpretations of the above-quoted verse. Here I shall give two of them as an example of the philological type of argumentation:

> (1) The verse may be paraphrased as: 'O our Lord! After having given us "guidance" to the right path do not subject us to a trial so bitter and severe as to induce our hearts to go astray'.
> When one has to undergo an unbearably severe trial, one's heart may lose faith under the pressure of the situation. To describe such a case it is quite admissible (i.e. grammatically) for one to make God the subject of the action (as the Koranic verse does) and to attribute to God the going astray of the heart.
> Now if we are asked to explain what we mean by God's making our hearts undergo an unbearably severe trial, we would answer: that occurs by God's making our desire extremely strong for anything which our Reason judges to be bad and evil, and His strengthening our tendency to shun our duties. (This, however, is not to be understood as an evil and malicious act on the part of God, because by His doing so) the moral duty upon us is made more difficult to accomplish, but the reward which we would merit (by accomplishing it) would be the greater.
> (2) The second possible way of interpretation is to take the verse as an earnest prayer to God on the part of Muslims so that He might keep their hearts firm and steady on the 'guidance', and strengthen them with His grace without

> which they could not continue to maintain *īmān* for a long time. (This interpretation is based on the Koranic thought that the human soul is by nature weak and prone to err.)
>
> Thus the verse may be paraphrased as: 'O Lord! Do not leave our souls alone without strengthening them with Thy grace. For without it we would surely lose the right path and go astray'.

Far more difficult is the situation of those who take the position that *kufr* is 'created', because, as we have remarked at the outset, this would raise immediately a most serious question: Does God will and desire *kufr*? For it is impossible for anybody to create anything without the will and desire to do so. And if they say Yes to this question, they would get involved in the difficulty of being forced to admit that God liked *kufr* and approved of it.

Ibn Ḥazm, in the passage we quoted at the beginning of the present section, introduced the key-word 'desire' or 'wish' *mashīʾah* (the corresponding verb is *shāʾa*, meaning 'to wish') in discussing the problem of the birth of *īmān* in man in relation to God's volition. The problem now is to see whether a similar relation holds or not between *kufr* and God's volition.[24] First of all, he formulates the Muʿtazilite thesis in the following way:

> When anybody becomes a Kāfir, or when anybody commits a grave sin and becomes a Fāsiq, or when anybody reviles God or kills a Prophet, all this has nothing to do with God's desire or wish. God never desires (*shāʾa*) such a thing. This is proved by the Koranic verse: 'God is not pleased with *kufr* on the part of men' (XXXIX, 7).[25]
>
> In general, whoever does what God wishes (man to do) is one who deserves reward because of his good deed. So if in truth God wished that a man be a Kāfir or that he commit a grave sin, and if the man really did so, he would have done what God wished him to do. In other words, he would have done a good thing and thus have merited Divine reward. (But this is absurd.)

Against this Muʿtazilite view, Ibn Ḥazm argues that, according to the view taken by the people of the Sunnah, the words 'will' *irādah* and 'wish' *mashīʾah* are equivocal in nature and are used in two different meanings according to actual context.

---

24. *Fiṣal* IV, pp. 142–143.
25. Cf. also XLVII, 28.

One of them is 'satisfaction' or 'good pleasure' *riḍá*, and 'approval' *istiḥsān* (which means more literally: 'considering something good'). In this first sense, these words cannot be used in reference to God regarding what He has forbidden.

The second meaning is that of wishing or willing the existence of a thing, whatever it may be. In this sense the words can be used in reference to God regarding every existent thing in the world, whether good or bad. We are entitled to say only in this second sense that God wished, desired, or willed such-and-such a thing, even if the thing in question be an evil like *kufr*.

The Muʿtazilites use these words sometimes in this and sometimes in that sense. But this is exactly what we generally understand by sophistry. It is clear then, so Ibn Ḥazm concludes, that they are using a sophistic method in their argument on this question.

> The right view of the people of the Sunnah is this: he who does what God wills (*arāda*) and desires (*shā'a*) cannot be considered thereby one who does a good thing and is praiseworthy. The real good-doer is a man who does that which God has commanded him to do and that with which He is satisfied.

In other words, *kufr* is an object of Divine will and desire in the second sense of these words as defined above, not in the first. Therefore he who does it does not by any means deserve Divine reward.

At this point Ibn Ḥazm takes the offensive more positively, and asks his opponents: Is God capable at all of preventing the Kāfir from *kufr*, the Fāsiq from *fisq*, the man who reviles Him from reviling, and the killer of a Prophet from killing, etc.? If the opponents answer in the negative, they would simply be attributing 'inability' *ʿajz* to God. This would of course be *kufr* itself, because it negates the divinity of God. If, on the contrary, they answer in the affirmative, that would amount necessarily to acknowledging that He (since He does not actually prevent all these things in spite of His ability to do so) wills that they remain in their *kufr*, and that He is the One who keeps the Kāfir and *kufr* as they are during the time in which the Kāfir remains in the state of *kufr*. And this is precisely what we mean when we say that He wishes the existence of *kufr*, without being at all satisfied with it. 'Without being satisfied' is here rather a weak expression. We shall rather say that 'He is angered' by what the man does.

> We know by necessity that he who is able to prevent something and yet does not do so wishes and desires the existence of that thing, for if he did not de-

sire it he would change it and prevent it without leaving it as it is.

Thus Ibn Ḥazm comes back to his favorite and basic thesis, namely that we must not measure the right and wrong of what God does by a standard which is valid only among human beings. God is absolutely free. Whatever He does, however He judges, He is just and wise. Only when the objects of God's will are materialized in the world of human reality and looked at from the human point of view, do some become good and others bad.

Now the most important point to notice in the above argument of Ibn Ḥazm is that he puts 'will' *irādah* and 'desire' *mashīʾah* together as one unit and isolates in it two different meanings. This is the point at which he differs basically from the Ḥanafites-Māturīdites. But before we come to this question, we shall do well to take a glance at Ashʿarī's position.

We have already seen how Ashʿarī deals with the problem of the 'creation' of *īmān* in quite a different context, namely as a cosmic event that infinitely precedes the birth of *īmān* as a personal existential matter of each individual man. As regards *kufr*, which is properly speaking but the reverse side of *īmān*, he deals with it as a purely individual and personal matter. But in addition to that, he considers the problem in an explicitly predestinarian context. To put it differently, he lays emphasis not so much on the problem of the 'creation' of *kufr* as on that of God's decree and predetermination of *kufr*.

To the question of whether he and his followers are satisfied with the idea that God has decreed and determined *kufr*, Ashʿarī answers:

> We are satisfied with the idea that God has decreed *kufr* as something evil and determined its nature as wrong. However (this does not mean that) we do approve of the fact that a man actually becomes a Kāfir thereby, because that is what God has forbidden man to do. Our expressing satisfaction with God's decree (*qaḍāʾ*, i.e. of *kufr*) does not necessarily mean that we are satisfied with *kufr* itself.[26]

Now to come to a more central point: Does Ashʿarī agree that the acts of disobedience were decreed and predetermined by God? Yes, he says, they were, in the sense that He has created them and has written them down and has informed

26. *al-Lumaʿ fī al-Radd ʿalá Ahl al-Zaygh wa-al-Bidaʿ*, ed. Richard McCarthy, Beirut, 1953, §104, p. 46.

us of their coming into being. However they were not decreed and predetermined in the sense that God has commanded us to do them.[27]

We have to conclude from this that God's decree concerns two kinds of objects: one is the right things (*ḥaqq*), like the acts of obedience, the doing of which God has not forbidden, and the other the wrong things (*bāṭil*), like injustice, *kufr*, and the acts of disobedience. Both are equally God's creation. But the one is right and the other is wrong. Thus 'decree' *qaḍā'* is to be differentiated from the 'object of decree' *maqḍī*. And the 'decree' in the former case is 'command' amr, whereas the 'decree' in the latter case, is just announcing, informing, and writing down. The 'decree' itself is in both cases right.

In the light of this, we must say that *kufr* (which is an object of decree) is essentially wrong, but the decree of *kufr* is right.[28]

We turn now to the Ḥanafite-Māturīdite position. The position has an important feature in common with the Ash'arite position which we have just analyzed. I am referring to the conception that there is nothing wrong with the creation itself of *kufr* by God. On this point Bayāḍī says as follows:

> The Divine creation of *kufr* is not at all wrong. What is wrong is that man gets qualified by that attribute through his own choice. (As Abū Ḥanīfah says,) God did not command it (i.e. *kufr*). How could this be, seeing that the Creator is infinitely wise? He never commands except that which will bring about a praiseworthy outcome. On the contrary He forbids it in accordance with his Wisdom.[29]

Basing himself on a statement found in Abū Ḥanīfah's *al-Fiqh al-Absaṭ*, Bayāḍī argues that if God punishes the Kāfirs, it is because of their voluntary choice (*ikhtiyār*) of *kufr*. God was pleased and satisfied with the creation of *kufr*, because He created it at the outset as a punishment for the bad choice (which human beings would make in future). If He had not been pleased, He would not have created *kufr*, particularly when He knew that it would be even stronger than His command.

Satisfaction with the creation itself of something, Bayāḍī goes on to say, does not necessarily imply satisfaction with the thing created. God was pleased to create *kufr*, but He was not pleased with *kufr* itself.

---

27. *Ibid.* §102, p. 45.
28. *Ibid.* §102–103, pp. 45–46.
29. *Op. cit.* p. 304.

> God 'wishes' for the Kāfirs (*kufr* because they voluntarily choose it), but He is not pleased with it. (As for his 'wishing' *mashī'ah* to create an evil thing like *kufr*, it is just the same as) His creation of Satan, wine and swine. He was pleased with His creating these things, (because creation of an evil thing is not in itself evil; on the contrary, it embodies something of Divine wisdom which is too deep for the ordinary human minds to comprehend.[30]

In connection with the word *mashī'ah* which occurs in the last quotation, we may remark that one important point is shared by the Māturīdite thesis and that put forward by Ibn Ḥazm. As we remember, Ibn Ḥazm uses the words 'desire' or 'wish' *mashī'ah* and 'will' *irādah* as important key-terms in the discussion of this problem. There is, however, a subtle but basic difference between the two positions. For Ibn Ḥazm *mashī'ah* and *irādah* are synonymous with each other. And within this single unit a distinction is made between the meaning of 'good pleasure' and the meaning of merely 'wishing the existence' of something.

In Māturīdism, *mashī'ah* and *irādah* are different concepts strictly to be distinguished from each other. Bayāḍī explains the distinction by the exegetical method.[31]

The first Koranic verse which he considers is: 'Even if We should send down the angels and the dead should speak to them, … they would not believe unless God wishes it (VI, 111).

> The meaning of this verse is that these people, even in the presence of Divine 'signs',[32] would never come to believe unless God desires (*mashī'ah*) their *īmān*. Here we have a definite proof that a Divine 'sign', however great it may be, does not coerce man to *īmān*.
> The truth of the matter is that in the case of a man of whom God knows that he is going to choose *īmān* voluntarily, He, on His part, wishes (*shā'a*) that for him, whereas in the case of a man of whom He knows that he is going to choose *kufr* or persistence in *kufr* (which he has chosen in the past), He wishes that for him. This is the opinion of Māturīdī in his great Commentary on the Koran.

---

30. *Ibid.* pp. 160–161. The words in parentheses are explanatory remarks of Bayāḍī.

31. *Ibid.* pp. 268–270.

32. Cf. my *God and Man in the Koran* in which a whole chapter is devoted to a discussion of the 'signs' of God. (Chap. VI, pp. 133–147)

Here Bayāḍī, following Māturīdī, points out God's *mashī'ah* as the decisive factor in the birth of *īmān*. He remarks, however, that *mashī'ah* is not a coercive power. *Mashī'ah* begins to be effective only when man, of his own accord, is ready to accept *īmān*. There is no coercion involved in the whole process. And the same is true of the birth of *kufr*. That *kufr* occurs only by God's *mashī'ah* is proved, according to Bayāḍī, by the next Koranic verse: 'It is not for us to go back to it (i.e. the old traditional idol-worship of the people) unless God should wish (*shā'a*) it.'

> The last clause means 'except when that is God's *mashī'ah*', or 'except when God's *mashī'ah* is to abandon us'. In any case, the verse is a clear proof that *kufr* occurs by God's *mashī'ah*, as Bayḍāwī has pointed out in his Commentary. The verse contains also a proof that *kufr* is not an object of God's love or His good pleasure.

Then Bayāḍī goes on to remark that *mashī'ah*, which is thus the determining factor in the process of the birth both of *īmān* and *kufr*, is neither to be confused with 'command' amr nor with 'will' *irādah*. On the basis of the verse: 'It is not for any soul to believe except by the permission (*idhn*) of God' (X, 100),[33] he argues that *īmān* occurs only by God's *mashī'ah*, His positive assistance, and that the word *idhn* here does not admit of being interpreted as 'command' amr, because actually it happens so often that those who are commanded to believe do not believe.

As regards the relation between *mashī'ah* and 'command' amr, which has just been mentioned, the *Creed* attributed to Māturīdī and the commentary on the *Fiqh Akbar* I[34] (also attributed to Māturīdī himself) express almost exactly the same view. I quote here from the *Creed* because it is more concise than the other source.[35]

> God created *kufr* and wished (*shā'a*) it, but He did not command it. However He did command the Kāfir to believe, though He did not wish it for him.
>
> To this one may raise an objection and say: (How is it conceivable that God

33. This verse was quoted at the beginning of the present section, together with Ibn Ḥazm's interpretation of it.

34. *Op. cit.* p. 21.

35. *'Aqīdah* §15, p. 14.

> should have 'wished' *kufr*?) Is not His *mashī'ah*[36] pleasing to Him? Of course it is pleasing, we answer. Then our opponent will say: Why should He punish (man) for (doing) what pleases Him?
> Our answer to this is: No, God (does not punish man for doing what He is satisfied with but) rather punishes him for what is not pleasing to Him. For, although His wish, His decree and all His other attributes are pleasing to Him, the act which is actually done by man is (not uniform in nature;) some acts are pleasing to Him, but some others are displeasing. The latter (which of course includes the act of *kufr*) are hateful to Him, and He punishes (man) for doing it.

Thus the opposition of 'wish' and 'command' in regard to *īmān* and *kufr* shows a complex structure in Māturīdism. For a man who happens to be a potential Believer, God 'wishes' *īmān*, though He does not 'command' it. And the man thereby becomes an actual Believer, without being coerced into it. Likewise in the case of a man who is a potential Kāfir, God 'wishes' for him *kufr*, but does not 'command' it. God 'wishes' *kufr* for such a man because of His eternal foreknowledge that this particular man will eventually end by making a wrong choice and taking *kufr* for himself.[37]

This last statement theoretically purports to save God's justice. It emphasizes that God does not 'wish' *kufr* for a potential Kāfir just arbitrarily, that His 'wish' is justified because He knew from eternity that the man would choose *kufr* for himself.

The same line of thought is followed regarding the case in which the man in question is not a potential Kāfir, but actually *is* a Kāfir. Concerning such a man Māturīdism takes that position that God 'commands' him to accept *īmān* (or *islām*) but does not 'wish' it. Here follow words ascribed to Abū Ḥanīfah on this problem as they are interpreted by Bayāḍī. As usual I put the explanatory remarks by the latter between parentheses.

> God 'commanded' the Kāfirs to accept *islām* (and imposed upon them the duty of choosing the latter voluntarily and of directing their ability and power

36. Note that in this sentence, put into the mouth of the opponent, *mashī'ah* refers rather to the 'object' of God's 'wish', while in the Māturīdite reply below, the same word designates the act itself of 'wishing'.

37. Bayāḍī, *op. cit.*, p. 163.

> toward it[38]), but He 'wished' for them, even before they were created, that they should be erring Kāfirs (without, however, coercing them into it, for God) pre-determined in accordance with His 'wish', and that 'wish' was based on His foreknowledge (about what each man was going to choose voluntarily. Thus His 'wish' worked in strict accordance with His knowledge about the particular choice of each man).[39]

The already complicated situation caused by various combinations of 'wish', 'command', and 'good pleasure' is made more complicated by the introduction of another very important concept, 'will' *irādah.*

The most remarkable feature of God's 'will', according to Bayāḍī, is that the object willed is bound to happen. Using the Koranic verse: 'If God so wished (*shā'a*), He could have gathered them (i.e. all men) together to the Guidance' (VI, 35), Bayāḍī asserts that 'God obviously did not "will" *īmān* for all men,' and that 'whatever He wills must necessarily come true'.[40]

This last point distinguishes 'will' from 'command', because what God 'commands', is often disobeyed, but what He 'wills' admits of no disobedience. And this makes clear the difference which exists between 'will' and 'wish', because 'wish' can very well act against 'command'.

As we have seen before, God 'commands' the Kāfirs to accept *īmān* voluntarily, and yet He 'wishes' that they should not do so. Such a thing is inconceivable with regard to the relation between 'will' and 'command'. If, instead of 'commanding' the Kāfirs to accept *īmān*, God 'willed' it, then it would simply be inconceivable that He should 'wish' them not to do so.

Besides, Bayāḍī continues, if *kufr* were an object of Divine 'will', man's doing it and actualizing it would be to respond to God's 'will' in the right way, and *kufr* would be a meritorious act of obedience to God. But this is a completely absurd conclusion.[41]

---

38. As we have remarked above (Note 18), this is a typically Māturīdite conception. Unlike the Ash'arites who assert that each 'power' *qudrah* in human beings is suitable for only one kind of work (the 'power' to do good things, for example, can never be used in doing evil things), the Māturīdites in general assert that 'power' is capable of being directed toward two opposites.

39. *Op. cit.*, p. 154.

40. *Ibid.* p. 268.

41. *Ibid.* pp. 155–156.

Here Bayāḍī affirms categorically that conformance with 'what is willed by the willer' is an act of 'obedience' *ṭā'ah*. In another place he says a slightly different thing about this problem.

> Not all conformance with what is willed by another person constitutes 'obedience'. ... 'Obedience' is rather conformance with a 'command'. And 'command' is different from 'will'.
>
> 'Obedience' turns round 'command', and in doing an act of 'obedience', it is inessential whether you know the 'will' (of the person whom you obey) or not. How could it be otherwise? 'Will' is always hidden; only 'command' is explicit. This is why in common parlance an authoritative leader is described as the one whose 'command' is obeyed, and not as the one whose 'will' is obeyed.
>
> However, it is also true that if a certain act done by somebody is in conformity with the 'will' of somebody else by sheer chance, and if the doer of that act is not at all aware of the (hidden) presence of 'will', the act is not regarded as 'obedience'.[42]

The Māturīdite argument which we have been trying to follow is of quite a scholastic nature. It is formally based on a sophisticated and subtle manipulation of a certain number of key-concepts: 'wish', 'will', 'command', 'decree', 'obedience' 'good pleasure', etc. And this discloses to our eyes a certain important aspect of Māturīdism. But the real theological point which they want to make by this scholastic manipulation of concepts is quite a simple one, namely that God created *kufr* by His 'wish' *mashī'ah* because He knew from the beginning that certain men would choose of their own accord the way of *kufr*; that He liked His creation of *kufr*, but He has been displeased with men's actually becoming Kāfirs by their choice of *kufr*.

It is undeniable that there is a conspicuous clumsiness in the content itself of this argument, too. But it is interesting as well as valuable as a concrete illustration of the tremendous intellectual effort made by the Māturīdites to safeguard God's justice within the boundaries of Orthodoxy, that is, without surrendering to Mu'tazilism. We must remember that the problem of the creation of *īmān* and *kufr* was raised first by the Mu'tazilites as a very serious problem of theodicy.

---

42. *Ibid.* pp. 158–159.

Before we close this chapter, mention must be made briefly of the question of *fiṭrah*, or the natural religious disposition of man, which obviously has a significant relation with the problem of the creation of *īmān*.

Historically, the problem of *fiṭrah* goes back to a very early period of Islam when the extremists among the Khārijites went so far as to propose (and to practise ruthlessly) the killing of the children of all those who did not agree with them in every detail about religion, whom they regarded as Kāfirs.

Against this extremism, some groups of the Khārijites (the *Ṣaltiyyah*, among the *ʿAjāridah*, for example) maintained that the children, whether born of believing parents or of Kāfir parents, were neutral, so to speak. When the children reach the age of discretion, they should be invited to embrace Islam. Only then, they maintained, would the real religious status of each person become definitely clear.[43]

Now there is a very famous Ḥadīth handed down to us concerning this particular problem. The Ḥadīth reads: 'Every child is born in the *fiṭrah*. But his parents turn him into a Jew or a Christian or a Parsi'. Here the word *fiṭrah* evidently means the natural religious disposition common to all men.

However, the Muʿtazilites understood *fiṭrah* in this Ḥadīth as completely synonymous with Islam. It was quite natural for them to do so because for the Muʿtazilites, religion was primarily a matter of Reason, and Islam *was* the true religion of universal Reason. In this interpretation, the Ḥadīth would mean that every child is born a Muslim.

Ibn Ḥazm agrees with this and maintains that even the children of the polytheists all deserve the name 'Muslim', and that in the Hereafter they would go to the Garden.[44]

The Ḥanafite-Māturīdite school prefers the neutrality thesis. In the *Fiqh Akbar* II, we read:

> God created all creatures free from both *kufr* and *īmān*. Then He addressed them, commanding them and forbidding them. As a result, some of them committed *kufr*. In this case their denial (of the Truth) and disavowal of it were caused by God's abandoning them. But some of them turned to *īmān* by their 'work', 'confession', and 'assent'. In this case, all this occurred because

43. Ashʿarī, *Maqālāt*, p. 97.
44. *Fiṣal* IV, pp. 130–131.

> of God's assisting them.[45]...
> God does not coerce any of His creatures into *kufr* or *īmān*. He does not create them either as Believers or Kāfirs, but He creates them simply as (responsible) individuals. So *kufr* and *īmān* are all 'works' of men.[46]

Strictly speaking, however, the Māturīdite understanding of *fiṭrah* is not perfectly 'neutral'. True, the *fiṭrah* is as yet neither *īmān* nor *kufr*. But it is a *good* religious nature. It is a kind of inborn quality which, if left alone without any interference from the parents, would lead the child to acknowledge by natural process of reasoning (*istidlāl*) the existence of his Creator.[47]

45. *Op. cit.* p. 44.
46. *Ibid.* p. 46.
47. *Creed* attributed to Māturīdī, §33, p. 19.

CONCLUSION

Contrary to what I did in two of my earlier works relating to Islamology, I have, in the present book, kept the methodological principles of semantic analysis in the background, and have tried to present only the results of the analytic process. But, in reality, all through the book it has been my aim to produce a consistent and systematic work of semantic analysis. In ending the book, I think I would do well to bring to light the methodological aspect of the matter and correlate it with some of the major results that have been presented.

The word 'semantics' is an extremely ambiguous and elusive expression And everybody who wants to speak at all of a 'semantic' study of any object with a measure of consistency must have recourse willy-nilly to a stipulative kind of definition, which cannot by nature avoid being arbitrary to a certain extent. 'Semantics', as I understand it, consists, briefly stated, in an analytic study of a segment or segments of a whole world-view, conducted through the analysis of the key-words that linguistically express the segment or segments in question. In a discipline like theology or philosophy, a 'key-word' corresponds to what is more generally called a technical term.

History of theological thought, which happens to be our immediate concern is, from the view-point of semantics, nothing but a history of technical terms, that is, the process of formation, extending over centuries, of key-words that correspond to main points of crystallization in theological thinking.

In the present work, I have tried to follow the key-word *īmān* through this gradual formative process. But we have to keep in mind the very important fact that no key-word stands alone and develops in isolation from other key-words of varying degrees of importance. Each key-word is accompanied by others, and together they form a complex network of key-words which we call in semantics a 'semantic field'. A semantic field is a more or less intricate network of key-words, which traces and duplicates linguistically a system of key-concepts.

A particularly important key-word gathers around itself at each stage of its development a certain number of key-words and forms one or more than one semantic field. The word *īmān* in Islamic theology proved historically to be one of those particularly important key-words. And in the course of the present work, several such semantic fields of *īmān* have been isolated.

Now briefly there are three major ways in which two or more than two key-words become closely associated with each other and come to form a closely-knit semantic network which we call 'field': (1) synonymous association, (2) antonymous association and (3) the splitting up of one key-concept into a number of constituent elements, each one of which is expressed by a key-word. Let us now try to examine in terms of these three categories the most important of the concrete facts that have been presented in the course of this book.

(1) Synonymous association

By 'synonymous' I do not mean an exact and perfect synonymity. I refer thereby to cases in which two (or more than two) key-words, say A and B, can be used more or less interchangeably without altering a semantic situation in a drastic way. The basic law of economy, however, does not allow the two quasi-synonymous key-words to co-exist peacefully. The result is that in cases of this kind, there develops ordinarily between A and B a tension situation, that of rivalry and competition for supremacy, and in most cases the rivalry ends up by A and B dividing the whole meaning area into two parts, and this new situation lasts until some new factor comes in to break the balance of powers.

This is roughly what happened to the two key-words *īmān* and *islām* in their mutual relation. At first, in the Koran, they are quasi-synonymous with each other. This can be perceived by the fact that in the majority of cases the two words are used almost interchangeably. A *muslim* (i.e. a man of *islām*) is roughly the same as a *mu'min* (i.e. a man of *īmān*) in the sense that both usually refer to one and the same person. In other words, they are synonymous with each other as far the denotation is concerned, although they are different in their connotation.

But already in the Koran a subtle but very important distinction between them is suggested in clear terms in connection with the religiously lukewarm

Bedouins 'who may be called *muslim*-s but not *mu'min*-s'. The thinkers in the post-Koranic periods tend to emphasize the aspect of difference rather than that of synonymity. Various attempts are made in the Ḥadīths to determine the relative importance of *īmān* and *islām*. Some make *islām* the more comprehensive concept, including within its area *īmān* as one of its constituents together with four ritual duties: worship, *zakāt*, fasting, pilgrimage. Others make *islām* an external matter, and *īmān* a matter of the heart. Some others again take the position that *īmān* represents a higher degree than *islām*.

All these things have been examined carefully in Chapter IV, and it would be meaningless to repeat what has been said earlier. The only point I would like to make in the particular context of this Conclusion is that *īmān* and *islām*, in whatever way one may understand the relation between them, represent two important rival concepts covering one and the same area of application. And this illustrates the way in which synonymous association of two or more words determines and delimits a meaning area which we technically call a semantic field.

The semantic field constituted by *īmān-islām* in Muslim theology is a very wide and comprehensive one which includes within it a number of sub-fields, and each one of the sub-fields is in itself a semantic field covering a certain area of its own and having a particular structure of its own, based either on synonymous association or antonymous association or conceptual splitting. For example, in the semantic field of the 'creation of *kufr*', which is itself a sub-section of the wider field of *kufr*, we saw in the last chapter a number of 'synonymous' key-words (*mashī'ah*, *irādah*, *amr*, *riḍá*, etc.) competing with each other for supremacy, as it were, and forming thereby an intricate system of combinations and repulsions.

(2) Antonymous association

This is best illustrated by the radical opposition of *īmān* (-*islām*) and *kufr*. A semantic field is formed when two major key-concepts stand totally opposed to each other. The semantic field standing on the basic opposition of *īmān* and *kufr* existed from the very beginning in Islamic thought, for the Koran constantly and emphatically put the Believer-Muslim in the sharpest opposition to the Kāfir. And theology inherited this semantic field directly from the Koran.

However, as we observed in Chapter I, under the surface of the same outward form (i.e. the opposition of *īmān* and *kufr*), a drastic inner change takes place in the structure of this field as it passes from the Koran to theology, because in the latter *kufr* no longer refers primarily to the unbelief of those who refuse to be converted to Islam, but concerns the unbelief occurring among the Muslims themselves, in the very midst of the Community.

Further, this semantic field presents a complex structure. For just as *īmān* forms a large independent field together with *islām* on the principle of synonymous association, so *kufr* too stands in a synonymous relation to its rival concepts such as *shirk*, i.e. polytheism, *fisq*, i.e. committing a grave sin, and *nifāq*, i.e. hypocrisy.

(3) As regards the splitting up of a key-concept into its constituents, Islamic theology presents a grand-scale illustration of the phenomenon, for this is precisely what the Murji'ites did with regard to the key-concept *īmān*. Four major elements were isolated: *maʿrifah*, *taṣdīq*, *iqrār* (or *qawl*), and *ʿamal*. We have seen in chapters VI-IX, how each one of these elements constituted a major problem in theology, causing endless heated discussions among the most brilliant minds in Islam.

Besides the three major principles of field formation which we have just surveyed, there are naturally a number of other ways in which a semantic field is developed. These secondary ways of field formation are largely dependent on particular historical circumstances and are therefore mostly of an entirely unpredictable nature. Semantic fields that are formed in this manner are conditioned by chance events and may reflect almost anything that attracts the attention of the people of a given age.

In the early days of Islam, for instance, the extremist Khārijites caused terror and spread havoc throughout the Community by murdering those who did not share their political and theological views. The people were horrified in particular at the sight of the Khārijites killing innocent children in the name of religion. On the higher intellectual level, this state of affairs raised the theoretical problem of the religious status of children, whether Muslim or pagan. And the problem, as we saw in the foregoing chapter, was crystallized in the key-word *fiṭrah*, i.e. the natural religious disposition. And this key-word gathered around itself a number of other words such as *īmān*, *islām*, *kufr*, *ṭifl* (i.e. child), and thus formed an independent semantic field.

The formation of a semantic field is often caused by a more theoretical circumstance. The Muʿtazilites, to give one example, were seriously concerned with the problem of the ethical responsibility of man. In order that human responsibility be upheld with theoretical consistency, the autonomy of man had to be established. Thus the Muʿtazilites came to maintain that whatever man did, whether good or evil, was his own work, and that God had no part in it. In the particularly Islamic context, this problem, which is in fact one of the most fundamental and therefore most universal problems in ethics everywhere, found its crystallization in the key-word 'creation' *khalq* (i.e. the 'creation of work' *khalq al-ʿamal* by man himself). Man was declared thereby the 'creator' of his own works. And the problem, once raised in this radical form, found repercussions in most of the important semantic fields in theology. The fields of *īmān* and *kufr* were no exception. The key-word *khalq* was soon brought into connection with *īmān* and *kufr* and thus a particular field (such as has been described in detail in Chapter XI) was formed within the larger fields of *īmān* and *kufr*.

As I have remarked more than once in the course of this book, *īmān* is originally a purely personal and existential affair. The very core of *īmān* is too personal and too deep to be talked about theoretically. There is something in *īmān* which to the last resists being theorized and rationalized. If, in spite of all this, one forces one's way toward an intellectual and rational grasp of the phenomenon, the throbbing life of *īmān* is of necessity lost. But of course the work is not without valuable recompense, for the analytic and intellectual grasp of *īmān* discloses the solid structure underlying the seemingly vague, elusive and purely psychological state. And this we have amply seen in the course of the present work.

All through this book we have been pursuing the process of the intellectualization of *īmān*, the process, in other words, by which the Muslims went on gaining an ever keener analytic and rational insight into the nature of *īmān*, as reflected in their own consciousness. By doing so they succeeded in laying bare the conceptual structure of *īmān*, but something deeply personal, something really vital, escaped the fine mesh of their analysis.

In the course of the history of Islamic theology some attempts have been made to restore the original living touch to the concept of *īmān*. The earliest systematic attempt of this sort was that made by the Murji'ites. We have seen earlier how most of the Murji'ite definitions of *īmān* contain 'love of God', 'fear of God', 'humble submission' and the like as part of the essence of *īmān*. The fact that most of the leading Murji'ites had to include these emotive attitudes in their definitions of *īmān* testifies to their deep personal piety which, even on the level of abstract rationalistic thinking, could not help seeking an expression.

Properly speaking, however, things of this kind were not the main concern of the theologians. This aspect of the matter was being developed, cultivated and even theorized mainly by the Mystics. If, therefore, one wishes to obtain a really comprehensive grasp of Belief or Faith in Islamic thought, one will have to conduct an analytic work similar to the present work on the nature and development of *taqwá*, i.e. 'pious fear of God', and other key-concepts in Sufism. Only when the results obtained on both sides, theological and mystical, are put together and coordinated with each other, can we hope to get a fairly complete picture of Belief as understood in Islam.

APPENDIX

A TRANSLATION OF THE

KITĀB AL-ĪMĀN

FROM THE *ṢAḤĪḤ* OF

ABU ʻABD ALLĀH MUḤAMMAD

IBN ISMĀʼĪL AL-BUKHĀRĪ

by

W. P. McLean

KITĀB AL-ĪMĀN

1. *Bāb* of *īmān* and the statement of the Prophet (May God bless him and give him peace): "Islām is built upon five (bases)". And *īmān* is speech (*qawl*) and work (*fi'l*), and it increases and decreases. God Most High said: "… *in order that they might add īmān to their īmān*" (48: 4); "*and We increase them in guidance*" (18: 12); "*and God doth advance in guidance those who seek guidance*" (19: 78); "*but those who receive guidance He increases in guidance and brings them their fear* (*taqwá*) *of God*" (47: 19). And God said: "*Which of you has it* (i.e. a Sūrah of the Revelation) *increased in īmān? As for those who believed, it increased them in īmān*" (9: 125). And God said: "*And it* (the truth) *only increased them in īmān and surrender* (*taslīm*)" (33: 22).

Loving God, as well as hatred for the sake of God, is part of *īmān*.

And ʿUmar b. ʿAbd al-ʿAzīz wrote the following letter to ʿAlī b. Adī:

> To *īmān* belong obligations (*farā'iḍ*) and commandments (*sharā'iʿ*) and forbidden practices (*ḥudūd*) and recommended practices (*sunan*). Whoever has perfected these things has perfected *īmān*, and whoever has not perfected them has not perfected *īmān*. And if I live, I will explain these requirements to you that you might be aware of them; and if I die (before I am able to do that), I do not desire your companionship.[1]

Ibrāhīm (on him be peace) said: "*But that my heart might be satisfied*" (2: 262).[2]

Muʿādh said: "Sit with us, that we might for a while believe".[3]

Ibn Maṣʿūd said: "Certainty (*yaqīn*) is the whole of *īmān*".

Ibn ʿUmar said: "The servant of God does not attain the reality of the fear of God until he abandons what he has concocted in his breast".

Al-Mujāhid interpreted the verse, "*He has prescribed for you as a religion what he entrusted to Noah*" (42: 11) to mean, "Oh Muḥammad, We have bequeathed to you and to him the same religion".

---

1. "I do not desire your companionship". This could perhaps mean that unless one is made aware of the requirements of *īmān* he must surely go to Hell.

2. I.e., made free from all doubt.

3. I.e., that we might for a while be free from the distractions which men are heir to.

Ibn ʿAbbās said that the words *shirʿah* and *minhadj* mean respectively *sabīl* (way or road) and *sunnah* (standard of conduct).

2. *Bāb*: Your call to God (*duʿāʾ*) is your *īmān*.

A. The Messenger of God (May God bless him and give him peace) said: "Islām is built upon five (bases): confession that there is no God but Allāh, and that Muḥammad is the Messenger of God, and the performance of *ṣalāt*, and the bringing of *zakāt*, and the *ḥajj*, and the fast of Ramaḍān".

3. *Bāb* of the matters relevant to *īmān* and of God's having said: "*Piety does not consist in directing your faces to the East or to the West, but the pious one is he who believes in God* (*āmana billāh*)…", and so on up to the point where He said, "*the God-fearers*" (*al-Muttaqūn*) (2: 172) and of God's saying: "*The believers have prospered*", etc. (23: 1).

A. The Prophet (May God bless him and give him peace) said: "*Īmān* consists in sixty-odd branches and *ḥayāʾ* is a branch of *īmān*".[4]

4. *Bāb*: The Muslim is he from whose tongue and whose hand the Muslims are safe.

A. The Prophet (May God bless him and give him peace) said: "The Muslim is he from whose tongue and hand the Muslims are safe and the *Muhājir* is he who avoids (*man hajara*) what God forbids".

5. *Bāb*: What kind of Islām is best.

A. According to Abū Mūsá who said: "They asked: 'Oh Messenger of God, what kind of Islām is best?' He said: 'The Islām of one from whose tongue and hand the Muslims are safe'."

6. *Bāb*: The giving of food is part of Islām.

A. A man asked the Prophet (May God bless him and give him peace): "What kind of Islām is best?" He said: "Feeding and greeting whom you know and

---

4. Note on *ḥayāʾ*: This word is translated in Lane-Poole as "the shrinking of the soul from foul conduct". While English words like "shame", "modesty", "scruples" and "diffidence" can carry perhaps the same meaning within a particular narrative context, no single English word can carry the proper connotation in a context like the one above.

whom you know not".

7. *Bāb*: It is part of *īmān* that a man desire for his brother what he desires for himself.

A. The Prophet (May God bless him and give him peace) said: "No one of you believes unless he desires for his brother what he desires for himself".

8. *Bāb*: The love of the Messenger (May God bless him and give him peace) is part of *īmān*.

A. The Messenger of God (May God bless him and give him peace) said: "(I swear) by Him in whose hand I am, no one of you believes unless I be more beloved to him than his children or his father".

9. *Bāb* of the sweetness (*ḥalāwah*) of *īmān*.

A. The Prophet (May God bless him and give him peace) said: "There are three things, the possessor of which finds the sweetness of *īmān*: that God and His Messenger be more beloved to him than anything else; that he loves a fellow man, loving him only for God's sake; and that he abhors (the fact) that he might fall back into infidelity (*kufr*) just as he abhors (the fact) that he might be thrown into Hell".

10. *Bāb*: The badge (*'alāmah*) of *īmān* is love of the *Anṣār*.

A. The Prophet (May God bless him and give him peace) said: "The sign of *īmān* is love of the *Anṣār* and the mark of hypocrisy (*nifāq*) is hatred (*bughḍ*) of the *Anṣār*".

11. *Bāb*: No *bāb* title.

The primary source of this account is 'Ubādah b. al-Ṣāmit who is qualified thus: "And he had witnessed Badr, and he was one of the leaders on the night of Aqabah".

A. "The Messenger of God (may God bless him and give him peace) said, while a group of his companions were (gathered) around him: Make your commitment to me that you will not steal or fornicate or kill your offspring, and that you will not come forth with slander that you have concocted, and that you will not disobey God. And whoever of you fulfills (these obligations), then his rewards are for God to decide, and whoever commits (of this list of prohibitions) anything will be punished in this world, this punishment being an expiation for his sins. And whoever commits anything (which) then God shields (from view), the punishment belongs to God. If He wills, He forgives him of it, and if He wills, He punishes him. And we swore our commitment to him on that basis".

12. *Bāb*: The flight from dissensions (*fitan*) is part of religion (*dīn*).

A. The Messenger of God (may God bless him and give him peace) said: "It can almost be said that the best property of the Muslim is the sheep with which he follows the peaks of mountains and the course of brooks, escaping with his religion from the dissensions".

13. *Bāb* of the saying of the Prophet (may God bless him and give him peace): "I know more about God than any of you", and of the fact that knowledge (*maʿrifah*) is the work (*ʿamal*) of the heart because of God's saying: "*But He will blame you for what your hearts have acquired* (*kasaba*)" (2: 225).

A. ʿĀʾishah is the primary source for the following.

The Messenger of God (may God bless him and give him peace) when he commanded them (i.e., the people), commanded them only to do things which they were able to do. They said: "We are not on the same level as you, oh Messenger of God: God has already forgiven you what has come to light of your sin (*dhanb*) and what has not yet come to light". Then he (the Prophet) became angry until the anger could be seen in his face, and he said: "I am more pious and know more of God than any of you".

14. *Bāb* concerning one who abhors (the fact) that he might return to infidelity (*kufr*) just as he abhors (the fact) that he might be thrown into Hell. This attitude is part of *īmān*.

A. The Prophet (may God bless him and give him peace) said: "Whoever has these three characteristics within himself finds the sweetness of *īmān*: Whoever loves God and His Messenger more than anything else and loves a fellow servant (of God), only loving him for God's sake, and abhors the fact that he might return to infidelity (*kufr*) just as he abhors the fact that he might be thrown into Hell".

15. *Bāb* concerning the ranking of the people of *īmān* in works.

A. The Prophet of God (may God bless him and give him peace) said: "The people of Paradise will enter Paradise and the People of Hell will enter Hell; then God will say: 'Take out (of the Fire) those in whose hearts there was the weight of a *mustard seed* of *īmān*'.[5] And they will be taken out of the Fire, already black, and thrown into the river of rain or of life (Mālik is not sure which). Then they will sprout, just as seeds sprout beside the torrent. Do you not agree that they will come up as saffron flowers, petals intertwined?"

B. The Messenger of God (may God bless him and give him peace) said: "While I was sleeping, I saw the people being paraded before me, and they were wearing shirts. The shirts of some of them reached the breast and others did not even reach that far; and ʿUmar b. al-Khaṭṭāb was presented to me and he was wearing a shirt that he was dragging behind him". They asked the Prophet: "So how do you explain that, oh Messenger of God?" He answered: "Faith".[6]

16. *Bāb*: *Ḥayāʾ* is part of *īmān*.

A. The Messenger of God (may God bless him and give him peace) passed by one of the Anṣār while he was upbraiding his brother about *ḥayāʾ*. And the Messenger of God said: "Leave him alone, because *ḥayāʾ* is part of *īmān*".[7]

17. *Bāb*: "*And if they repent and perform the ṣalāt and bring the zakāt, then let them go*". (9: 5)

A. The Messenger of God (may God bless him and give him peace) said: "I am commanded to fight a people until they confess that there is no God but Allāh and perform the *ṣalāt* and bring the *zakāt*. And if they do that, they have saved from me their blood and their property, except what rightfully belongs to Islām (or except what is required of them by the right or law of Islām); and their accounting belongs to God".

18. *Bāb* of those who say that *īmān* is a "work" (*ʿamal*) because of God's saying: "*And this is the garden which I cause you to inherit because of what you were doing*" (43: 72). And a number of the learned said that God's saying, "*And*

5. According to another version, the expression should be "mustard seed of good".

6. The relatively great length of ʿUmar's shirt is a symbol here of his superiority in religion.

7. *Ḥayāʾ* is not a virtue that appears heroic. The discomfiture of the pious man when confronted by evil can be mistaken for timidity or weakness.

by your Lord, we will surely ask all of them about what they were doing", (15: 92–93) concerns the saying of *lā ilāha illā'llāh*, for He said: "*Let those who act do the like of this*" (37: 59).

A. The Messenger of God (may God bless him and give him peace) was asked: "Which work is best?" He said: "*Īmān* in God and His Messenger".

"Then what?"

"*Jihād* for the sake of God".

"Then what?"

"A faultless *ḥajj*".

19. *Bāb*: When Islām is not real but is based upon threat or fear of being killed, referring to God's saying: "*The Bedouin say: We believe. Say: You have not believed; rather say. We have submitted*" (49: 14). And when it is sincere Islām, the reference is to God's saying: "*The religion acceptable to God is Islām*" (3: 17); "*as for whoever seeks other than Islām as a religion, it will never be accepted from him*" (3: 79).

A. ʿĀmir b. Saʿd b. Abī Waqqās is the original source and narrator of the following.

The Messenger of God (may God bless him and give him peace) gave (gifts) to a group while Saʿd was sitting (in the Prophet's presence), and he (the Prophet) ignored a man who was the most remarkable of them as far as I was concerned. So I said: "Oh Messenger of God, what do you have against so and so? For by God I see him as a believer (*mu'min*)".

He said: "Or as a Muslim".

And I was silent for a while. Then what I knew of him (i.e., of the man in question) overcame me and I returned to my thesis. I said: "What do you have against so and so? For by God I see him as a believer".

Then he said: "Or as a Muslim".

And I was silent for a while. Then what I knew about him overcame me and I returned to my thesis. And the Messenger of God (may God bless him and give him peace) reiterated what he had said: Then he said: "Oh Saʿd, I give to a man (while others are more beloved to me than he) in fear that God might throw him into Hell".

20. *Bāb*: The universal greeting is part of Islām. And ʿAmmār said: "Those who combine three things in themselves, possess *īmān*: rigorous justice towards

oneself; greeting the whole world; and spending money for others while in a condition of poverty".

A. A man asked the Messenger of God: "What kind of Islām is best?"

He (the Prophet) said: "You will feed and greet whomever you meet, whether you know him or not".

21. *Bāb* of ungratefulness toward the husband and of the particular kind of *kufr* inherent in it.

A. The Prophet (may God bless him and give him peace) said: "I was shown Hell (*an-Nār*) and most of its people were women. They are guilty of *kufr*".

It was asked: "Are they guilty of *kufr* with respect to God?"[8]

He (the Prophet) said: "They are ungrateful toward the husband, and they are ungrateful for the doing of good deeds. If you have done good to one of them for a very long time, (and) then she experiences something because of you (that she does not like), she says, 'I have never had anything good from you".

22. *Bāb*: The rebellious deeds which are the remnants of the Jāhiliyyah; and whoever commits them is not declared to be a *Kāfir* for committing them except for *shirk*, because of the saying of the Prophet (may God bless him and give him peace), "You are a man who has within him a bit of the Jāhiliyyah", and God's saying, "*God does not forgive that* (*anything*) *be associated with Him, but He forgives anything else to whomsoever He wills*" (4: 51), and "*if two parties of believers fight with one another, make peace between them*" (49: 9); and He called them "the believers".

A. From al-Aḥnāf b. Qays we have the following.

I went to help a certain man and Abū Bakr met me, and he asked: "Where are you going?"

---

8. The Arabic word *kufr* is usually translated "unbelief". This translation leaves out the equally important aspect of the Arabic word which this *Ḥadīth* illustrates. *Kufr* is an attitude of *ungratefulness* toward the one God who is the giver and sustainer of all life. In the view of this *Ḥadīth*, a chronic failing of women is that they are ungrateful toward their husbands and tend always to forget kindnesses done to them. But this attitude of women is only a particular expression of a fundamentally wrong attitude toward life. The husband and his solicitations are part of God's bounty, and the woman's ungratefulness towards these gifts is but a particular expression of ungratefulness toward God.

I said: "I will help a certain man".

He (Abū Bakr) said: "Go back! Because I heard the Messenger of God (may God bless him and give him peace) saying: 'If two Muslims encounter in a swordfight, the killer and the one killed are in Hell'."

"I said: 'Oh Messenger of God, so much for the killer, but what is the condition of the slain?"

"He said: 'He was bent upon the death of his brother'."

B. From al-Maʿrūr we have the following.

I met Abū Dharr in Rabadhah and he was wearing a rich new suit of clothes and his young slave was wearing a rich new suit of clothes (like that of his master). So I asked him about that and he said: "I was exchanging insults with a man, and I reviled him about his mother, and the Prophet (may God bless him and give him peace) said to me: 'Oh Abū Dharr, do you revile him about his mother? Behold, there is a bit of the Jāhiliyyah in you.[9] These servants whom God has placed under your power are your brothers. And anyone who has his brother under his power should feed his brother from what he himself eats, and dress him from what he himself wears. And do not impose upon your servants a task that overcomes them. Further, if you do impose such a task, relieve them of the burden'."

23. The *Bāb* of one kind of transgression as distinct from other transgressions.

A. From ʿAbd Allāh we have the following.

When the verse, "*Those who believe and do not confound their īmān with transgression* (*ẓulm*) …" (6: 32) was revealed, the Companions of the Messenger of God (may God bless him and give him peace) asked: "Which of us has not transgressed?" Then God revealed the verse, "*Lo polytheism* (*shirk*) *is indeed a great transgression*" (31: 12).

24. The *Bāb* of the marks of the hypocrite (*munāfiq*).

A. The Prophet (may God bless him and give him peace) said: "The mark of the hypocrite consists in three things: When he speaks, he lies; when he promises, he breaks his promise; and when he is trusted, he violates the trust".

B. The Prophet (may God bless him and give him peace) said: "There are

9. In the Jāhiliyyah period, a verbal assault on a man often took the form of insulting his mother.

four traits which make anyone having them a downright hypocrite. Indeed, anyone having a single one of these traits has an element of hypocrisy until he abandons that trait: when he is trusted, he violates the trust; when he speaks, he lies; when he makes a compact with someone, he betrays the agreement; and when he disputes, he uses unjust means".

25. *Bāb*: Wakefulness on the Night of the Decree is part of *īmān*.

A. The Messenger of God (may God bless him and give him peace) said: "Past sins will be forgiven anyone who is wakeful on the Night of the Decree, in *īmān*, and anticipating a future reward".

26. *Bāb*: The *Jihād* is part of *Īmān*.

A. The Prophet (may God bless him and give him peace) said: "God promised anyone who goes out to fight for His sake, going out only because of "faith" (*īmān*) in Him or belief (*taṣdīq*) in His Messengers, that He will bring him back with what he has gained of pay or spoil, or He will bring him into Paradise.[10] And if I would not have made my community anxious by going, I would not have remained behind a single expedition. And indeed, I wish that I might be killed for the sake of God, then brought back to life, then killed, then brought back to life, then killed".

27. *Bāb*: The voluntary (or supererogatory) wakefulness during Ramaḍān is part of *īmān*.

A. The Messenger of God (may God bless him and give him peace) said: Past sins are forgiven anyone who is wakeful during Ramaḍān in *īmān*, and anticipating a future reward.

28. *Bāb*: (Participation in) the Fast of Ramaḍān, while anticipating a future reward, is part of *īmān*.

A. The Messenger of God (may God bless him and give him peace) said: "As for anyone who fasts during Ramaḍān, in *īmān*, and anticipating a future reward, God forgives him his past sins".

---

10. I have in this sentence translated the first person Arabic in third person English for sake of smoothness.

29. *Bāb*: The (demand of) Religion (*al-Dīn*) is moderate and the saying of the Prophet (may God bless him and give him peace): "The religion most beloved to God is the Hanifitic Religion, the indulgent religion".

A. The Prophet (may God bless him and give him peace) said: "The (demand of) religion is moderate (*yusr*), and whenever religion is imposed upon someone in a severe form, it will overcome him. So aim (at the right goal) and come as close as you can and rejoice. And seek help from God in the early morning and the early evening and a little at night".

30. *Bāb*: *Ṣalāt* is part of *īmān* and the saying of God: "*And it was not God's intention to waste your īmān*". (2: 138), meaning, your *ṣalāt* toward the House (i.e. the Temple of Jerusalem).

A. The Prophet (may God bless him and give him peace) immediately after he arrived in al-Madīnah settled with his grandparents (or his maternal uncles of the *Anṣār*) and he prayed facing the Temple at Jerusalem sixteen or seventeen months. And he was wishing during this time that his *qiblah* were toward the Kaʿbah. And a people prayed with him. Then a man of those who prayed with him went out and passed before the people of the mosque while they were bowing in prayer, and he said: "I testify by God that I have prayed with the Messenger of God (may God bless him and give him peace) facing toward Makkah". Then they turned about, still bowing, to face toward the Kaʿbah. And the Jews had been pleased when he used to pray facing the Temple at Jerusalem and the People of the Book also (had been pleased), and when he turned to face toward the Kaʿbah they denounced that.

B. From Al-Barā' We have the following:

"Men were killed before the *qiblah* was changed, and we did not know what to say about them (i.e., whether they will be in Hell or Paradise). Then God revealed the verse: '*And it was not God's intention to waste your īmān*' (2: 138)".

31. *Bāb*: The authenticity (*ḥusn*) of the man's Islām.

A. Abū Saʿīd al-Khudrī said that he heard the Messenger of God (may God bless him and give him peace) saying: "If the worshipper submits (*aslama*) and his Islām is authentic, God forgives him (*kaffara*) every evil deed (*sayyi'ah*) that he has committed. And after that is the settlement of accounts (i.e., after that the Muslim once again begins to acquire a balance of merits and demerits), the good deed (being weighed) by ten times its value up to seven-hundred-fold, and the evil deed (being weighed) according to its value, unless God disregards it".

B. The Messenger of God (may God bless him and give him peace) said: "If one of you makes his Islām authentic, every good deed which he does will be recorded for him at ten times its value up to seven-hundred-fold; and every evil deed will be recorded against him according to its value".

32. *Bāb*: The religion most beloved to God is the most constant.

A. From 'Ā'ishah is the story that the Prophet (may God bless him and give him peace) came in upon her while a woman was with her. And he said: "Who is this?"

She ('Ā'ishah) said: "So and so", mentioning her assiduity in prayer.

He said: "Easy now! You must do only what you are able to do. God does not become impatient until you become weary, and the religion most beloved to Him is that in which its adherents can persist (i.e., not the most strenuous)".

33. *Bāb* concerning the increase of *īmān* and its decrease and God's saying: "*... and we have increased them in guidance*" (18: 12), and God's saying: "*... in order that those who believe might increase in īmān*" (74: 31). And God also said: "*Today I have completed for you your religion* (*dīn*)" (5: 5). If anyone abandons anything of the completeness, he is the loser.

A. The Prophet (may God bless him and give him peace) said: "Whoever says, 'There is no God but Allāh' while having in his heart a barley seed of *good*[11] will be brought out of Hell; and whoever says, 'There is no God but Allāh' while having in his heart the weight of a wheat seed of good will be brought out of Hell; and whoever says there is no God but Allāh, while having in his heart the weight of a particle of good, will be brought out of Hell".

B. From 'Umar b. al-Khaṭṭāb we have the account of an encounter with a Jew who said to him: "Oh Commander of the Faithful, there is a verse in your Book which the people are reciting. Had it been revealed to us, a community of Jews, we would surely have adopted the day in which it was revealed as a religious festival".

'Umar asked: "Which verse?"

The Jew answered: "*Today I have completed for you your religion, and I*

11. According to another version the phrase is "*of īmān*".

have perfected My blessing to you. And I approve of Islām for you as a religion". (5: 5)

Then ʿUmar said: "We know that day and the place in which it was revealed to the Prophet—at ʿArafah on a Friday".

34. *Bāb*: *Zakāt* is part of Islām and God's saying: "*And they are only commended to serve God, offering him sincere devotion as "Hanīfs" and to perform the ṣalāt and bring the zakāt and that is the true religion*" (98: 4).

A. On the authority of ʿUbayd Allāh we have the following:

A dishevelled man from the people of Najd came to the Messenger of God (may God bless him and give him peace). The sound of his voice was heard, but we did not understand what he was saying until he came close to us, and lo! he was asking the Prophet about Islām. And the Messenger of God (may God bless him and give him peace) said: "Five *ṣalāt*s during the day and night (are required)".

And he asked: "Do I have any obligation beyond that?"

He said: "No, unless you do (it) voluntarily" (meaning, anything beyond the stated number is supererogatory).

Then the Messenger of God said: "And the fast during Ramaḍān (is required)".

He asked: "Do I have any obligation beyond that?"

He said: "No, unless you do it voluntarily".

And the Messenger of God (may God bless him and give him peace) mentioned the *zakāt*.

The man of Najd asked: "Do I have any obligation beyond that?"

He said: "No, unless you do (it) voluntarily".

Then the man turned away saying: "By God, I will neither exceed nor lessen this".

The Messenger of God (may God bless him and give him peace) said: "If he speaks the truth, he will thrive".

35. *Bāb*: The following of the funeral bier is part of *īmān*.

A. The Messenger of God said: "Whoever has followed the bier of a Muslim in *īmān* and anticipating a future reward, and was with him until he was prayed over and interred, returns with two measures of reward, each measure equivalent to Uḥud. And whoever prays over him, then returns before he is interred, returns with one measure".

36. *Bāb* concerning the fear of the *Mu'min* that his action might be of no avail while he is unaware of the fact. And Ibrāhīm al-Taymī said: "I never compare my speech with my action without fearing that I might be shown to be a liar"; and Ibn Abī Mulaykah said: "I had personal contact with thirty Companions of the Prophet and each of them was afraid of *nifāq* in himself; not one of them was saying that he had attained the *īmān* of Jibrīl or Mīkā'īl". And it was recalled about al-Ḥasan (al-Baṣrī) that he said: "Only a *mu'min* is afraid of it (*nifāq*), and only a *munāfiq* feels secure about it". (And the *Bāb* of) bewaring of persistence in *nifāq*[12] and disobedience without repentance, because of God's saying: "*And they have not knowingly persisted in* (*the wrong*) *they did*" (3: 129).

A. Abū Wā'il was asked about the Murji'ah and he cited this saying of the Prophet.

The Prophet (may God bless him and give him peace) said: "The revilement of a Muslim is disobedience (*fusūq*) and fighting him is unbelief (*kufr*)".

B. The Messenger of God (may God bless him and give him peace) went out to make known the Night of the Decree. Then two Muslims quarreled and he (the Prophet) said: "I came out to tell you about the Night of the Decree and so-and-so quarreled with so-and-so, and I forgot what I was going to say. But (on reflection), it might be better for you to expect it on the twenty-seventh, or the twenty-ninth, or the twenty-fifth (day of the month)".[13]

37. *Bāb*: The questioning of the Prophet (may God bless him and give him peace) by Jibrīl about *īmān* and *Islām* and *iḥsān* and the knowledge of the Hour and the statement of the Prophet (may God bless him and give him peace) to him. Then he said: "Jibrīl came to teach you your religion". And he established all of it as religion. And what the Prophet (may God bless him and give him peace) made clear to the delegation from 'Abd al-Qays about *īmān*, and His (God's) saying: "*Whoever seeks other than Islām as religion, it will not be accepted from him* (3: 79)".

A. From Abū Hurayrah we have the following:

---

12. Krehl's text reads *taqātul*, "mutual struggle", "quarreling".

13. The event might fall on any of these days. The Muslims must be very careful.

The Prophet (may God bless him and give him peace) was standing one day before the people and a man came to him and asked: "What is *īmān*?"

He answered: "*Īmān* means that you believe in God and His Angels and His Meeting (i.e. that you will be confronted by God in the Hereafter) and His Messengers and that you believe in the Resurrection (*al-baʿth*)".

He asked: "What is *Islām*?"

He (the Prophet) answered: "*Islām* means that you serve God, that you do not associate anything with Him, and that you perform the *ṣalāt* and bring the required *zakāt* and that you fast during Ramaḍān".

He asked: "What is *iḥsān*?"

The Prophet answered: "That you serve God as though you see Him, for if you do not see Him, He certainly sees you".

He asked: "When is the Hour?"

The Prophet answered: "The one asked doesn't know any more about it than the one asking the question, but I will tell you about its signs (*ashrāṭ*). When a slave girl gives birth to her lord, and the black camel-shepherds take on royal airs in fine houses (the Hour will be near). All this is included in the five things which only God knows about".

Then the Prophet (may God bless him and give him peace) recited the Qur'ānic verse, "*With God is the knowledge of the Hour*". (31: 34)

Then the man slipped away and the Prophet said: "Bring him back". But they could not see anything of him.

The Prophet said: "This is Jibrīl who came teaching the people their religion".

Bukhārī adds: "The Prophet made all the things mentioned above parts of *īmān*".

38. *Bāb*: Abū Sufyān said that Hiraqla said to him: "I asked if they increase or decrease and you claimed that they increase, and likewise *īmān* (increases) until it is complete, and I asked you does anyone apostatize out of discontent for his religion after he has entered into it and you said 'no'. And likewise when the joy of *īmān* blends into hearts, no one can be displeased".

39. *Bāb* of the excellence of whosoever abstains for the sake of his religion.

A. An-Nuʿmān b. Bashir heard the Messenger of God (may God bless him and give him peace) saying: "Lo, the permitted (*ḥalāl*) is clear and the forbidden (*ḥarām*) is clear, but between these two categories are uncertainties which many of the people do not know. And whoever is on guard against the uncertainties refrains for the sake of his honor (*ʿirḍ*) and his religion. And whoever falls among the uncertainties is like a shepherd on the periphery of the sanctuary, about to encroach upon it. Verily, every king has a sanctuary. The sanctuary of God in his earth consists in the things that He has forbidden. In the body is a small chunk, which if it be healthy, the whole body is healthy, and if it be corrupt, the whole body is corrupt. Lo, it is the heart (*qalb*)".

40. *Bāb*: The rendering of the fifth is part of *īmān*.

A. Abū Jamrah said: I was staying with Abū ʿAbbās and he made me sit down on his couch and he said: "Abide with me until I give you a portion of my property". So I stayed with him two months.

Then he said: "Behold a delegation of ʿAbd al-Qays when they came to the Prophet (may God bless him and give him peace), he said: 'Who are the people?' (or 'who are the delegation?')

"They said: 'Rabīʿah'."

"He said: 'Welcome to the people (or the delegation) who come without shame or remorse'."

"Then they said: 'Oh Messenger of God, we are unable to come to you except in the Holy Month, because between us and you is this tribe of unbelievers, Muḍar. So command us with a conclusive command about which we can inform those who live beyond us and by which we might enter Paradise'. And they also asked him about beverages.

"Then the Prophet commanded them to do four things and he forbade them four. He commanded them to *īmān* in God alone. He asked: 'Do you know what *īmān* in God is?"

"They replied: 'God and His Messenger know best'."

"He (the Prophet) said: '*Īmān* consists of the witness that there is no god but Allāh and that Muḥammad is the Messenger of God'. And (he commanded them) also to perform the *ṣalāt* and to bring the *zakāt* and to fast during Ramaḍān and to hand over a fifth of the spoils.[14]

---

14. While the Tradition says that the Prophet commanded four things, the list contains five. A. J. Wensinck's *The Muslim Creed* (Cambridge, 1932) pp. 14–16 treats an alternate form of this Tradition.

"And he (the Prophet) forbade them four things: the *ḥantam*, the *dubbā'*, the *naqīr*, the *muzaffat* and perhaps he said the *muqayyar*.[15]

"Then the Prophet concluded by saying: 'Guard those commands and prohibitions and tell those who live beyond you about them'."

41. *Bāb* concerning what has been handed down in the Tradition to the effect that works (*a'māl*) and the accounting for reward and punishment are by intention (*niyyah*), and to every man belongs what he intends. This statement applies to *īmān* and *wuḍū'* and *ṣalāt* and *zakāt* and the *ḥajj* and the fast of Ramaḍān and (all other) statutes.

And God said: "*Say: each one acts according to his intention* (*shākilah*)" (17: 86), i.e., according to his *niyyah*.

And the Prophet (may God bless him and give him peace) said: "But a *jihād* and an intention (*niyyah*) ...,"[16] and the Prophet also said that even a man's expenditure for his family, in anticipation of a future reward from God, would be rewarded by God as though it were an act of charity.

A. The Messenger of God (may God bless him and give him peace) said: "The works (*a'māl*) are evaluated by God according to the intention behind them and to every man belongs what he intends. Whoever journeys toward God and His Messenger will be judged according to the intended goal. The same thing may be said of the man who journeys in search of the things of this world or a woman whom he marries. Man's 'flight' (*hijrah*) is weighed in terms of its intended goal".

B. The Prophet of God (may God bless him and give him peace) said: "Even if a man spends (his money) on his family while anticipating a future reward, God will reward him as though this were an act of charity".

C. The Messenger of God (may God bless him and give him peace) said: "You will never spend anything by which you are seeking the face of God without being rewarded for it, even if you put it into the mouth of your wife".

42. *Bāb* of the saying of the Prophet (may God bless him and give him peace): "The true religion is being loyal to God and His Messenger and the *Imāms* of

15. The Arabic terms listed here all refer to wine containers. Thus the "prohibitions" together make up an elaborate denunciation of wine drinking.

16. Reference to another Tradition of the Prophet.

the Muslims and the common people", and of God's saying: "... *when they are true to God and His Messenger* ... (9: 92)".

A. Jarīr b. ʿAbd Allāh said: "I swore commitment to the Messenger of God on the basis of performing the *ṣalāt* and bringing the *zakāt* and being true to every Muslim".

B. From Ziyād b. ʿAlaqah we have the following:

I heard Jarīr b. ʿAbd Allāh on the day al-Mughīrah b. Shuʿbah died. He stood up and praised God and lauded Him and said: "What is required of you is the fear of God alone, not associating anything with Him, and the dignity of peace of mind until an Amīr comes to you—and he is coming even now". And he said: "Ask forgiveness for your Amīr (i.e. the dead one) because he used to love to forgive". Then he said: "Now then, I came to the Prophet (may God bless him and give him peace) and I said: 'I swear my commitment to you to Islām', and he imposed the additional condition upon me of being true to every Muslim. And I swore my commitment to him on that condition. By the Lord of this mosque, I am indeed true to you". Then he asked forgiveness and descended (left the *minbar*).

INDEX OF PERSONS AND SECTS

A

ʿAbbād b. Sulaymān 94, 119 (note), 172, 218
ʿAbd al-Karīm b. Abī al-ʿAwjāʾ 23
Abū al-Muntahá al-Maghnīsāwī 73, 75
Abū Bakr (Caliph) 2–3, 33, 133, 206
Abū Bakr al-Aṣamm 172
Abū Dharr 48, 54, 80
Abū Ḥanīfah 73, 98–99, 101, 109, 115–118, 120, 122–123, 126–129, 132, 161, 196, 207, 224–225, 227, 235, 238
Abū Hudhayl 43, 119 (note), 172
Abū Hurayrah 175
Abū Shimr 94, 105, 107, 109–110
Abū Thawbān 95, 107, 110
Abū ʿUdhbah 44, (120–121), 123–125, 134 (note), 211, 224–225
Abū ʿUthmān al-Ādamī 115
Abū Yūsuf 122, 127
Aḥmad Amīn 3
ʿĀʾishah 211
ʿAjāridah 241
ʿAlī (Caliph) 3–6, 12, 131 (note)
Aristotle 32, 197
Ashʿarī 5, 16, 17 (note), 28–29, 42–43, 51, 53, 56, 61, 68, 72–73, 92, 94, 99–100, 104, 107, 115, 119, 121, 131–132, 134 (note), 152–158, 159, 161, 172 (note), 173, 215, 220–223, 225, 229, 234, 241 (note)
Ashʿarites 29, 120–121, 126, 131–132, 136, 140, 207, 210–211, 239 (note)
Awzāʿī 211
Azraq, Nāfiʿ b. 13
Azraqites (*Azāriqah*) 13–14, 40, 46

B

Baghdādī 4, 13, 15 (note), 16, 17 (note), 23, 40 (note), 46, 50, 67 (note), 95 (note), 96 (note), 101, 104–105, 107, 131 (note), 132, 143, 155, 168, 217 (note)
Bakr, nephew of ʿAbd al-Wāḥid 19, 61
Bāqillānī 28, 28 (note), 68–69, 72
Barāhimah 31 (note)
Bāṭiniyyah 37
Bayāḍī 121, 123, 125, 127 (note), 128–129, 224, 226–227, 235–240
Bayḍāwī 237
Bayhasiyyah 15
Bishr al-Marīsī 42, 100, 105
Bukhārī 48, 57, 64 (note), 67 (note), 88 (note), 108 (note), 109, 183

D

Dahriyyah 31
Ḍirār b. ʿAmr 26

F

Falāsifah 31

Fuḍaylites (*Fuḍayliyyah*) 161

G

Gabriel (*Jibrīl*) 64–65, 73, 83, 102
Ghassān 100–101, 105, 108–109
Ghassāniyyah 101
Ghaylān 96–97, 104–105, 109, 117
Ghaylāniyyah 96–97
Ghazālī 28–37, 133–135, 197–198, 210–211

H

Ḥafṣah 38
Ḥafsiyyah 17, 17 (note)
Halkin, Abraham 167 (note)
Ḥanafites 163
Ḥanbalites 27–28
Ḥasan al-Baṣrī 45, 52, 56–61, 181, 211
Hishām al-Fuwaṭī 172
Ḥusayn b. Iskandar 208–209

I

Ibāḍiyyah 16, 17, 17 (note), 46, 56
Iblīs 90, 93, 98
Ibn Abī al-Ḥadīd 131 (note)
Ibn Abī Mulaykah 58
Ibn al-Faḍl 225
Ibn ʿAsākir 223
Ibn Ḥanbal, Aḥmad 2, 36, 66, 186, 211, 215–216, 220
Ibn Ḥazm 14, 16 (note), 17 (note), 19, 46, 49, 51–52, 54–55, 58–60, 76–77, 93 (note), 99, 136–142, 151–153, 161, 164–165, 171, 175–177, 193–196, 209–210, 228–229, 232–234, 236, 241
Ibn Karrām 100, 104–106, 115, 161, 164, 171
Ibn Kaysān 34
Ibn Kullāb 213 (note), 214, 220
Ibn Masʿūd, ʿAbd Allāh 40–41, 210–211, 215
Ibn Shabīb, Muḥammad 94, 97–98, 105, 107–110, 117
Ibn Sīrīn 211
Ibn Taymiyyah 1, 66, 68–69, 72–73, 77–83, 92 (note), 165–167, 178–192, 198–199, 212–216
Ibn ʿUyaynah 211, 215
Ibrāhīm (= Abraham) 129
Ibrāhīm al-Sindī 22
Ibrāhīm al-Taymī 57
Ismāʿīl b. al-Ḥusayn al-Zāhid 225

J

Jabrites (*Jabriyyah*) 226
Jaʿfar b. Ḥarb 220
Jaʿfar b. Mubashshir 43
Jāḥiz 131
Jahm (b. Ṣafwān) 20 (note), 21, 92, 105, 109, 115, 153, 171, 185, 187–188, 205, 212, 215, 217, 226
Jahmites (*Jahmiyyah*) 20, 69, 71–72, 90, 92, 93 (note), 163–166, 172, 176, 185, 212–213, 223
Jesus 20, 75
Joseph (Yūsuf) 184
Jubbāʾī 43, 53, 172
Junayd b. Muḥammad 186

K

Kaʿbī 5
Karrāmites (*Karrāmiyyah*) 70, 72, 100, 134 (note), 143, 160–161, 162–170, 176, 185 (note)
Khārijites (*Khawārij*) 1–4, 5–17, 19, 39, 41–42, 45–47, 47 (note), 48–50, 58, 72, 91, 102, 111, 161, 171–172, 241

Khayyāt 21 (note), 23 (note)
Kullābites 214

L

Laoust, Henri 114 (note)

M

Makkī 44, 220
Malaṭī 6, 13, 20, 22, 23 (note), 25, 46–47, 113–114, 176
Mālik b. Anas 211, 215
Maqrīzī 61 (note), 95 (note)
Marīsiyyah 100
Māturīdī 51 (note), 120 (note), 121, 125, 132 (note), 143–144, 147–149, 160, 163, 211, 224, 236–237, 242 (note)
Māturīdites 26 (note), 27 (note), 51 (note), 52, 120–130, 142–144, 206–207, 210, 220–221, 223–228, 234, 240
Moses 20, 75, 152
Muʿādh b. Jabal 202
Muʿāwiyah 3–4, 12
Muḥakkimah 6–7, 12, 14
Muḥammad 8, 31, 33, 69, 70–71, 75, 83–84, 97, 114, 116, 132, 137, 139, 141, 149, 156, 177, 184, 189, 193, 195, 208–209, 225
Muḥāsibī, Ḥārith 220
Muqātil b. Sulaymān 175
Murdār, Abū Mūsá 21–22, 26
Murji'ites (*Murji'ah*) 42–43, 45, 47 (note), 48–51, 57, 58 (note), 68–69, 82, 88 (note), 90–120, 154, 174, 175–176, 179, 181, 185, 188–193, 210 (note), 213
Murtaḍá, al-Sharīf 168–170, 175, 218, 229–232
Muslim (Ibn al-Ḥajjāj) 20 (note), 40 (note), (41), 54 (note), 55 (note), 64 (note), 67 (note)
Muʿtazilites (*Muʿtazilah*) 20–23, 27–29, 32, 37, 42–45, 52–55, 71–72, 108, 119–120, 121 (note), 123–125, 130–131, 133–134, 134 (note), 149, 171–172, 174–175, 217–220, 223, 229, 233, 240–241

N

Nader, Albert 43
Najdah 16
Najdites (*Najadāt*) 5, 16, 41, 46
Najjār 95, 109
Najjārites (*Najjāriyyah*) 95, 223
Nasafī (Najm al-Dīn) 26 (note), 73, 75, 149, 159, 196
Nawbakhtī 49, 49 (note)
Naẓẓām 24, 34, 97, 119 (note), 172
Nūḥ b. Abī Maryam 225

P

Pharaoh 90
Plato 190, 204–205

Q

Qadarites (*Qadariyyah*) 23, 149, 229
Qarmatians (*Qarāmiṭah*) 25
Qushayrī, Abū al-Qāsim 134 (note)

R

Rawāfiḍ 6 (note), 23, 161
Rāzī (Fakhr al-Dīn) 75 (note)
Ritter, H. 56

S

Ṣāliḥī, Abū al-Ḥusayn 93, 105, 107 (note), 109, 188

Ṣāliḥiyyah 93
Ṣāliḥ Qubbah 229
Ṣaltiyyah 241
Samnānī 136
Shāfiʿī 211, 215
Shahrastānī 21, 23 (note), 95 (note), 131, 154–159, 164, 173–174
Shīʿites (*Shīʿah*) 3–4, 34
Shimriyyah 94, 97
Spitta 220 (note)
Ṣufriyyah 15, 46, 161
Shakkākiyyah (or *Shakkākah*) 210, 213
Sufyān al-Thawrī 211, 215

T

Ṭabarī, Muḥammad b. Jarīr 136
Taftāzānī 26, 46, 54 (note), 73, 75, 149–150, 159–160, 172, 196–197, 205–206
Thawbāniyyah 95
Tritton 95 (note), 210 (note)
Tūmanī, Abū Muʿādh 99, 108–109
Tūmaniyyah 99

U

ʿUmar (Caliph) 211
ʿUmar b. Abī ʿUthmān al-Shimmazī 98–99, 115–116
ʿUthmān (Caliph) 3, 5

W

Waʿīdites (*Waʿīdiyyah*) 172–174
Wāṣil b. ʿAṭāʾ 19, 26 (note), 52, 61
Waqīʿ b. al-Jarrāḥ 185
Wensinck, A. J. 9 (note), 41, 51 (note), 65 (note), 67 (note), 73, 80 (note), 120, 132, 162 (note), 208 (note), 210, 224 (note)

Y

Yūnus 93–94, 105, 107–109
Yūnusiyyah 93

Z

Zamakhsharī 172, 174
Ziyād b. al-Aṣfar 15
Zurqān 97, 117

INDEX OF ARABIC WORDS

A

abrār (sg. *bārr* or *barr*) 81
ʿādah ilāhiyyah 130
ʿadhāb 126
ʿadl 95, 108, 217
aḥkām (sg. *ḥukm*) 72 (note)
ahl al-ḥall wa-al-ʿaqd 34
ahl al-Sunnah 24
aḥwāl 187
aḥwāl īmāniyyah 185
ʿajz 233
ākhirah 57
ālah 123
ʿālam 23 (note)
ʿālim 37
āliyyah 124 (note)
Allāh al-aḥad 117
ʿamal (pl. *aʿmāl*) 47 (note), 51, 55, 57, 74, 86, 91, 103–104, 110, 112, (119), 132, 153, 159, 162, 167, 171–206, 221
aʿmāl al-qalb 82, 86, (89), 182–184, 186, (191–192), (201–202)
āmana 180
amānah 180
amr 229, 235, 237
ʿaqd (*bi-al-qalb*) 153, 157, 164, 192
ʿaql 107, 119, 120–130, 195
ʿaql bi-al-fiʿl 122
ʿaql bi-al-malakah 122
ʿaql bi-al-quwwah 122
ʿaql gharīzī 122
ʿaql hayūlānī 122
ʿaql mustafād 122
ʿaraḍ (pl. *aʿrāḍ*) 24
ʿārif (pl. *ʿārifūn*) 121
arkān 67, 103, 154
aṣḥāb al-yamīn 188
aṣl (*al-īmān*) 143, 186
asmāʾ (sg. *ism*) 72 (note)
āyah (pl. *āyāt*) 127
ʿaẓīm 41 (note)
ʿazm 43

B

badan (*jamīʿ al-badan*) 45
baqāʾ 28
bāṭin 187
baṭn 45
bidʿah 34, 37, 165
birr 80–81
burhān 36–37, 138, (140)

D

dāna (*dīn*) 83
dār al-Islām 14
dār al-kufr 14
ḍarūrah 136,
ḍarūrī 97, 104, 131

ḍarūrīyyāt 122
da'wá 136
dhikr 135
dhimmī 113 (note), 114
dīn 65, 75, 80, 83–84, 97, 98 (note), 195
dunyā 57

F

faḥshā' 79
farā'iḍ 96
faraq 57
farḍ kifāyah 129
farj 45
fasaqa 100
fāsiq 22, 39–55, 47 (note), 54 (note), 60, 70, 100, 110–111, 131, 137, 173–174, 232–233
fatwá 34
fiṭrah 241–242
fiqh 30
fisq 47, 55, 77, 146, 233
fu'ād 144–145
furū' 33

G

ghayb 212

H

ḥalāl 17, 31, 51–52
ḥaqq 235
ḥarakah (pl. *ḥarakāt*) 24
ḥarām 46, 51
ḥawādith 23
ḥayā' 108
hidāyah 224, 226
hijrah 13
ḥukm 6–7, 12

I

idh'ān 75–76
idhn 228, 237
iḍṭirār 96, 104
iftirā' al-kadhib 178
iḥsān 65–67
ihtidā' 224
ījāb 130
ijmā' 34, 107
ijmāl 199–200
ijtihād 30, 37
ikhrāj 219
ikhtiyār 149, 235
iktisāb 97, 131
'ilm 97, 117, 136
imām (*jā'ir*) 5, 15
īmān 4, 11, 15, 21, 24, 31, 47–48, 50–51, 53 (note), 55–57, 59, 63–118, 133–136, 138–141, 143–161, 163–228
īmān bi-al-taqlīd 26, 120, 130–142
inqiyād 68
in shā'a Allāh 89 (note), 207
inshirāḥ al-ṣadr 136
iqrār 51, 73, 86, 92, 94, 96 (note), 97, 103, 105, 111, 143, 155, 159, 162–170, 185–186
iqrār fard 167
irādah (verb *arāda*) 232, 234, 236–237, 239
irjā' (verb *arja'a*) 49–50, 91, 103
ishtirāk 197
iṣlāḥ 78
islām 7–8, 63–90, 99, 133, 140, 144, 146, 153, 177, 179–180, 182, 192, 209–210, 238
iṣrār 44
istidlāl 120, 128, 130, 133, 134 (note), 136–137, 141, 242
istighfār 44
istiḥsān 233
istikbār 93, 101

istiʿrāḍ 14
istiʾṣāl 126
istislām (*istaslama*) 77, 83, 86
istithnāʾ 207–216
iʾtimān 180
iʿtiqād 136, 149
iṭlāq 216

J

jahālah 147
jāḥid 61
jāhil 35, 148, 203
jahl 92, 93
jihād 183

K

kabīrah (pl. *kabāʾir*) 16, 40–45, (akbar) 41, 46–47, 52, 61
kadhaba (*kadhdhaba*) 179
kadhib 194
kāfir (pl. *kuffār*) 4, 7–16, 19–37, 45–47, 51, 55–56, 58, 92–111, 131–133, 136, 140–142, 149, 152, 158, 173–174, 187, 208, 211, 214, 218, 225, 229–230, 232–233, 238–241
kāfir dīn 16
kāfir niʿmah 16
kalām (= *ʿilm al-kalām*) 11, 134, (135)
kalām 106, 219
kalām nafsī 225
kasbī 149
kayfiyyāt 194
khafiyy 145
khalīfah 2–3
khalq al-qurʾān 219–220
khashyah 184
khaṣlah (pl. *khiṣāl*) 53, 53 (note), 68, 88 (note), 108
khātimah 211–212
khawf 57, 92
khilāfah 2
khinzīr 118
khuḍūʿ 92, 96 (note)
kufr 4, 6, 10–12, 15–17, 19–37, 41–43, 47–48, 50, 56, 59–61, 77, 87, 93–94, 96, 99–100, 121, 138, 141, 147–148, 153, 155, 161, 164, 178, 180, 182, 185, 208, 211–212, 214, 218, 226–228, 228–242
kufr al-ʿāmmah 130–136
kufr shirk 16

L

lawāzim 86
lisān 45

M

maʿdūmāt 23
maḥabbah 101
maḥall 51 (note), 142
māhiyyah 190
makhlūq 220
manāzil 187
manzilah bayna al-manzilatayn 52, 131
maqāmāt 187
maqḍī 235
maʿrifah 17, 86, 90, 92–93, 97, 100, 103–105, (106–108), 110, 113–118, 122, 135, 135 (note), (139), 144, 149, 153 (note), 155, 157, 161–162, 184, 186, (201), (202–203)
maʿrūf 78–79
mashīʾah (verb *shāʾa*) 228–229, 232, 234, 236–238, 240
maʿṣiyah (pl. *maʿāṣī*) 40, 43, 229
mawḍiʿ (*al-īmān*) 143
mawjūd 37

miṣbāḥ 145
mishkāt 145
mūbiqāt 41
mufaṣṣal 204
muḥarramāt 17
muḥsin 65
mujmal 204
mujtahid 37
mukadhdhib 32–33, 35, 37, 61, 148
mukhṭiʾ 35
muʾmin 4, 7–8, 12, 52–53, (58), 65, (69–71), 81, (87), (89–90), 91, 93, 102, (110), 111, 130, (131–132), 132, (135–136), (140), (142), (156), (158), (160–161), (172), (173), (178), 179, (182), (185), (187), (195–196), (203), (207–208), 209, (211–212), (214), 222–223
munāfiq 52, 55–61, 74, 84–85, 100, (106), (108), (157), (162), (165), 165, (170), (174), (182)
munkar 78–79
muqallid 137
muqarrab 187
muqayyad 78
murtakib al-kabīrah 4–5, 45–61, 172
muṣaddiq 152, 177, 179, 193
mushrik 13–17, 45–47, 56, 132, 141, 152
muslim 7, 45, 65, (69–71), 77, 86–87, 89–90, 114, 132, (136), 144, 161, 180, 182, 185, 241
mustadill 139
mutakallim 130, 133–134
muthul aflāṭūniyyah 205
muṭīʿ 40
muṭlaq 78
muttaqī 81
muwāfāt 211–212, 214–215
muwāẓabah 198

N

nāfiqāʾ (al-yarbūʿ) 60
nafs 20
naqala 151
naẓar 115, 128
naẓariyyāt 122
nifāq 56, 58–61, 87–89, 108, 182
niyyah 103, 185, 192
nubuwwah 66
nūr 133–134, 218
nūr al-hidāyah 145

Q

qaḍāʾ 234–235
qādhif 15
qadīm 222
qalb 45, (*ṣālih*) 57, (*salīm*) 57, 82, 142–146, 183, 186, 191
qawl 153, 158, 161, 173, 221
qawl al-qalb 186
qawl fī al-nafs 156
quʿūd 14
quwwah 122

R

rāshidūn 139
riḍá 233
rijl 45
risālah 66
rūḥ 25
rukn (pl. *arkān*) *al-īmān* 159, (162), (172–173), 226
ruʾyah Allāh 20

S

sababiyyah 124
ṣadaqa 78, 179
ṣaddaqa (*yuṣaddiqu*) 154, 180–181
ṣadr 144–145
ṣaghīrah 16, 39–40, 46–47
ṣalāt 15, 79, 93, 113, 181
ṣāliḥāt 79, 82
sāriq 15
shahādah 8, 64, 67 (note), 69, 71, 84, 135, 156–158, 160–161, 170, 213, 225
shajarah 145
shakk 208
shākk 22, 140, 194
shanāʿah 114
sharʿ 121–130, (134)
shayṭān (*ʿābid li-*) 61
shirk 15–17, 19, 26–27, 40–41, 44–45, 48, 54, 56, 121, 176
shuʿbah (pl. *shuʿab*) 88, 108
ṣidq 194
sirr 145
sulṭān (*jāʾir*) 5, 15

T

ṭāʿah (pl. *ṭāʿāt*) 40, 69, 96, 98, 103, 155, 196, 240
tabarruʾ 77
tabaʿʿuḍ 108
tabdīʿ 34
tafāḍul (*fī al-īmān*) 192
tafṣīl 199–200
tafsīr 98
taghṭiyah 148
taḥallī 181
takdhīb 30, 32–35, 61, 89, 148, 155, 179–180
takfīr (*or ikfār*) 5, 6 (note), 12–15, 19–37, 46, 50, 51, 61, 91, 131, 172
takfīr al-ʿāmmah 26, 130–131, 133, 158
takhfīf 174
takhṭīʾah 34
taʿlīq 208
tanāsukh 23
taqiyy 146
taqiyyah 6 (note), 153, 164
taqlīd 131 (note), 132–133, 136–140
taqwá 57, 80–81, 135, 146
taqyīd 216
taṣawwur 75 (note)
taṣdīq 31, 51, 55, 69–70, 73–76, 82, 86, 89–90, 96–97, 100, 103, 105, 138, 140, 147–160, 162–167, 173, 177–198, 201–203, 221
tashbīh 21, 108
taslīm 74, 75
tasmiyah 15, 59, 177
tawajjuh 122
tawakkul 186
tawfīq 224
tawḥīd 56, 74, 95 (note), 108, 145–146, 162, 177, 186, 221
taʾwīl 32, 35–37
tawlīd 130
taʿẓīm 92, 101
tazkiyah al-nafs 216
thamarah (*al-īmān*) 191
tumaʾnīnah 148

U

ʿubūdiyyah 211
ulūhiyyah 144
ummah 8–10, 12, 110
ʿuqūd arbaʿah 146
uṣūl 33

W

waʿd 119
waḍʿ (*al-lughah*) 155
waḥdāniyyah (*Allāh*) 117 , 145
wāḥid 37
waʿīd 15, 42–44, 119
wājibāt 128
wālī 15

Y

yaqīn 84, 197

Z

ẓāhir 36, 187
zakāt 64, 66–69, 81, 83, 107–108, 135, 176, 189
zānī 15
ziyādah (*al-īmān*) 192–206
zujājah 145
ẓulumāt 218
zunnār 113 (note)

THE CONCEPT OF BELIEF IN ISLAMIC THEOLOGY

A Semantic Analysis of *Īmān* and *Islām*

2016年2月25日　初版第1刷発行

著　者――――井筒俊彦
発行者――――古屋正博
発行所――――慶應義塾大学出版会株式会社
〒108-8346　東京都港区三田2-19-30
TEL〔編集部〕03-3451-0931
〔営業部〕03-3451-3584〈ご注文〉
〔 〃 〕03-3451-6926
FAX〔営業部〕03-3451-3122
振替　00190-8-155497
URL　http://www.keio-up.co.jp/
装　丁――――中垣信夫＋北田雄一郎［中垣デザイン事務所］
印刷・製本――萩原印刷株式会社
カバー印刷――株式会社太平印刷社

Printed in Japan　ISBN 978-4-7664-2288-7